Beverly's Best

A Distinctive Saratoga Springs Cookbook
BEVERLY REEDY

Always have a goal !
Beverly Reedy

The Greenfield Review Press
Greenfield Center, New York

The Greenfield Review Press
PO Box 308
Greenfield Center NY 12833

ISBN: 0-87886-145-9

Library of Congress control number 2003115970

Cover painting by Dan Maciag
Cover and interior design by Sans Serif, Inc.

Manufactured in the United States

This book is dedicated to my oldest son, Mark, who worked as Promotion Art Director for Good Housekeeping Magazine before he passed on. He always wanted me to pursue my dream and encouraged me to compile these recipes, and my story, into a cookbook that could be shared. This is for you Mark.

In 1988 Mark gave me a Good Housekeeping Cookbook for Christmas, and this is what he wrote:

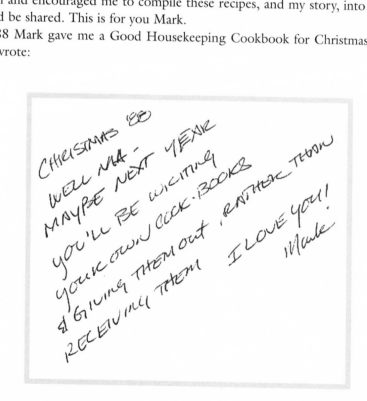

CHRISTMAS '88
WELL MA -
MAYBE NEXT YEAR
YOU'LL BE WRITING
YOUR OWN COOK-BOOKS
& GIVING THEM OUT, RATHER THAN
RECEIVING THEM   I LOVE YOU!
Mark

$1.00 from the sale of this book will be donated to an organization supplying food to people with AIDS and their families.

Contents

"Ahead of ones time," is a phrase often misused in our society, but perfectly apropos in the case of the talented and delightful Beverly Cone (Reedy). Nearly two decades ago, a small shop, in an out of the way location on Phila Street, in Saratoga Springs, began displaying imported olive oils, balsamic vinegars and dozens of other exotic products that were all but impossible to find in our area at that time.

As an executive chef and having just purchased the legendary Siro's in Saratoga, I was thrilled to hear about this place and rushed right down to see what it was all about. The wonderful sweet smells of baking cakes and pastries began in the parking lot and on entering through rack after rack of beautifully presented exotic wares I caught my first glimpse of a very beautiful but somewhat harried Beverly covered head to toe in flour. Let the laughter begin.

Through the years that sense of humor along with exquisitely prepared foods and an ever changing array of fabulous retail products have become the hallmark of Beverly's Specialty Foods. Now part of the fabric of Saratoga Springs, Beverly and her namesake shop continue to provide a classic culinary destination for residents and visitors to Saratoga alike. I know that the recipes in this book will bring the passion and joy of Beverly's cooking to your table as they did to mine.

Tom Dillon
Proprietor
Siro's of Saratoga Springs

Acknowledgements

I wish to thank the following people who have played important roles in my career:

- My children, Mark, Kimberlie, Michael, Tammy, Rob and Melissa, for standing by me all these years of experimenting with food and businesses. I love you all.
- My father and mother, for allowing me to get an early start in cooking and baking.
- Constance Boardman, for helping me to come into my own.
- All the customers at Beverly's Specialty Foods for testing all my new recipes and ideas.
- The many friends that have encouraged me to write this book and have enjoyed the successes and failures of my food preparations.
- Friend, Priscilla Toth for editing the first rough draft.
- Friend, Kate O'Connell for proof reading the first and second proof.
- My Publishers and good friends, Joe and Carol Bruchac for keeping me in line, and for being honest and supportive.
- The people I have worked for and with, who influenced me and perhaps unknowingly contributed to this publication.

Introduction

I believe we are all blessed with a God given talent. It is up to us to discover it, pursue it, nurture it and share it to the best of our ability. It has taken me years to get to this point, and I'm anxious and excited to share my talent with you. There are four important factors in my life; Faith, Family, Friends and Food. Without any of them, I would not be complete or even survive in a healthy life.

First, let me tell you about myself. I was born and raised in rural western Pennsylvania to Thomas Reedy and Mary Mills-Reedy. They met in Templeton, Pennsylvania where he was a friend of her schoolteacher's. They married and were together fifty years before my father passed away twenty six years ago. My father was a schoolteacher all of his life and my mother was a homemaker. They raised five children; three boys and two girls. I, being the youngest, am sure there was more hardship than I realized, although I do remember the tail end of the ration stamps and receiving government surplus cheese, canned meats and other staples. Our humble country home was homey and clean. I can see plainly the kitchen which was equipped with a wood and coal fired Kalamazoo® cooking stove, pale green and ivory in color, a corner cupboard, and a sink with no running water (we hand carried our drinking water one quarter mile from a spring in the woods). For washing clothes and dishes, we collected rainwater or melted snow. Also in the kitchen was a table with six chairs and a bookcase with glass doors that my brother Harold retrieved from a moving job he had. The walls always shone with clean white enamel. The ceiling was very low and shining also. A little gas stove in the corner helped to heat the kitchen.

There was a black potbelly stove in the living room at the bottom of the stairway which heated the living room and the upstairs. My father always got up first to get the stoves going before he awakened the rest of the family. Our favorite place to dress for school, in the winter,

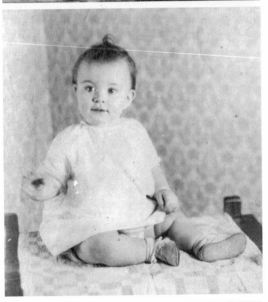

2

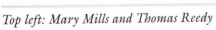

Top left: Mary Mills and Thomas Reedy
Top right: Paul and Louise
Right middle: Dick, Harold, and Beverly
Right bottom: Beverly in Smudge Pot
Above: Baby Beverly

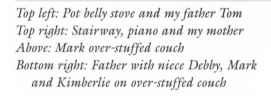

Top left: Pot belly stove and my father Tom
Top right: Stairway, piano and my mother
Above: Mark over-stuffed couch
Bottom right: Father with niece Debby, Mark
*   and Kimberlie on over-stuffed couch*

was behind the corner stove because it was the warmest spot in the house. There was a very small bedroom upstairs and one that was large enough to have two double beds, a couple of dressers and a closet in the corner that my mother had built. There was also a small bedroom downstairs off the living room, which was my parents. The living room, in addition to the black coal stove in the corner, contained a very large over-stuffed maroon couch and chair, which was very scratchy and adorned with crocheted doilies that my Grandma Mills had made. There was also an end table and light that had been a reward for saving S&H Green stamps. In the other corner was a beautiful upright player piano that we always had fun with. The piano lessons that I was exposed to didn't really last much longer than a few years. It was much easier to put a paper roll in and *pump* out the tunes! My mother still has that piano. The player doesn't work now because there are holes in the ballast, but someday I hope to have it restored and move it to New York.

*Top left: Front porch, Mother,
    niece Debby and Beverly*
*Top right: Grandma Mills and
    Mother front porch*
*Left: Back porch with washing
    machine sister Louise, niece
    Debby and Mother*

Even though our house was very small and seemingly full, my mother always kept it wall-papered, but she never removed the old paper because it helped to insulate the walls. If the old paper cracked, she would patch it with flour bags. There were so many layers of wall-paper on the walls that the corners were rounded. We made the wallpaper glue from flour and water, which worked very well. I learned so much about making do with as little as possible.

There was a front porch on that little house, which we almost never used, and a back porch, where the laundry was done (except in the winter and at that time it was one more function for the kitchen). The old wringer washer was pushed up against the red asbestos-shingled outside wall of the house but on laundry days; it was pulled out and filled with water that had been heated on the stove in large pots. We sorted the dirty laundry into piles of whites and colors and washed in order of their color and dirtiness. The throw rugs were always last because the water was never replaced with fresh. In addition, the tub of rinse water was then used to scrub the floors or water the flowers and gardens. It seemed I helped a lot with the household chores. I remember getting my hand caught in the wringer of the washing machine and before I knew it, my arm was in it up to my shoulder. No real damage done but it was scary.

We hung the clean laundry on clotheslines that strung from tree to tree, to garage corner to porch post, summer and winter. Sometimes the clothes would freeze before we got them on the line. Talk about freeze-dried! However, they smelled wonderful, especially the bed linens. I still hang laundry outdoors as often as I can but not in the freezing temperatures of the northeast. If it rained, we strung the clothes line upstairs. We also had a ten prong clothes rack that hung on the room divider upstairs over the open stairwell. When in use it was pulled up and fastened with a metal lever; when not in use it folded flat against the doorframe. The clothes were also hung over the banister. Monday was always laundry day and a busy one at that! Nothing else seemed to be done because doing laundry for a family of seven in those conditions, once a week, was a big enough job.

When we were running low on bread, my dad would mix up a batch of bread dough in a big dishpan, (which I still have) before leaving for school. My mother would take over at that point and finish the procedure throughout the day. It was a beautiful thing when we arrived home from school to the smell of fried dough. I understand that, when my mother was expecting me, she was in the middle of mixing a batch of bread dough when she went outside for some reason and fell, leaving my father to finish the procedure. Ever after, he was not only the breadwinner but also the bread maker and what a bread maker he was!

We raised all of our own vegetables, apples, pears, grapes, a few chickens, a pig or two and family pets here and there. In the early summer, we went to the woods to pick wild strawberries. What a terrible thing to make your children do! They weren't any bigger than

My father making bread

your thumb nail and made your hands and nails red, but oh when we sat down that evening for a full meal of homemade sweet biscuits topped with sugared fresh wild strawberries and fresh from the farm whipped cream, it made it all worth while. Almost as tasty was the next morning's breakfast when we smothered big thick slices of my dad's home baked bread with the congealed foam from the strawberry jam that my mother had made. You see when you make jam there is a foam that develops on the top, and since we didn't (or should I say were not allowed to) waste a thing, we were permitted to eat the foam immediately. The good stuff we saved for guests or for "putting up" for the long winter months ahead. It seemed that is what we did *all* summer—prepare for the winter.

Another family outing was to put on long pants and long-sleeved shirts (this is the only time the female members were allowed to wear trousers). After putting on our armor to protect us against briars, ants, snakes and the blistering hot sun, we would grab a bucket or basket and head for the wild huckleberry, blueberry and blackberry patches, where we would pick until the cows came home. Not really—that's one animal we didn't have room for. The huckleberries and blueberries were much easier to pick than the wild strawberries because they grew on knee to waist-high bushes. We would pick gallons and gallons of them. When we got home, we would sit in the shade of the silver maple tree, in the front yard, and pick through the berries for green ones, stems or any other foreign objects that were not conducive to good taste or to tasting good. We would then put them into quart baskets, place the baskets on a table out by the road with a sign that said "Fresh Blueberries 50 cents a quart". We had a coffee can for our customers to put their money into. We didn't

have a freezer in my young days, but we would can them for later use, and of course eat as many as we possibly could. The wild berries seem so much tastier than the big cultivated ones but not nearly as easy to pick.

In the fall, we would get up very early on Saturday mornings, sometimes even before dawn, pack a large basket of food and go down toward Pittsburgh, to an apple orchard named Treesdale Farms, where we would pick apples all day long for 20 cents a bushel. Sometimes my mother and father would pick one hundred bushels each. It seemed, at that time, to be so much money. There are times to this day when I smell a fresh picked apple, that I am right back there at Treesdale Farms with the ice cold dewy apples and wet morning grass with apple trees all around me as far as I can see. Then the sun would come up and dry everything up, and it wouldn't be long until we were very hot, tired, thirsty, and hungry. Then we would start to whine, "Are we done yet? Is it time to go yet?" When I wouldn't get the answer I was looking for, I would either go back to picking or more likely find a spot to hide and rest for awhile. Sometimes there were other kids with us, and then we would play or do something to entertain ourselves so the time would go faster. My niece, who was just a baby, would also be with us. My mother would put her in a wooden apple box to keep her from wandering away. Looking back on it now, it is a fond memory, although at the time, it was hard work.

My father was born in 1904 and as I mentioned before, was a schoolteacher. He was a wonderful, soft-spoken, gentle man that everyone adored. At that time teachers didn't make much money. He and my sister had extensive health problems, so he always had to

Top: My father in garden
Bottom: Picking berries with Grandma Mills, niece Debby, Mother Mary and Father Tom

supplement his teaching salary with summer work to cover medical expenses. He was an inspector for road building jobs and would come home after working in the hot sun all day and do gardening until dark.

Our home was very small but was always very pleasant and inviting. Incidentally, I was born in that house, and when I was very young, we really did not have many of the conveniences of life. For instance we didn't have indoor plumbing, so therefore we had a "path to the bath", equipped with the latest edition of the Sears Roebuck catalog to either read or use page by page and hope and pray the ink didn't rub off. The catalogs were much better to use than newspaper for just that reason! Having a roll of toilet paper was a real luxury. Every once in awhile my mother would whitewash or paint the inside of that old privy, just to freshen it up. If the smell got a little to bad, we either added wood ashes or lime to disguise the aroma. When the hole got full, my father and brothers would dig a new one, move the old privy onto that new hole, fill in the old one and then, another flower bed was born.

My mother was born in 1911. Her life was not an easy one. She has worked very hard and we always had wonderful home-grown and homemade food. I learned so much from the exposure to the whole process of growing, cooking and preserving food, and that has proven to be beneficial. It would be impossible to find a school that could teach me what I learned in our humble kitchen as a child and a teenager.

I remember the first thing I ever cooked. My mother was not feeling well, so I decided to make her something to eat. We had a tiny iron skillet, which looking back, was probably really an ashtray, however, no one smoked in our house. My father smoked, but never in the house and absolutely never in front of my Mother. Well I proceeded to make her some home fried potatoes and eggs in that little skillet. She survived so I have to assume it was okay. That was the beginning of my cooking career. Today, I am very partial to iron skillets. Do you suppose that is the reason?

I don't remember my childhood being an extremely happy one, but it wasn't unhappy either. Our family life was full of challenges. My parents were hard workers and struggled for everything. My mother was religious and my father was easy-going and accepted things as they came.

I don't totally agree with the way we were disciplined, but at a point in my life I came to realize that they did whatever they did because they believed it was the best way. It is so easy to blame our parents for whatever happens to us, but at some point we have to take responsibility for our actions. We can either accept our childhood, move on and try to improve ourselves, or we can choose to be angry and disturbed about it all of our lives. I choose to accept it, better my life and move on.

My first four grades of school were held in a one-room schoolhouse and my teacher's name was Cora Unverzagt.

In 5th grade, I moved right next door to another one-room schoolhouse. These schools were in the country, and we had to take a school bus to get there. My second teacher's name was Katherine Mahood.

When I went to 6th grade, I wanted to go to the school where my father taught. I'm not sure that attending my father's class was a very good idea, because I was expected to be the perfect example which I was not and that caused a few problems. I did survive the 6th grade however. Then on to junior and senior high school at Hooker High, Hooker, Pennsylvania. Yes, I attended "Hooker High". I became involved in band, girls chorus, mixed chorus, 4 H, Home Economics, all of which I took through my junior and senior high school. Since my father was a schoolteacher, I really wish now that he

Michael, Kimberlie, Mark—not happy in Birmingham, AL

would have put some pressure on me to be a better student.

My last year of high school I sent to Cincinnati, Ohio, to a Bible School. That is where I met my first husband, who was studying to become a minister. It makes me nervous just to think of it: the school, the education, the experience and my own innocence.

That was where it all began: growing up and facing adult problems, which I wasn't prepared for in the slightest. I wasn't permitted to face the everyday problems of being a normal teenager, much less getting myself into a situation where I had to deal with adult feelings and choices. I came to the realization some years later, and after several years of therapy, that my parents raised us the way they did because they thought they were doing it the right way. They wanted to protect us from the big bad world, whatever was out there to harm us and led us down a path of sin, or perhaps to protect us from what they had experienced themselves.

My newfound love, John Bowman, and I thought we were in love and planned to be married after I graduated from high school, and we were. I turned eighteen in June, he was twenty two in July, and we married in August. The next August we had our oldest son, John Mark; the next September we had our oldest daughter, Kimberlie; the next October we had our next son, James Michael; and

twenty eight months later our second daughter and fourth child; Tammy was born. Up to this point, we had lived in Ohio, Indiana, Illinois, Pennsylvania, Louisiana and Alabama, including several moves within the state of Louisiana. When we lived in Louisiana and Alabama, he was pastoring at a church.

The first three children were born in Louisiana, and Tammy was born in Alabama. While living in Louisiana, we lived with John's sister, Dot, for a while, where I learned about southern cooking. She was great and helped us as much as possible.

We moved to Birmingham, Alabama, then back to Ohio where we lived until we divorced three years later. Many things happened in and to that marriage, however, I think it failed because we were both so immature, and not at all ready for the family we had. My husband had come from a family of nine children, and had some extremely hard times. He continued his education for many years after we married which made it difficult.

One of his brother's-in-law was manager of a grocery store, and periodically he would bring us bags of canned goods that had lost their labels and couldn't be sold. I really never knew whether it would be dog food or soup until I opened it. Growing up the way I did and with the imagination, willingness and necessity to be creative with food and the products I had to work with, certainly became challenging. I look at it now as a great education in creativity, managing and in the production of food, but not with the dog food of course!

Being a northern girl, I was very excited about the different kinds and tastes of food to be found in the deep south. I had some wonderful mentors and one was my sister-in-law, Dot. She was the best cook and knew how to make all those delicious southern dishes like crayfish bisque, shrimp gumbo, dirty rice with pork chops, jambalaya and pralines. However, the best fried chicken came from my mother-in-law. She used any kind of grease she had on hand, from bacon grease to lard to cooking oil, but that chicken always came out the juiciest and tastiest chicken you could ever imagine. Now today we wouldn't think of using bacon fat or lard even if we did splurge on our diets and *fry* our chicken. She also made awesome oatmeal cookies.

Then there was a friend in Alabama who taught me how to make the most tender, flaky biscuits you could ever want. In addition, her cornbread and blackberry cobbler was to die for. Looking back now, I understand why I took such an interest in food. This is my talent and I was a quick, easy study

I mentioned earlier about moving to Ohio. Besides taking care of four children, I reached a point when I wanted to get out of the house, so I got a job at a private German Club that was very interesting and served delicious food. Then I got a job at Sanginitis, the oldest Italian restaurant in Akron, which was owned by four brothers. The food was incredible. I was a waitress, but I was very interested in the food we served so I always asked questions about what was in each dish and how they were prepared. I learned how to make the best Caesar salad tableside, how to de-bone a whole cooked pickerel tableside, how to create wonderful beef stew, marinara sauce, Italian salad dressing, great salad platters, and much more. I also learned about fine dining and serving of fine foods. That was my first experience with the elegance of dining in style.

It was at this restaurant that I met my second husband, Walter Cone. He worked for the Los Angeles Times Syndicate, and I was his waitress. You know the scenario—the traveling salesman and the waitress. I saw him at the bar, asked who he was and arranged for him to be seated in my station. And, as the saying goes, "The rest is history". We fell head over heels in love.

Seven years after my fourth child was born, our son, Walter Robert Cone, Jr. was born in Akron, Ohio. He was my third son and Walt's first. Five years later our daughter Melissa was born in Kingston, New York, my third daughter and his fifth. At this point, we had ten children, four of which were mine, four were his and two were ours. His children didn't live with us, so we only had six at home.

We had many rocky years, some together and some apart, however it did endure for thirty two years. He continued to travel and I continued to work and take care of the children. We did have some wonderful times together. We traveled a lot with the children and sometimes without. We had a travel trailer that we used while traveling with him across the country. We were in every state together, except Alaska.

One of the jobs we had, and I say *we* because I worked along side Walt, was at a newspaper in Blairsville, Pennsylvania. We lived in Greensburg at the time. He bought the weekly newspaper with a friend of his, Tom McGrath, and another partner. I believe we had that venture for two years. What a disaster! Walt used to call it the Blairsville Disgrace, actually the name of the paper was the *Blairsville Dispatch*. The best thing that came out of that was my friendship with Tom and Marlene McGrath. We did lose contact with them for quite awhile, but in the past few years, we have become very good, close friends again.

Walt changed jobs a lot so we moved a lot, and, sometimes we just moved because he wanted to. When we first got together, we lived in several different places in Ohio. We lived in Los Angeles for six weeks then back to Ohio. We made several more moves in Ohio, then on to Greensburg, Pennsylvania, Saltsburg, Pennsylvania, and then to a farm in Parker, Pennsylvania. I believe Charleston Beach, Rhode Island, was the next move (into a summer cottage that belonged to his brother), then to Fleischmanns, New York, for three years. From there we moved to Roxbury, New York, for four years, then to Stepney, Connecticut, down to Orlando, Florida from there, and then to Saratoga Springs, New York.

The kind of background I came from made it rather exciting to live in so many different places. I do have to thank him for exposing me to a lifestyle I may never have seen or been a part of. At times it was glamorous, however, he always seemed to be on the verge of one financial disaster or another.

Six Weeks after we moved to Fleischmanns, Melissa was born in Kingston. I will never forget that move. We were moving from a farm in Parker, Pennsylvania, to a beautiful farm on Hog Mountain Road in Fleischmanns, New York. We were loaded down with horses, chickens, dogs, five children and a pregnant woman. All we needed was a rocker tied to the top with Granny sitting in it. We pulled into the Northland Motel and Restaurant where Peter Ruhe was a server. He told me later that he wasn't too sure about us, where we were coming from or how we would fit in there. In the near future, he and my older children became good friends and his mother, Marie, and I became best friends. It was a good move, I loved the place, the Catskill Mountains, and

the people we met there have remained lifetime friends. I can't say enough about the friendliness and hospitality we found there. If I ever had to move again, I would want it to be back to the Margaretville area.

We then bought a farmhouse in Roxbury, which I loved and worked very hard at remodeling. I even hung sheet rock. The foyer was 18 feet high, which I wall papered from a scaffold. It was beautiful. I painted, spackled, refinished, laid floors, wired lights and did just about everything.

My newfound friend, Marie, and I decided to go into a little business together. We were very excited about being the proud owners of The Cheese Barrel of Margaretville, New York, and what fun we had organizing and planning that little venture. It was only four hundred square feet. It was in Binnekill Square and the Binnekill Square Restaurant was behind it. I worked there also. We were partners for two and a half years, and, eventually, I sold out to Marie and moved to Connecticut. Marie kept the business, moved it to a larger location up the street and after seven and a half more years sold it to a girl named Sue who still runs it very successfully. It is amazing to me how this little gourmet food store survived all these years in such a small town. It took a lot of hard work and a huge amount of determination. Marie and her husband, Skip Ruhe, both retired some years ago, sold their beautiful house in High Mount and bought a small ranch north of San Diego, California, where I visit every couple of years. It is wonderful to have friends with whom you can pick up the friendship whenever and wherever the opportunity presents itself. A few more friends from that area are, Marcia and Charlie Geehrer, Aggie and Milt Laub, Bob and Carolyn Hubbell and Jackie and Walter Keller.

Mark, Kimberlie and Michael graduated from Margaretville High School. Tammy, the last child of my first four children, graduated from Roxbury High School. When Mark, the oldest, and Kimberlie the next one down, graduated from high school, they had attended thirteen different schools. They are well-adjusted people at this point, I think, but I'm sure it took a lot of work for them.

When we lived on Hog Mountain Road and Melissa was one and half years old, I got a job at Roxbury Run Restaurant, in Roxbury, NY, owned by a Swiss couple, Jackie and Walter Keller. The food they prepared and served was incredible. I have not had escargot that would even come close to his. They bought another restaurant in Margaretville, New York. The name of it is Binnekill Square Restaurant. (The movie "You Can Count on Me", that was released in January of 2001, was filmed in Binnekill Square Restaurant and in the towns of Margaretville and Phoenicia.)

I worked for them for six years and learned so much about fine food. Many ideas you will find in this book came from Walter Keller. I have to give him some credit for what I have accomplished. I was so interested in the kind of food he was preparing and serving that it wasn't an effort to learn about the preparation and presentation of food. I was a waitress and bartender. If only I had been directly exposed to his talent, in the kitchen, it would have made my career easier. I also learned from Jackie about how to set a table properly and the correct way to serve. I refer back to her teachings often when catering a function.

We left Roxbury, New York, and moved to Connecticut where I opened another little Gourmet Food Shop and called it Cheese Etc. From there, an unhappy move to Orlando, Florida, followed by a job offer for Walt in Glens Falls, New York. I had hoped to move to the Hyde Park area so I could attend the Culinary Institute of America but that was not to be. Walt found a house near Loughberry Lake, in Saratoga Springs, which we purchased, and where we lived for thirteen years.

When we came to Saratoga Springs, I had made up my mind if I liked it here, I would stay and finally put down some roots. We made the move in March of 1986. After I settled in and unpacked yet one more time, I started to look for a location to open another cheese and gourmet food store. However, I wanted this one to be a little different from the other two. It should offer gourmet foods, cheeses, pâtés, shelf goods and catering but also a bakery and café. After doing much research and searching for the right location, I decided that the initial cost and the lease prices were much more than I could afford. I had no money and I wanted to do this on my own. Therefore, I went to plan B. I decided to do some baking at home, so I made sample desserts in small sizes and took them around to different restaurants for them to try. Actually, my youngest son, Rob, was then a dishwasher at the Old Bryan Inn and that was my first stop. They liked, they bought. That gave me courage to peddle my wares elsewhere. I baked for Sweet Temptations, Chez Pierre, the Wishing Well, The Elms, The Tradewinds, Siros, and several other Saratoga Springs restaurants. I took many classes in special occasion and wedding cake decorating and absolutely loved it. I also did some catering from home and did all of this for two and a half years. In the meantime, I was looking for a reasonably priced location to lease. With the money I was making in my little home-based business, I bought restaurant equipment and supplies and stored them in our two-car garage, which was filled to the doors when I finally found the perfect place. That perfect place was and is Beverly's located at 47 Phila St. in Saratoga Springs, New York.

While stock piling in my garage, I knew I still needed cash to open a business. I was looking for investors and was turned down several times. I had no credit of my own, and what credit I had jointly with my husband was not that good. I got the bright idea to talk to a contractor, Tim Reed, to ask him if he would be interested in doing the renovating of a location, as an investment. I would pay him back, with interest of course, on a monthly basis. Much to my surprise, he agreed. That took care of that problem, but I still needed operating capital and cash for inventory. I know one should never borrow money from a relative, but I did. My mother took out a loan on her house, and I made the payments on $13,000.00. I still needed about that much more. I tried everything I could think of. I didn't want to go through the Small Business Association, because I didn't want to wait as long as it would take. I had set a deadline for myself, and if I didn't have all the financing in place by that date, I was going to forget the whole idea and have a garage sale of restaurant supplies. The day before the deadline, I received a phone call from Roger, the boyfriend of my daughter Kimberlie's friend Carol, from Hawaii. Roger said Carol had told him that I was an excellent cook, that she believed in me and that I needed a little more money. I couldn't believe it. Talk about things working out just at the wire. Needless to say, I was so grateful! He received a few gift baskets as a "thank you". We worked out a payment plan, and away I went to find a location.

Shortly after that I was at Suburban Propane buying some cake pans and learned that Eartha's Kitchen had purchased and was moving to a location on Court St. I immediately went to see Selma Neemer, then owner of Eartha's, and asked if it was true. She verified the fact but wondered how I found out, since she hadn't even told the landlord yet. Oh, the wonders of a small town! Especially in the restaurant business, word, good or bad, travels quickly. The property owners were Sandy and David Silverhart. I met with them, signed a lease on Memorial Day weekend, the end of May, totally renovated it from front

Top: Kimberlie's friend Carol
Bottom: Renovations by daughter Melissa

Tim Reed—hard at work constructing Beverly's

door to back door and opened for business on July 1, 1989. Tim was anxious to get Beverly's going. He did a wonderful job, and I will always be grateful to him for his part in making Beverly's Specialty Foods a success. Can you believe the beginning rent was $595.00 a month?

I was determined to do this on my own. I had a plan to execute within ten years. I was fifty years old when I opened Beverly's Specialty Foods, and my plan was to have a successful business, invest some money, become independent, and in ten years sell.

During the 10 years of owning Beverly's Specialty Foods, it was not easy, especially in the beginning. Since I started on a shoestring, I had to do as much as I could myself. In the early days, it was not as it is today. It was a gourmet food store with shelf goods along the right wall, a deli case to the left of the front door with over one hundred different varieties of cheese, eight kinds of pâté, lox to be hand sliced and also a whole prosciutto sliced to

order. Then there was a bakery case that was filled to overflowing with homemade muffins, cookies, cakes, pies, quiche, tarts and eight different kinds of fresh baked croissants.

On the upper level, I had a few little tables. I only wanted to serve fresh ground and brewed coffee, tea and my homemade baked goods. However, I made the mistake of doing a few little breakfast specials, that went so well I did a few more. Then my son Mark, who was a graphic design artist, designed a small menu, then a bigger one, and the first thing I knew we were moving the shelf goods to the front of the store and putting more tables in the back. Then Michael came onboard and he convinced me to get rid of the retail goods all together and go for a full-fledged breakfast and lunch restaurant. That was generating income and the money was not tied up in something sitting on the shelf.

One of the reasons the gourmet foods were selling so slowly was because the grocery stores had begun carrying specialty foods. It

Early days in Beverly's

was easier for the consumer to buy it all in one place. And, of course the price was much better at the bigger stores. Therefore, the retail went and the counter and more tables came in. This didn't happen in a few years—it was over the course of seven or eight.

The catering business grew and grew as well and I loved it! I was also doing special occasion cakes and all kinds of baking. (I did turn down a few questionable requests though.)

In the evolvement of it all, I had to hire more and more people to help me. I just couldn't do it all myself anymore. That was a hard thing to do, because I was loosing control of the range and ovens. Many of the cooks and chefs that I hired knew much more than I about things, but I still insisted that they do it my way. I did, however, learn something from every one of them, even the bad ones. If they could show me a better way to do something, I would listen, and then I would decide. I had created everything that was on the menu and the items were all prepared from my own recipes, so there was one thing I insisted on: *always* follow the tried

and tested recipes for the menu items, then be as creative as you want to be on the specials. Some of the chefs that worked for me are very talented and have moved on to more challenging positions, some have their own restaurants, some went back to construction, some to prepping some place else and some just went. A few didn't, by the largest stretch of the imagination, live up to the way they presented themselves on their résumés. I found, by working in restaurants and from having chefs work for me, that many of them have large egos and don't respect the wait staff. That is something I couldn't and wouldn't tolerate. We were all there for the same reason, to do the job we were being paid to do and to perform it to the best of our abilities.

One of the dishwashers would throw things away if he didn't want to clean them. After all my pastry bags and a few large pans disappeared, I figured out what was happening. Another dishwasher, on his first day, went out for a smoke, took off his apron and kept going, Yet another time, one of the line cooks, again

Above: Michael and Beverly
Beverly's waitresses forever Michelle and Melissa

on his first day, went out for a smoke, said he was going to move his car and kept on going.

I will never forget in the very beginning after I decided to do breakfast, a person came to me looking for a chef's position. He said he had been head chef at The Russian Tea Room in NYC. I took him at his word, after all I was new in the restaurant business and believed what he said. On a Sunday morning, I went to church with my family, and we stopped on the way home from church to have breakfast. When I walked in the front door, every table was full and the waitress Kristin Hurtado, (who happened to be one of my all time favorites) told me that the chef was out back smoking. None of the tables had been served, and the people I was trying to impress from the Adirondack Trust Bank were sitting there very patiently waiting for their meal. I went straight through

the restaurant to the kitchen and relieved him of his smoking position. The next day I called the Russian Tea Room, spoke with the manager only to hear, "I think there was a bus boy a few years ago by that name". After that, I learned to check references. Unfortunately since Sundays were my busiest days, I now felt it necessary to be there myself, so I wasn't able to go to church much for ten years.

I have done many interesting catering jobs but one of the most exciting, was the weekend I was hired by the Canadian Pacific Railway. There was a merger being discussed with another line, and they needed a caterer on board the train. We left Saratoga Springs on Friday morning for Montreal and returned on Sunday afternoon.

That train had the best-equipped kitchen I have ever worked in, and everything was at my fingertips. My son, Michael, Chef Steve Knopf and I worked well together to supply fifty guests with breakfast and lunch on Friday, then breakfast and lunch on the return trip on Sunday. While in Montreal for two nights, we were supplied with a hotel room and expense money. That was a gig I will never forget.

I loved my business but I was getting very tired, so at sixty I decided to sell to my son, Michael. In less than a year, I divorced, stopped smoking, sold a house, bought a house, moved, sold my business, turned sixty and spent the winter in Key West. It was a beautiful thing. I can't begin to tell you how my life has changed and my happiness grown. Not because I sold the business but because I finally took charge of my life. It was, and still is, an empowering and wonderful feeling.

The home I purchased is in the foothills of the Adirondacks on two and a half acres, and I absolutely love it. The grounds were like a bare canvas with not a flower in sight. What a blessing! I am an avid gardener, so the first thing I did was to purchase a tiller and get busy making flower gardens. I am surrounded with beautiful forests and all the wild creatures that come with it. Every morning I have wild turkeys in my compost pile. I love the sounds and smells of nature.

After returning from Key West, in the spring of 2000, I thought I would work at a few different places for the summer. I baked and cooked at several Saratoga Springs restaurants, they included Sperry's two mornings a week, Eartha's, for Carolyn Male, two nights a week, and I helped Michael at Beverly's two days a week. It was a busy schedule but it was achievable and I liked the diversity. Baking is a passion of mine, so I really enjoyed the job at Sperry's. Working with the staff and for Ridge Qua, the owner, was a treat. Of course, it was nice to be back at Beverly's, but in a different role as an employee. I also enjoyed working with Carolyn and her employees at Eartha's.

The summer of 2000, my ex-husband, Walt, then living in North Carolina with our son Rob, was diagnosed with terminal cancer. Arrangements were made for him to return, and I would take care of him until he died in November. That was not an easy thing for me to do, but I am thankful that I had the opportunity to do so. It healed many hurts and mended many bad feelings.

I decided to take time off from working and to concentrate on writing this book. Living where I am living, that's a hard thing to do. I love my gardens, and while seated at my computer I can see them through the window, and they seem to call my name. Gardening is wonderful therapy for me.

After retiring for a year, I was hired at Putnam Market as a baker. I enjoyed it and was in their employ for more than a year. Kathy Hamilton and Gloria Griskowitz are wonderful, kind and understanding women who are eager to work *with* their employees through all kinds of problems. They have a great staff, also.

I didn't work much on my cook book while employed, but there was a large force pushing me to finish it. I set a goal for myself that it

Top: Beverly, Rob, Mark, Michael, Kimberlie, Melissa, Tammy
Bottom: My family plus son-in-law and grandson

was to be finished by the spring of 2003. It is now June of 2003 and I am proud to say, it is complete.

Beverly's Specialty Foods was very good for me and I loved it. I met my best friends here in Saratoga Springs through my business. The business was my life for ten years. My children were supportive in this venture, and they all, at one point or another, worked for Beverly's. They have all done well and I am very proud of each one of them.

Breakfast & Brunch

A Perfect Poached Egg

I like to use a flat stainless steel or coated skillet
   Fill with water leaving room for the eggs.
   Add 1 tablespoon white [only] vinegar. Don't use too much or your eggs will taste pickled.
   Bring the water and vinegar to a boil. Add the eggs. Cook to your liking. Remove with slotted spoon onto whatever you would like.

I learned this little trick from Walter Keller—Binnekill Square Restaurant, Margaretville, N.Y.

❈

Absolute Best Pancakes

1½ cup Whole Wheat Flour	¼ cup Sugar
4 cups Flour	4 Eggs
4 tbs Baking Powder	5 cups Milk
2 tsp Salt	1⅓ cup Butter

Sift dry ingredients into a large bowl, set aside.
   Melt butter in microwave. While doing so, whisk eggs, add milk, whisk to combine, add to dry mixture, continue to whisk until all is combined. Fold in melted butter. Place onto a heated, seasoned grill in 2 or 3 oz size cakes. When bubbles start to form on top, flip over and continue to cook until the under side is golden brown.

Some tasty serving suggestions:
   Serve with warm maple syrup or fresh fruit of your choice.
   After placing on grill, add chopped walnuts and bananas.
   Sprinkle with **Great Granola,** before flipping.
   Add Jarlsberg and sliced apples, before flipping.
   Top with **Bev's Berry Sauce** after cooking.

I have been told many times, that Beverly's has the "absolute best" pancakes ever tasted. This recipe is one of my originals, which took me several months or maybe even years to perfect. I know you will agree that they are unbelievable and somewhat healthy, and the combination of ingredients makes their flavor unique. Enjoy them but please continue to purchase pancakes at Beverly's; it is with much hesitation that I surrender this recipe to you.

❈

Best Ever Oatmeal

4 cups Water
½ tsp Salt
½ cup McCanns® Irish Oatmeal, regular
1½ cup Quaker Oats®, rolled, not quick or instant

Bring water and salt to boil. Slowly add the McCanns®, while stirring. Reduce heat, cover and simmer for 30 minutes, stirring every 10 minutes. Remove from heat. Add the Quaker Oats® and stir well. Cover and let sit, off the heat, until the oats has absorbed the liquid. Stir every so often. The oats will be flaky and crunchy, not gooey. This reheats quite well in the microwave.

My father used to make oatmeal this way, only without McCanns®. I never did like oatmeal as a kid, but his wasn't too bad. I just remember the flaky and crunchy consistency of it. Of course, we always topped it with brown sugar and butter which made it acceptable.

Did you ever have *Fried Oatmeal?* Well it's a good way to use up that leftover oatmeal, (another good way is the *Lazy Daisy Oatmeal Cake*).

I always use an iron skillet to fry it, heating it very hot. Cover the bottom with butter or oil. Slice the COLD, not cool, oatmeal about 1 inch thick. Place in the hot oil, brown without disturbing for about 10 minutes. Turn over and brown the other side. Serve with maple syrup.

This idea came from my mother, who never wasted a thing. It also happens to be a favorite of my daughter Melissa.

❈

Bev's Berry Sauce

2 lbs Mixed Berries
1 cup Sugar
⅓ cup Cornstarch

1 cup Water
2 tbs Butter
½ tsp Salt

Place all ingredients into a heavy saucepan. Stir to combine and cook over medium heat until thick, stirring often. Remove from heat. Serve on *Waffles, French Toast, Pancakes* or on that *Best Ever Oatmeal* with bananas.

This is one of the breakfast favorites at Beverly's Specialty Foods.

❈

Cajun Salmon Cakes with Fresh Salmon

2 lbs Fresh Salmon Filet
½ cup Dry White Wine
¼ cup Lemon Juice

1 tsp Aunt Jane's Crazy Salt®
¼ tsp Dill Weed

Rinse salmon filet and remove skin and all bones with clean pliers [They will pull right out]. Place salmon onto a shallow baking pan that has been sprayed with non-stick spray. Pour wine and lemon juice over salmon, sprinkle with salt and dill weed. Cover with foil and bake in a 400 degree oven for 20 minutes, cool.

½ cup Celery, diced small
½ cup Spanish Onion, diced small
½ cup Red Pepper, diced small
½ cup Green Pepper, diced small
1 tsp Garlic, minced
½ cup Butter
¼ cup Parsley, chopped fine

1 cup Soft Bread Crumbs
2 Eggs, slightly beaten
½ cup Hellmann's® Mayonnaise
¼ tsp each Oregano, Thyme,
    Cayenne, White Pepper and Black
    Pepper
Salt to taste.

Remove salmon from the baking pan, cool and break it into a mixing bowl. Do not use the juice.

Melt butter in skillet; add celery, onion, garlic and the peppers. Sauté until just transparent, add to salmon along with the parsley, bread crumbs, eggs, mayonnaise and the seasonings. Mix completely. From here you can use this in several different ways. To make croquettes, use about ⅓ cup mixture; form into a cone shape. Coat with flour, dip in a milk/egg mixture and then in seasoned breadcrumbs. Deep-fry to golden brown and serve with a dill sauce as a main course.

Or you could shape it into half dollar size patties, brown and serve as an hors d'oeuvre with a spicy mayonnaise dipping sauce. One of my favorite ways to serve this dish is to form into patties large enough to hold a poached egg. Brown patties in a buttered skillet. Place a poached egg on the patty and top with a roasted red pepper hollandaise sauce.

This dish, a proven customer favorite, I created for Sunday Brunch at Beverly's.

Salmon Cakes with Poached Eggs

Use the *Cajun Salmon* recipe found in this chapter.

Grill the Salmon Cake to reheat. While this is being done, poach the eggs. Remove salmon cakes to heated plates, top with poached eggs. Since the salmon cakes are Cajun, I like to serve this dish with either the **Roasted Red Pepper Hollandaise** or **Jalapeno Hollandaise**.

Top each of the poached eggs with either of the sauces, or just plain **Hollandaise**. Serve immediately with home fries.

This dish is definitely a Brunch favorite.

French Toast

This is the one you've all been waiting for. If it shows up in any other restaurant, Michael will be looking for my head. However, I'll take the chance.

12 Eggs
1 cup Milk
2 tsp Vanilla
½ cup Sugar
½ tsp Cinnamon

1 tsp Lemon Rind
1 Loaf French Bread, sliced diagonally across loaf 1½ inch thick

Mix cinnamon and sugar together in small bowl. This keeps the cinnamon from being lumpy in the batter.

Beat eggs in mixer, until completely incorporated. Add milk, mix very well, then add the remaining ingredients. Mix until sugar is dissolved.

Place one layer of bread, cut side up, in a flat container. Pour the egg mixture over bread; marinate overnight. Be sure to use enough of the liquid to saturate the bread ALL the way through. I like to use french bread. Actually, my *Baguettes* are the best. A good solid bread works much better than a light fluffy one.

Heat a shiny aluminum skillet until hot (I say shiny because the bread is less apt to stick). Melt butter in skillet, place one layer of soaked bread slices into the hot skillet. Brown both sides. Place in oven to finish. Depending on the thickness of the bread, it will take 12 to 15 minutes. Remove from oven, place on a serving plate, sprinkle with powdered sugar and serve immediately.

Some suggestions to compliment the french toast are:

Serve with fresh sugared peaches or strawberries; or coat with coconut before browning; or serve with fresh mango and pineapple. Try *Bev's Berry Sauce*, or just serve with real maple syrup.

Your guests will love this dish and it's one you can prepare partially the night before.

✳

French Pancakes—Bev's Style

2 cups *Beverly's Best Pancake Batter*

Add milk to the batter until it is a pouring consistency.

With a large spoon, place the thinned batter onto a hot griddle, to make a cake about the size of a saucer and ⅛ inch thick, when light brown on one side, turn to brown the other. This will happen quickly.

Place the pancake on a plate and roll up using 3 or 4 per serving.

Top with fresh sugared strawberries, fresh sugared peaches, *Bev's Blueberry Sauce* or your favorite fruit or topping. Sprinkle with powdered sugar, spritz some whipped cream on top and you have a wonderful breakfast treat. This is a fun dish to offer on a buffet table. Just place the rolled up cakes in one serving container and several different toppings in others along with the whipped cream.

❋

Corned Beef Hash

8 lbs Corned Beef	7 or 8 Potatoes, boiled
6 large Carrots	White Pepper
½ head Celery	Thyme
2 large Onions	

You will need a grinder with a course blade for this, or you may hand cut the beef, but it will take a long time. I have never used the processor for this dish but I suppose if you watched it carefully and didn't over process the mixture, it would be okay.

In a large pot, place the corned beef and contents of the seasoning packet that comes with it. Cover with water. Bring it to a boil, reduce heat, cover and simmer until fork tender (about 4 to 5 hours). Add more water as needed. Or, you could buy a pre-cooked corned beef but the flavor isn't the same.

Peel the carrots and onions. Wash the celery. Cut them into 1 inch chunks not having to be uniform at this point. Place the three veggies in a pot, cover with water and cook until tender. Don't salt the vegetables yet, because you don't know how salty the corn beef may be.

Cook the potatoes separately. When everything is cooked, cut the corned beef into pieces that will fit into the grinder. Put all the veggies, including potatoes and the corned beef through a meat grinder letting it fall into a large mixing bowl. After everything has been ground, sprinkle with white pepper and thyme, about a tsp of each to start. Mix completely and thoroughly. Taste and season to your liking. If you need to add salt, do so at this time.

When ready to serve, fry the hash in a hot skillet until brown and crisp on the bottom then turn over and brown the other side. Serve hot with pouched eggs and home fries.

The idea of this dish and the method of preparing it came from one of my ex-employees, Scott Fitzgerald. It has been on the "Best Sellers" list at Beverly's ever since. Thank you, Scott!

❋

Corn Muffin with Grilled Tomatoes and Poached Eggs

2 Corn Muffins   4 Eggs
1 Tomato   *Roasted Red Pepper Hollandaise*

This is a great way to use up leftover corn muffins.

Slice the muffins in half across. Lightly butter each half and grill. You may need to cut the top off so it will lay flat on the plate.

Slice tomato in ¾-inch slices and grill.

Poach the eggs.

Lay grilled corn muffins on heated individual plates, grilled side up. Place a slice of grilled tomato on each muffin half, then the poached egg. Top with warmed *Roasted Red Pepper Hollandaise Sauce.*

Serve immediately with fruit or home fries.

This is one of my originals. Trying to do something different for weekend brunches for 10 years is bound to bring out the creativity in one.

❋

Frittata

There is so much one can do with a frittata, and it's a great way to use up leftovers. I remember my mother using leftover spaghetti and green beans. I loved it!

My definition of a frittata is "an egg pizza" or open-faced omelette.

For each person use 2 or 3 eggs and 1 tbs water. Whisk until very well mixed and light.

In a hot non-stick pan, place some butter or olive oil. I prefer the latter.

Sauté the veggies, meat, pasta or whatever you desire. Add the egg mixture and stir with a rubber scraper until the eggs start to set.

Top with cheese of your choice, place in a 375 degree oven until the frittata is puffed, cooked through and lightly browned.

Serve immediately or take it on a picnic. This is great for a crowd. Using a larger skillet, after cooking, place on a large platter and cut into wedges, serve hot or at room temperature.

❋

German Apple Pancake

4 Eggs	Sprinkle of Nutmeg
1 cup Milk	2 tbs Butter
1 cup Flour	1 Apple, your favorite variety

For this recipe, you will need a heavy, non-coated, 10-inch, aluminum skillet with rounded sides.

In a mixing bowl, whisk milk and eggs until totally combined. Add flour and nutmeg, then whisk until just incorporated. Set aside.

Peel apple, slice into ¼-inch slices.

Place skillet onto burner and heat until very hot. Add butter and melt. Add apples and sauté slightly. Pour 1 cup of the batter over the apples [not all in one spot] and put into preheated 400 degree oven immediately. Bake at least 20 minutes. until it is *completely* golden brown. It will puff up around the edges and also in the center If taken out of oven too soon, it will not hold it's shape and will be a little doughy as opposed to crispy.

Remove from skillet to a serving plate. Sprinkle with powdered sugar. Serve with a lemon wedge and real maple syrup. This is one of the best things you will ever eat!!!!!!!

I have also made this with strawberries, cranberries, raisins and walnuts. Or, any combination.

When I worked at Roxbury Run Restaurant, in Roxbury, NY, this recipe was thumb tacked to a doorframe, in the kitchen. I suppose it was there for all to use. I'm not the only employee that "borrowed" it. But, I'm sure Walter Keller didn't expect it to be served in another restaurant. I have, however, seen this recipe in print elsewhere. Thank you again, Walter.

❋

Granola

4 cups Old Fashioned Oats	1½ tsp Cinnamon
3 oz Coconut	1 tsp Nutmeg
½ cup Sunflower Seeds	½ cup Honey
½ cup Sesame Seeds	½ cup Vegetable Oil
½ cup Toasted Wheat Germ	

Place all dry ingredients into a large mixing bowl. Mix thoroughly. Combine the oil and honey. Pour over the dry mixture and mix until all is coated with honey and oil. Spread no more than 1-inch-thick onto baking sheets. Place into preheated 300 degree oven. Stir every 15 minutes bringing granola in from sides and scraping off bottom. This mixture will brown very quickly and needs to be watched closely at the end. Remove from oven when granola is golden brown. Using a metal pancake turner, scrape granola from the bottom while still hot. If allowed to cool before scraping bottom, it will stick. When cool it should be crunchy.

Stored in airtight containers, it will keep very well. If it does get damp and chewy, place it back on baking sheets and freshen in oven for 10 minutes.

Some suggestions for serving:

Of course one of the most likely is with milk and raisins or fresh fruit.

Sprinkle on fresh fruit bowl that has been topped with nonfat yogurt.

Sprinkle on top of a bowl of **Best Ever Oatmeal** with **Blueberry Sauce**. It gives the oatmeal a little added crunch.

How about sprinkling it on top of **Pancakes,** before you flip them over.

Also goes quite nicely on top of those wonderful **Waffles**. Have fun and enjoy!

We will thank my daughter, Tammy, for this recipe. Everyone at Beverly's has enjoyed this for many years, actually since the beginning of Beverly's. Tammy lives in Los Angeles now but graduated from Sullivan County Community College in Hotel and Restaurant Management.

❈

Lemon-Poppy Seed Pancakes

1½ cup Flour	½ cup Sour Cream
2 tbs Sugar	2 tsp Lemon Zest
1 tbs Poppy Seeds	2 tsp Lemon Juice
1 tsp Baking Soda	1 Egg
½ tsp Baking Powder	1 Egg white
¼ tsp Salt	2 tbs Butter, melted
¾ cup Milk	

Sift dry ingredients together into a mixing bowl.

In a smaller bowl, combine remaining ingredients except the butter. Mix very well to incorporate the eggs. Add wet ingredients to dry ingredients. Stir to blend. Fold in melted butter. Brush griddle with melted butter or oil before using it. Be sure the griddle is hot before brushing.

Serve these with Lemon Honey.
    1 cup Honey
    ¼ Lemon, sliced thin

Cook over medium heat until hot and lemony. Serve with the above pancakes.

Lobster Hash

2 lbs Lobster Meat, chopped fine	¼ cup Butter
½ cup Onion, diced small	¼ tsp Thyme
½ cup Carrot, peeled and shredded medium	¼ tsp Rosemary, crushed
1 cup Potato, cooked and diced small	Salt and Pepper to taste.

Sauté the carrot and onion in the butter until the onion is opaque. Add the potato and the seasoning. Stir to combine and continue to cook over low heat until the flavors have blended, then stir in the lobster meat. Heat and serve immediately with poached, scrambled or fried eggs and home fries or whatever breakfast sidedish you like.

My friends, Carol, Kate, Claire and I went to the Cape for a few days. Of course you can't go there, or to Maine, without having lobster. We found a fish market that would cook and crack the lobsters so we ordered four 2-pounders. Needless to say, we had leftovers, so this is the dish I prepared for breakfast the next morning.

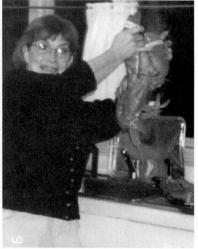

Left: Tammy, Kimberlie, Michael and Mark. Right: Beverly at Cape

My Father's Waffles

This is not a belgium waffle recipe, but one that is used in the home waffle iron that everyone has stuck on the bottom shelf someplace. Well, dig it out and clean it up. You'll want to try it one more time with this recipe.

6 cups Flour	1½ cup Crisco®
2½ tbs Baking Powder	6 Eggs, separated
1½ tsp Salt	4 cups Milk

Preheat waffle iron. If you haven't seasoned your iron, read the instructions on how to do so, or brush lightly with melted butter.

Sift dry ingredients together. Cut Crisco® into flour mixture. Set aside.

Separate eggs. Beat egg whites to stiff peaks. Set aside.

Beat egg yolks and milk together. Add to the flour and Crisco mixture and mix until well blended. Fold in the egg whites until just incorporated. Place a scoop in center of hot iron, close lid, holding lid down for a few seconds to allow the batter to reach all the corners. Cook until most of the steam has escaped or until it reaches the crispness you desire.

My father made these when we were children and could hardly make them fast enough. Sometimes we would have them for supper with fresh homemade sausage. YUM! When I got married and had children, they also enjoyed this treat. Sometimes I would place pieces of bacon on top of the scoop of batter before the lid came down. At that time, I used raw bacon. Today I would use crisp, well-drained bacon. However, some of my kids still like the crispness that the bacon grease gives. By the time the waffle is done, the bacon is cooked.

Another addition I would recommend is chopped pecans [without the bacon]. I discovered this tasty treat after I moved to pecan country, Louisiana.

If you do not have a waffle iron, this recipe will make you want to buy one.

❈

Mark, my Father Tom, Kimberlie

Pumpkin Pancakes

1 cup Whole Wheat Flour	2 tsp Baking Soda
3 cups Flour	4 Eggs
1 tsp Salt	2 cups Yogurt, plain
½ cup Brown Sugar	3 cups Milk
2 tsp Cinnamon	3 cups Canned Pumpkin
2 tsp Nutmeg	½ cup Butter, melted
2 tsp Ginger	

Sift dry ingredients together into a large mixing bowl.

Mix the wet ingredients together, EXCEPT the butter, in a separate bowl.

Add the wet mixture to the dry mixture. Whisk until totally incorporated. Add melted butter and fold in. Grill immediately or it will keep in the refrigerator for a few days.

Now remember the pancake will be a lot moister than regular pancakes, so don't try to cook them until they are dry because it won't happen. Try adding some chopped toasted pecans to the batter.

Cafe Beaujolais' gets the credit for this idea. They are located in Mendocino, CA.

I always served these with a caramel sauce, at Beverly's. I never wrote down the recipe but I'll try to remember. Actually, it's only three ingredients. Try this:

½ cup Butter
2 cups Brown Sugar
¾ cup Heavy Cream

Melt butter in a heavy pan, and add brown sugar and cream. Stir over medium heat until combined. Lower heat and simmer until sugar has melted and it reaches the consistency of a sauce. You want it thick enough to stay on top of the pancakes, not thin to soak into them.

This dish is definitely not low cal or low fat but it is delicious. Some of my customers would start asking for these as soon as summer was over.

❀

Raspberry Butter

In bowl of mixer, place as much butter as you like. Whip it until it is very light and fluffy, almost like whipped cream. Add enough raspberry jam to color it and flavor it. Continue to whip until light in color and all is incorporated.

I have also made this with honey, maple syrup or strawberry jam. You could actually make it with any of your favorite jams.

This Raspberry Butter is perfect with your morning pastries, pancakes, waffles, french toast or *Scones.*

My daughter, Tammy worked in a hotel in Orlando where they served this butter with croissants and morning pastries. Try it. You will be the hit of the Brunch Bunch.

Quiche Filling

This recipe will make five 10-inch quiche.

2½ doz Eggs
2 qts Half and Half
1 tsp each Black Pepper, Salt,
   Paprika, Dry Mustard

¼ tsp Fresh Ground Nutmeg
3½ lb Imported Emmenthaler,
   shredded

Crack eggs into bowl of mixer, whisking with wire until totally blended. Add half and half. Mix all the spices in a small cup to break up any lumps, then add to above and whisk to blend. For each quiche, I use ¾ lb imported swiss such as Emmenthaler. The imported cheese gives a much better flavor. Sometimes I will mix ½ lb Emmenthaler and ¼ lb gruyere, or maybe some cheddar, but never only cheddar, as it is too oily and sharp.

The traditional Quiche Lorraine has bacon, onion and ham added (just enough to flavor). There are many different things you can add, just let your imagination and taste buds lead you. The combinations are endless. One of the favorites is shrimp, crab or chicken with a little tarragon. Almost any kind of vegetable works.

Using the *Pie Dough* recipe, line the baking pans with rolled-out dough. Crimp the edges. Mix the cheese and additions of your choice and place in the unbaked pie shell. Stir the egg mixture and ladle enough onto the cheese mixture to bring it up to the bottom of the crimped edges. Place the filled shell onto a baking sheet to prevent overflow in the oven. Bake at 375 degrees for about 40 minutes or until golden brown and the mixture is cooked in the center.

Savory Bread Pudding

8 cups Stale Bread, 1-inch cubes
½ cup Spanish Onion, diced
¼ cup Red Pepper, diced
½ head Broccoli,
   cut into florets

1 cup each Zucchini and yellow
   squash, cut into 1 inch cubes or
   desired size
½ lb Cheddar, shredded,
   reserve ½ cup for top
1 Recipe of *Quiche Mixture*

Any breakfast meats you would care to add. It is delicious with or without.

Sauté onions. Place all ingredients [except the quiche mixture] into a large mixing bowl. Stir to mix then add as much of the *Quiche Mixture* as needed to saturate the bread. Mix very well. Let stand for about 45 minutes to allow bread to absorb as much liquid as possible. Pour mixture into a greased baking dish. If there is not enough liquid to come to the top, add some milk or cream over all. You don't want the mixture to be totally covered but you do want enough liquid in it to prevent it from being too dry.

   Sprinkle the ½ cup cheddar on top. Place in a preheated 375 degree oven for about an hour. It will puff up like a soufflé and become golden brown and crispy on top.

This is a great dish to serve at a breakfast or brunch buffet and has been a very successful dish in my catering business. Several years ago, I made this dish for a wedding brunch thinking I was being VERY creative. Well the Italians came up with it a long time ago. They even gave it the name of Strata. Whoever created it—it's great and a wonderful way to use up those little pieces of vegetables, stale bread, left over sausage, bacon and almost dried up cheese. Enjoy!

❋

Scottish Eggs with Whole Grain Mustard Sauce

8 Hard Boiled Eggs
¾ cup Oats, uncooked
8 slices Bacon, crisp and cooled
½ cup Flour

Salt and Pepper
½ cup Milk
¼ cup Whole Grain Mustard
1 cup Heavy Cream

Process oats and bacon together until coarsely ground. Place in a bowl.

Cut hard-boiled eggs in half lengthwise.

Season the flour with salt and pepper. Place in a small bowl.

Put milk into a small bowl.

Roll each egg half in the flour then in the milk and then into the oat mixture. Press it on with your hands so it will stay. Repeat until all the eggs are coated. Place eggs into a buttered baking pan. Place in a preheated 400 degree oven for 10 to 12 minutes or until they are heated through.

To make the Mustard Cream Sauce:

Place cream into a heavy saucepan or skillet. Add whole grain mustard. Stir and bring to a boil. Reduce heat and simmer stirring occasionally until it reduces to a sauce consistency. Spoon the sauce onto the center of warmed plates. Arrange four egg halves on top of the sauce on each plate, cut side down. Garnish with minced parsley around the edge of plates.

This is a wonderfully delicious brunch dish, a little time consuming, but worth every minute.

The credit for this dish goes to Scott Fitzgerald again. Thank you, Scotty!

Vegetable Hash

Cut into 1-inch cubes equal parts of the following vegetables. Keep each one separate.

Zucchini
Yellow Summer Squash
Eggplant
Spanish Onions
Carrots
Sweet Potatoes

Half the amount of Mushrooms, sliced
Butter, Melt in a large skillet, amount according to the quantity of vegetables
Salt, white and black pepper, and thyme.

Sauté onions in the butter. Add the squashes and eggplant, then mushrooms. Sauté just until cooked through. Place into colander to drain, *reserving* the liquid.

In the meantime, place carrots in one pot and sweet potatoes in another. The cooking times are different for each of these, so cook them separately. Cook until tender. Drain, reserving the liquid. In one of the pots, combine all the reserved liquids. Bring to a boil, lower heat, continue to simmer until the liquid has reduced to a thick syrup. Mix all of the well-drained veggies and the syrup together in a large mixing bowl.

Adjust the seasoning to your own taste. Place into a large skillet. Continue to sauté until all the moisture is evaporated.

This is another original from Beverly's Kitchen and has become a very popular item for our catered brunches. It's great topped with poached eggs. You can make a small quantity for home use. I suggest you don't use any of the cabbage family veggies as they are rather strong and they cook up too quickly. It is rather time consuming but well worth it if you're looking for something a little different.

Whole Wheat Apple Walnut Pancakes

2 cups Wheat Flour
½ cup Flour
¼ cup Brown Sugar
½ tsp Salt
1 tbs Baking Powder
1 tsp Baking Soda
2 cups Milk

1 tsp Vanilla
2 Egg
½ cup Walnuts, diced medium
2 cups Apple, peeled and shredded
¼ cup Vegetable Oil or Melted
    Butter

Sift dry ingredients together into a mixing bowl. In a smaller bowl, combine eggs, vanilla and milk. Add wet ingredients to the dry and stir to combine. Fold in apples and walnuts. Gently combine the oil or butter with the batter. Bake on a hot griddle that has been brushed with melted butter or oil. When bubbles form on the surface, gently turn them over. The pancake is done when the underside is golden brown.

Serve with warm maple syrup.

All in One Christmas Breakfast Biscuit

1 ¼ cup Flour
⅔ cup Sugar
½ cup Grape Nuts® Cereal
1 tsp Baking Powder
½ lb Bacon, cooked crisp and
    crumbled

½ lb Butter, soft
1 Egg
1 tbs Frozen Orange Juice
    Concentrate
1 tbs Orange Rind, grated

Mix flour, sugar, grape nuts and baking powder. Add bacon, butter, egg, orange juice and rind. Mix well. Drop by level tablespoons 2 inches apart onto a ungreased cookie sheet. Bake 10 to 12 minutes. Yields 2½ doz.

Thank you to daughter, Kimberlie, for this interesting, tasty morsel.

The Christmas biscuit maker daughter Kimberlie
and granddaughter Abigail

Apple Nut Bread

3 Eggs
1 cup Vegetable Oil
1 cup Sugar
1 cup Honey
2 cups Apples, grated course
1½ cup White Flour
1½ cup Wheat Flour

1 tsp Baking Powder
1 tsp Salt
1½ tsp Baking Soda
2 tsp Cinnamon
½ tsp Nutmeg
1 cup Raisins (optional)
1 cup Walnut pieces (optional)

Sift dry ingredients together and set aside. In the large bowl of your mixer, place the eggs, oil, sugar and honey. Beat until very creamy. Add the grated apples and mix just to blend. Add the flour mixture and mix until all is blended. Place into 1 large, or 2 medium size loaf pans that have been brushed with *Pan Grease*. Bake in preheated 350 degree oven for 35 to 45 minutes or until a toothpick comes out clean when inserted in the center of the loaf. Remove from oven and cool on cooling rack for 10 minutes. Remove from pan and cool on rack before wrapping or eat immediately.

Sour Cream Blueberry Bread

4 cups Flour
1 tsp Baking Soda
1 tsp Salt
½ lb Butter
2 cups Sugar
4 Eggs

2 cups Bananas, ripe,
    mashed or processed
1 cup Sour Cream
2 cups Blueberries
1 cup Pecans, chopped

Prepare 10-inch round tube pan or 2 loaf pans by brushing them generously with *Pan Grease*. Mix dry ingredients, except the sugar, together and set aside. Cream sugar and butter together then add eggs and continue to cream until light in color. Add the dry ingredients alternately with the sour cream and bananas mixing well after each addition. Fold in the blueberries and pecans. If you use frozen blueberries, stir them in very quickly as the color melting into the batter will turn it a very ugly gray and they will take longer to cook. If you use fresh blueberries, stir in gently to prevent them from breaking up. Pour into prepared pans and place them in 350 degree preheated oven. Bake for 45 to 50 minutes depending on size of breads.

Check for doneness before removing from oven. Cool on rack for 10 minutes before removing from pan.

This recipe came from *The American Breadbook* and it is very moist which makes it a great keeper.

Banana Bread

¾ cup Sugar
½ cup Oil
2 Eggs
1 cup Banana, mashed
  or processed

1½ cup Flour
2 tsp Baking Powder
½ tsp Baking Soda
½ tsp Salt
½ cup Walnut pieces (optional)

Sift the dry ingredients together and set aside. In bowl of mixer, place the sugar, eggs and oil. Beat until frothy. Add bananas and blend thoroughly. Fold in the dry ingredients just until blended. Place the batter in a loaf pan that has been brushed with **Pan Grease**. Bake in preheated 325 degree oven for 45 minutes or until toothpick comes out clean when inserted in center of loaf.

My father used this recipe when I was a child. I remember thinking it was the best thing I had ever tasted. I'm not sure where he got it but by the looks of the tattered page I am copying from, it's been used a lot.

❈

Biscuits

2 cups Flour
1 tsp Salt
3½ tsp Baking Powder

½ cup Crisco® (any other shortening
  does not work for me)
¾ cup Milk

Place the dry ingredients into a bowl and stir just to mix. Add Crisco® and rub between hands to form sheets of shortening. This helps to create flaky biscuits. Rub until all the shortening is worked in. Add milk. Stir with either wooden spoon or a rubber spatula, until flour is mixed in. Turn out onto a lightly floured worktable. Pat out to 1½-inches-thick and then fold into thirds. Pat out again and repeat 2 times. This also creates flaky biscuits. Do not overwork, as it will make the biscuits tough. Cut with floured round cutter. Place onto baking pan just touching each other. Brush the tops with either cream or milk. This helps the tops to brown more evenly. Bake in preheated 400 degree oven for 15 to 20 minutes or until golden brown. Remove from oven and serve immediately with my homemade **Orange Marmalade** or **Raspberry Butter**. These can also be served with sausage gravy, fried chicken or whatever you like.

When I lived in Alabama, a friend of mine, who had 8 children and lived in a trailer, (back then it was called a trailer not a mobile home) taught me how to make these biscuits. She didn't measure a thing and that's the way I learned but, when I opened Beverly's Specialty Foods, I had to write down all the recipes I had in my head. That was not an easy thing to do.

When my children were small if I had any biscuits left over from the night before, I would split them in half, butter each half, sprinkle each half with cinnamon and sugar, place them under the broiler for a few minutes and bingo have instant little coffee cakes. They loved them then and they still do.

Boston Brown Bread

This is a large recipe but will freeze very well and even keep unfrozen in the refrigerator quite well. You will need six 1-lb coffee cans.

6 cups Buttermilk	3 cups Corn Meal, I always use
6 Eggs	yellow but I suppose you could
2¼ cups Molasses	use white
1½ cups Vegetable Oil	2 tbs Baking Soda
5 cups Whole Wheat Flour	1 tbs Salt
1 cup White Flour	3 cups Dark Raisins

Prepare coffee cans by brushing them very generously with **Pan Grease**.

Combine all the dry ingredients and set aside. Place the eggs, molasses, buttermilk and oil into a bowl and mix with whisk until completely incorporated. Add the flour mixture in several additions, mixing well after each addition. Stir in raisins. Divide the batter equally into the 6 coffee cans. Cover each can with foil and tie or tape the foil down so the steam can't escape. Place the coffee cans into a pan large enough to hold them and add hot water to come up about halfway on the cans. Place in 325 degree preheated oven and bake about 2½ to 3 hours. Remove from oven and cool for 10 minutes before removing from cans. If it seems to be difficult to remove the breads, open the bottom end of the can with a can opener and push the bread out.

This bread is so worth the effort and time it takes to make it. It's one of my favorite sweet breads. I'm really not sure where I got this recipe, but I think I combined several and this was the outcome. You are going to love it, too.

Breadsticks and Baguettes

½ cup Whole Wheat Flour
6 cups White Flour
1 tbs Salt
2 cups Warm Water
1 tbs Sugar

1½ tbs Yeast
2 tbs Vegetable Oil
Garlic Salt
Kosher Salt
Parmesan Cheese

Dissolve sugar and salt in warm water. Add yeast and stir to moisten. Allow to set until the yeast starts to form a sponge. In the meantime, measure the flours into the bowl of mixer. Add the sponge to the flours along with the oil and mix with dough hook on low speed for 8 minutes. Place in a lightly oiled bowl, cover with plastic wrap, place in a warm place and allow to double in bulk. Remove plastic wrap, work down with hands and knead for a minute or two. Replace plastic and return to warm spot allowing it to rise again. To make breadsticks, when double in bulk, divide the dough into two pieces. Place onto a floured surface and form into a rectangle. Let stand for 8 to 10 minutes. Roll dough out to about ¾-inch-thick then cut into 5-inch long by 1-inch wide strips. Place onto a baking sheet that has been lined with parchment paper. Cover lightly and allow strips to rise again until double in size. Very gently brush the top with olive oil then sprinkle with garlic powder and kosher salt. Place into a 400 degree preheated oven for 15 to 20 minutes or until the bread sticks are lightly browned. Remove from oven and sprinkle with parmesan cheese. Serve hot. They can be kept in the freezer and re-heated as needed.

To make baguettes, divide the dough into thirds. On a lightly floured surface, form each piece of dough into a baguette form. Place onto a baking sheet that has been sprinkled with cornmeal. Place pan in a warm spot and allow loaves to rise until double in bulk. Very gently, brush the surface with beaten egg white. With a very sharp knife, make three slashes diagonally across the loaf. Place into a 375 degree oven and bake for 20 to 25 minutes or until golden brown and crispy.

Years ago, our family went on a 2-week cruise on the QE2. My daughter Tammy's favorite thing for breakfast was their *French toast*. They made it with baguettes cut diagonally about an inch thick. They marinated them and then coated each piece with sugar twin for her because she was diabetic. That process stayed with me, so when I opened Beverly's I used the same procedure, except I didn't coat the *French Toast* with sugar twin. I did, however, make my own baguettes using this recipe. [Look in the Breakfast Chapter for the *French toast* recipe.] Then I went in a different direction using the same dough for bread sticks, which we served with the salads and specials.

This is a great recipe but because there are no preservatives in it, the shelf life is not very long, but they can be wrapped and frozen successfully.

❋

Chocolate Zucchini Bread

½ cup Vegetable Oil
1¾ cup Sugar
2 Eggs
2½ cups White Flour
4 tbs Cocoa
½ tsp Baking Powder
1 tsp Baking Soda

1 tsp Cinnamon
1 tsp Cloves
1 tsp Vanilla
½ cup Sour Cream
2 cups Zucchini, grated course and
   squeeze out the excess liquid
½ cup Chocolate Chips

Prepare 2 loaf pans by brushing them with **Pan Grease.** Mix dry ingredients together and set aside. Beat the eggs, sugar and oil together until creamy, then add the flour mixture gradually with the sour cream and vanilla. Mix well after each addition. Fold in the zucchini. Mix well and pour into prepared pans. Sprinkle chocolate chips on top. Bake in 350 degree oven for 35 to 45 minutes. Check for doneness before removing from oven.

When I came to Saratoga, some 15 years ago, I needed something to do so I looked in the Saratogian and found an announcement for a Katrina Trask Garden Club meeting. I went and was graciously accepted. Later some of us broke away and started the Heritage Garden Club. When I got involved with Beverly's Specialty Foods, I resigned, but, I'll always remember some of those women. One of them was Lottie who gave me this recipe. Try it! It's great! Now that I'm retired maybe I should go back to the Garden Club.

❊

Cinnamon Rolls

½ cup Mashed Potatoes
¼ cup Butter, melted
¼ cup Sugar
¼ tsp Salt
½ cup Milk
½ tsp Vanilla

1 tsp Yeast
2–3 cups Flour
1 Egg
1 cup Raisins (optional)
1 cup Pecans (optional)

To prepare pan, brush a square or rectangular pan generously with **Pan Grease**. Sprinkle about ¼-inch of brown sugar on the bottom, then enough water just to dampen the sugar. This gives you the syrup on the bottom of the cinnamon roll. At this point, you should add the nuts, if desired. Heat milk, cool to body temperature. Add sugar, salt, vanilla and yeast. Stir until dissolved, then let stand to allow yeast to begin to work. Add egg, potato, butter and 2 cups of the flour. Stir until smooth and elastic. Continue to add flour until it is no longer sticky. The dough will be soft but shouldn't be sticky. Turn out onto floured work service and continue to knead until very smooth. Oil bowl and place dough into bowl then turn oiled side up. Cover with plastic wrap, then a clean kitchen towel. Place in a warm place to rise. When double in size, punch down, Let rest for 10 minutes. Turn out onto floured work surface again and roll into rectangular shape about ½-inch thick. Sprinkle with butter mixture, and raisins, if desired. Roll up like jelly roll starting at edge closest to you. Roll away from you but not too tight. Slice into 1½-inch pieces and place cut side up onto prepared pan. Let rise until doubled in size again. Bake in preheated 375 degree oven for about 20 minutes or until golden brown on top. Remove from oven to cooling rack for 3 or 4 minutes. Turn upside down onto a baking pan that is lined with waxed paper to catch the syrup. If syrup runs off return it to the bottom of the roll until it cools and stays on

✳

Butter Mixture:

½ lb Butter
1½ tsp Cinnamon

1¾ cup Brown Sugar
½ cup Flour

Mix the flour, cinnamon and sugar together. Work in the butter until crumbly.

If you want to ice the top of these, omit the sugar and water on the bottom of the pan in the beginning. Turn out of pan. Turn upright and when cool spread with powdered sugar glaze.

✳

Powdered Sugar Glaze

1½ cups Powdered Sugar
1 tsp Corn Syrup
½ tsp Vanilla

Half and Half (enough to
bring to a drizzling
consistency)

Stir all together and drizzle over cooled cinnamon rolls.

The potatoes and egg in this dough gives the finished product a very soft texture. I have always loved working with dough, yeast or otherwise. Therefore, it is fun for me to experiment with it. I think you will like this recipe very much. In can be increased at no risk.

Cinnamon bun fans–grandchildren Zachary and Abigail.

Raisin-Pecan Cinnamon Rolls

This recipe is a little different than the other one. It's equally as soft but does not require potatoes.

4½ to 5cups Flour
1 pkg Dry Yeast
1 cup Milk
⅓ cup Butter
⅓ cup Sugar
½ tsp Salt
3 Eggs
¾ cup Brown Sugar

¼ cup Flour
1 tbs Cinnamon
½ cup Raisins, light or dark,
or diced apples
½ cup Pecans
1 tbs Half and Half
1 recipe Powdered Sugar Glaze

In a large mixer bowl combine 2½ cups flour and the yeast. In small saucepan heat milk, butter, sugar and salt just till warm and the butter is melted, stirring constantly. Add to the flour mixture along with the eggs. Beat with an electric mixer on low speed for 30 seconds, scraping sides of bowl constantly. Beat on high speed for 3 minutes. Using a wooden spoon, stir in as much of the remaining flour as you can.

Turn dough out onto a lightly floured surface. Knead in enough of the remaining flour to make a moderately soft dough that is smooth and elastic, 3 to 5 minutes. Shape into a ball and place into a lightly oiled bowl, turning once. Cover and allow to rise in a warm place until the dough has doubled in size.

In another bowl combine the following cutting in the butter until the mixture is the consistency of course cornmeal:

¾ cup Brown Sugar
¼ cup Flour
½ cup Butter

Prepare 13×9×2-inch baking pan by brushing liberally with *Pan Grease.* Punch the dough down. Place the dough onto the floured work surface and allow to rest for 10 minutes. Roll the dough out to a 12-inch square. Sprinkle the dough with the above mixture, raisins and pecans. Roll up as jelly roll starting with the side closest to you. Don't roll too tightly, as the cinnamon rolls will pop up in the center during baking. Slice dough into 1½ inch slices. Arrange in prepared pan, cut side. Cover loosely with plastic wrap and allow to rise, in a warm place, until double in size (about 45 minutes). Brush with half-and-half. Bake in preheated 375 degree oven for 25 to 30 minutes or until golden brown. Remove rolls from oven. Cool just a minute. Place a wire rack on top of pan and carefully turn both at the same time to invert the rolls onto the rack. Cool slightly. Invert again onto a serving platter. Drizzle with *Powdered Sugar Glaze* found in *Cinnamon Rolls* recipe.

❋

Corn Bread

2 cups Corn Meal	3 Eggs
3 cups Flour	3 cups Milk
2 tbs + 1 tsp Baking Powder	½ cup Vegetable Oil
1 tsp Salt	¼ cup Jalapenos (optional)
¼ cup Sugar	

Mix dry ingredients together, add the remaining ingredients and stir to combine.

Pour batter into an iron skillet that has been preheated on stovetop with an additional ⅛ cup veggie oil. Place hot skillet and batter into preheated 400 degree oven until golden brown on top (about 15 minutes). Remove from oven and turn upside down onto a serving plate. The bottom will be very crisp and delicious.

I learned this method of cooking cornbread in the south. It's not as sweet and cakey as other cornbread recipes. I especially enjoy this type with greens and beans. It also makes great corn sticks. If you have cast iron corn stick pans, you can use the same method.

❋

Orange Cranberry Walnut Bread

1 cup Cranberries, chopped	1 tsp Salt
½ cup Walnuts, chopped	½ tsp Baking Powder
4 tbs Orange Rind	⅓ cup Butter, melted
2 cups Flour	¾ cup Orange Juice
1 cup Sugar	1 Egg
1½ tsp Baking Soda	

Brush 9×5×3-inch loaf pan with **Pan Grease.** In a bowl big enough to mix all, place the flour, sugar, baking powder, salt and baking soda. Cut in the butter. (Rub it together as if you were making pie dough). Stir in orange juice, egg and orange peel just to moisten. Fold in cranberries and nuts and spoon into prepared pan. Bake in 350 degree preheated oven for 45 minutes to 1 hour.

This recipe is right off the package of Ocean Spray cranberries and is the best cranberry bread recipe I have tried.

Cranberry Zucchini Bread

1 cup Zucchini, shredded course	½ tsp Baking Powder
1 cup Cranberries, chopped	3 cups Flour, if desired use ½ whole wheat and ½ white
2½ cups Sugar	
1 cup Vegetable Oil	½ cup Nuts, chopped medium (it doesn't matter what kind but pecan are good in this)
3 Eggs	
2 tsp Baking Soda	
1 tsp Salt	

Prepare 2 loaf pans by brushing them with **Pan Grease**. Mix dry ingredients together and set aside. In the bowl of mixer, place the sugar, eggs and oil and mix until creamy. Stir in the cranberries and zucchini. Add the flour mixture gradually, mixing well after each addition. Fold in nuts and spoon into prepared pans. Bake in 350 degree preheated oven for 45 to 50 minutes. Check the doneness by inserting a toothpick into center of each loaf. If it comes out clean, it is done. Remove from oven and cool on rack for 10 minutes before removing from pans.

I created this recipe just to have one a little different from just zucchini or just cranberry. It is quite tasty.

Date and Nut Bread

8 oz Dates, pitted and chopped
1½ cups Boiling water, pour over
   prepared dates and let stand
2¾ cup White Flour
1 tsp Baking Powder
1½ tsp Baking Soda

1 tsp Salt
1 Egg
1 cup Sugar
4 tbs Butter
1 tsp Vanilla
1 cup Walnuts

Prepare large loaf pan by brushing generously with **Pan Grease**. Stir dry ingredients, except the sugar, together and set aside. Cream the sugar and butter together, add the egg and continue to cream until light in color. Add the cooled date mixture and the vanilla then mix well. Add the flour mixture and stir until well blended. Stir in the nuts, spoon into prepared pan and bake in preheated 350 degree oven for 40 to 45 minutes. Check for doneness by inserting toothpick into center of bread. If it comes out clean, the bread is done.

If you like dates, you will love this bread. It's a great holiday season treat.

Dill Rolls

2 oz Sugar
1 oz Onion, grated
½ oz Salt
¼ cup Oil
1 oz Dill Weed
2 Eggs

1 tbs Horseradish
2 tbs Dry Yeast
3 cups Warm Milk
3 lbs Flour
Cream
Kosher Salt

Dissolve the yeast in the warm milk with 1 tbs of the sugar. The sugar helps to activate the yeast. Place all the dry ingredients together in the bowl of a mixer with the dough hook in place. Stir to combine. Add the remaining ingredients, except 1 cup of the flour. Turn mixer on low to blend, then, increase the speed for 5 minutes. Add flour until the dough is not sticky. (You want it soft but not sticky.)

If you don't have a mixer with a dough hook, mix by hand with wooden spoon until the dough gets too stiff to continue, then, finish with your hands by turning it out onto a floured work surface and continue to knead until the dough is very smooth and elastic. Place into an oiled bowl turning once. Cover with plastic wrap, place in a warm spot and let rise until double in bulk. Punch down, oil lightly, cover and let rise again. When double in size again, shape dough into round balls about the size of a golf ball or into oval shapes. Place onto a greased baking sheet about 2 inches apart. Cover and let rise until double the size. Very lightly brush the surface with cream, sprinkle with kosher salt and slash diagonally about ¼-inch deep. Put baking sheets into a preheated 350 degree oven for 12 to 15 minutes. Serve hot. These can be reheated very nicely.

When my youngest son Rob attended the New England Culinary Institute, this recipe was one he had to prepare. I have learned a lot from him and I like to think he has learned a lot from me too. Thank you Rob and NECI.

Irish Soda Bread by Aggie

4 cups Flour	1 tsp Baking Powder
6 tbs Crisco	1¾ cup Buttermilk
2 tbs Sugar	1 cup Dark Raisins
1 tsp Salt	2 tbs Caraway Seeds
1½ tsp Baking Soda	

Sift the dry ingredients together. Add the shortening and work with hands until it has disappeared. Add the raisins and caraway seeds. Stir to combine. Add the buttermilk and stir until all the ingredients have been worked together. Turn out onto floured working surface. Knead 10 times. Divide the dough into 2 or 4 equal pieces, depending on how big you want the loaves. Form into balls and place onto greased baking sheet. Cut an × on the top of each loaf and place pan into a preheated 350 degree oven. Bake for 50 to 60 minutes until golden brown or when the bottom is tapped and it sounds hollow.

A very good Irish friend, Aggie Laub, from Fleischmanns, NY, gave this recipe to me. Her husband, Milt, was also Irish and a retired firefighter from New York City. They hosted some really good St Patrick's Day parties at their house. She and I became friends when I went to work at Roxbury Run Restaurant, where she was employed at the time. Her oldest child, Danny, and my youngest child, Melissa, are the same age. We don't see much of each other, since I moved away from that area, but when we do, it's like we've never been apart. She is now employed by the New York State Education Department as Director of Mathematics in a West Chester County school. Thank you, Aggie, for this recipe. I hope you don't mind being in print.

Melissa and Danny

45

Muffins—Carrot

2½ cups Vegetable Oil
3 cups Brown Sugar
8 Eggs
1 cup Molasses
4½ cups White Flour
1 cup Whole Wheat Flour
3 tsp Baking Powder

4 tsp Baking Soda
1½ tsp Salt
4 tsp Cinnamon
2 lbs Carrots, peeled and shredded
  fine
1 cup each Raisins, Coconut and
  Walnuts

This recipe makes 24 very large muffins but could be cut in half. Prepare muffin pans by brushing cups and top surface with *Pan Grease*. Sift the flours, salt, baking powder, baking soda and the cinnamon together and set aside. Place eggs, brown sugar, oil and molasses into mixer bowl, then mix until very creamy. Add the dry ingredients. Mix thoroughly. Add the shredded carrots and combine until totally incorporated. Add the raisins, coconut and walnuts, and mix to combine well. If you don't have a large mixer you will either have to finish mixing this by hand or cut the recipe in half, which would work just fine. The batter will keep in the refrigerator for 2 or 3 days also. Place batter into prepared muffin pans by filling about ¾ full. Place into preheated 425 degree oven for 10 minutes. Reduce heat to 375 degrees. At this point, you should rotate the pan and continue baking for about 15 minutes longer or until top on muffin responds to touch by springing back. When baked remove from oven and cool in pan for 10 minutes. Remove from pan to a cooling rack. Serve warm. These freeze very well in an airtight container also.

Years ago when I started adding a variety of muffins to our bakery list, I bought a bucket of "Scoop and Bake Glorious Morning Muffin" batter. They didn't taste too bad but I thought I could make them much better and less expensively. So, I did just that. I got out my carrot cake recipe, which I had perfected for the Old Bryan Inn, and added some other ingredients, took some away and finally came up with this recipe for Carrot Muffins. I think they are excellent and I'm sure you will too.

❈

Muffins—Corn

1½ cup White Flour
½ cup Yellow Corn Meal
1½ tbs Baking Powder
½ tsp Salt
⅓ cup Sugar
1 cup Milk
1 Egg

½ cup Vegetable Oil
1 Jalapeno (optional)
¼ cup Cheddar, shredded (optional)
¼ cup Corn (optional)
¼ cup Red Pepper, diced (optional)
1 cup Blueberries (optional)

Prepare muffin pan by brushing the entire top and cups with *Pan Grease*.

Sift dry ingredients together into a larger bowl. In a smaller bowl, combine the egg, oil and milk. Add the egg mixture to the dry ingredients and stir just to combine. At this point, you could add the corn, jalapenos, peppers and cheese, *or* the blueberries, depending on what flavor you desire. Divide batter into prepared muffin pan. Place pan into 375 degree preheated oven. Bake for 15 to 18 minutes. Let stand for 5 minutes and remove to rack to cool.

This is just a basic cornbread recipe but it's tasty. Try the options. Serve the jalapeno and cheddar variety with chili.

❋

Muffins—Bran Raisin

1¼ cups White Flour	1½ cups Milk
½ cup Sugar	2 Eggs
4 tsps Baking Powder	¾ cup Vegetable Oil
¼ tsp Salt	1 Orange, grated rind of
2 cups All Bran® Cereal	1 cup Raisins

Pour milk over bran and let set to absorb and soften. Prepare muffin pan by brushing with **Pan Grease**. Brush even the top of the pan, in case the muffins rise over the cup, or use muffin papers. Sift together flour, sugar, baking powder and salt. Set aside. In large bowl, combine softened bran mixture, egg and oil. Beat well. Add flour mixture, stirring only until combined. Add raisins and the orange rind and stir lightly. To obtain a very light, tender muffin, stir as little as possible but still combine ingredients. Don't *ever* beat your muffin batter. Portion batter evenly into muffin cups. I like to fill them almost to the top for a big full muffin. If there is an empty cup left in the pan, place a couple of ice cubes in the cup to prevent the pan from getting too hot in that area. Place the pan in a 400 degree preheated oven for 10 minutes. Reduce the heat to 350 degrees to finish the baking process. (The high heat to start gives the muffins a hot shot to rise quickly in the beginning and then the reduced heat allows a more even baking throughout.)

This is basically the recipe from the box of All Bran® but I have altered it to make a lighter, more moist muffin and the bit of orange adds a lot. If you like bran muffins, you will love this recipe.

❋

Muffins—Blueberry or Apple Walnut

4 Eggs
2 cups Brown Sugar
1½ cup Vegetable Oil
3 tsp Vanilla
½ tsp Nutmeg [for Apple Walnut use also 2 tsp Cinnamon]
1½ tsp Salt
2 cups Half and Half or Heavy Cream

4½ cups White Flour
1 cup Whole Wheat Flour
3 tbs Baking Powder
3 cups Blueberries, frozen [or Diced Apples]
1 cup Walnuts [for apple walnut]
Crumb Topping

Prepare muffin pan by brushing the entire top and the cups with **Pan Grease**, or use muffin papers. Sift flours and baking powder together and set aside. In the bowl of mixer, place the eggs, brown sugar, oil, vanilla, salt and nutmeg. (Add cinnamon for apple walnut version). Mix until very creamy and light. Add the cream. Stir just to mix. Add the dry ingredients, mixing with spoon just until flour has disappeared. Do not over mix. Add the frozen blueberries. (do not thaw or you will have discolored batter), or the apples and walnuts. Fold in just until combined. Spoon batter into prepared pans. Top each muffin with crumb topping. Place on center rack of oven, which has been pre-heated to 425 degrees. Bake for 10 minutes, then reduce heat to 375, rotate muffin pan and continue to bake for another 15 to 18 minutes. Check for doneness before removing from oven. Place on a cooling rack and cool in pan for 10 minutes—no longer. Carefully remove the muffins from pan and allow to cool on rack or serve them immediately with your favorite jam and/or **Raspberry Butter**. These freeze very well in airtight containers.

Crumb Topping

1 cup each:
    Brown Sugar
    White Sugar

Flour
Oatmeal
Butter

Mix together with hands until butter has totally disappeared.

This is great on fruit pies. You can also add nuts, if you desire.

Muffins—Cooked Oatmeal and Wheat Germ

4 Eggs
2 cups Brown Sugar
1½ cup Vegetable Oil
2 tsp Vanilla
2 cups Half and Half or Heavy
   Cream
1½ cups Oatmeal, cooked (a great
   way to use up left over oatmeal)

1 tsp Cinnamon
1½ tsp Salt
1 cup Whole Wheat Flour
1 cup Wheat Germ
3 cups White Flour
3 tbs Baking Powder

Prepare muffin pans by brushing the cups and the top of pan with **Pan Grease** or using muffins papers. Sift dry ingredients together and set aside. In bowl of mixer, place the eggs, brown sugar and the oil. Beat until it is very creamy. Add the oatmeal and mix until incorporated. Add the vanilla and the cream and combine. Add dry ingredients and mix just until dry ingredients have disappeared. Do not over mix or you will get a tough muffin. Place in prepared muffin pans. Bake in a 350 degree oven for 20 to 25 minutes.

When my son, Mark, visited the West Coast, he frequented a little cafe called Cafe Beaujolais. He said it reminded him of my place, Beverly's Specialty Foods. He bought two cookbooks for me and one of them is "Morning Food-Cafe Beaujolais". This recipe isn't directly from that cookbook but some of the ideas that went into it are. I have never been to the restaurant but if you ever get to Mendocino, CA look it up. I certainly will.

Muffins—Oatmeal

1⅓ cup Flour
1 cup Oats, uncooked
½ cup Brown Sugar
1 tbs Baking Powder
½ tsp Salt

1 tsp Cinnamon
1 cup Milk
1 Egg
4 tbs Vegetable Oil
1 cup Blueberries (optional)

Prepare muffin pan by brushing the cups and top of pan or use muffin papers.
   Combine the dry ingredients and set aside. Mix the egg, milk and oil in a small bowl. Add the egg mixture to the dry ingredients. Stir just to incorporate. Fold in the blueberries. Divide into medium size muffin cups. Place pan into preheated 425 degree oven for 10 minutes. Reduce the temperature to 350 for the remaining 10 to 12 minutes. You can sprinkle the top with **Crumb Topping** before baking, if desired.

Muffins—Vegetable and Cheese

2 cups Flour
2 tbs Sugar
1 tsp Salt
1½ tbs Baking Powder
½ cup Vegetable Oil
1 Egg

1 cup Milk
½ cup Vegetables of your choice, diced
¼ cup Cheddar, Swiss, Mozzarella or cottage cheese
¼ tsp Dill Weed (optional)

Prepare muffin pans by brushing very generously with **Pan Grease**, including the top of the pan or use muffin papers. In a large bowl, combine the dry ingredients. In a smaller bowl, whisk the milk, egg and oil together then add the veggies and cheese and stir to combine. Add the egg mixture to the dry ingredients and stir just to combine. Place into prepared muffin pans. Bake in 375 degree oven for about 15 to 20 minutes. Check for doneness before removing from oven. Allow to cool in pan for 10 minutes but no longer. Remove to cooling rack and serve while still warm.

Some combination suggestions:
    Zucchini, cottage cheese and dill
    Tomato, mozzarella and fresh basil
    Broccoli and cheddar
    Green beans and swiss
    Asparagus, mushroom and swiss

The combinations are endless. Just pick your favorite vegetables and put them in the muffin. This is a great muffin to serve with soup and salad for lunch.
    This is another original from Beverly's Kitchen.

My Father's Dark Bread

4½ cups White Flour
1 cup Whole Wheat Flour
½ cup Bran Cereal
½ cup Wheat Germ
¼ cup Molasses

2 cups Water, heated to 120 degrees
1 tbs Salt
2 tbs Sugar
1½ tbs Dry Yeast
¼ cup Vegetable Oil

Add the sugar, salt and yeast to 1 cup of the water, stir and allow to sit to form a sponge. Pour 1 cup water over the bran cereal, letting stand to soften.
    Place the white flour, whole wheat flour and the wheat germ in a large bowl. Stir to mix. Make a well in the center of the flour. Combine the yeast mixture, molasses, oil and the cereal mixture. Gently pour that mixture into the well in the flour. Working with a

large wooden spoon, very gently stir the mixture pulling a little of the flour at a time, into the yeast mixture. Stir as you go until all is combined. When the mixture gets too stiff to work with spoon, knead with hands.

Place dough on floured work surface and continue to knead, adding flour as needed. Knead until dough is elastic and smooth but not sticky. Place in a lightly oiled bowl, turning once to oil the top. Cover with plastic wrap and a clean kitchen towel. Place in a warm spot to rise until double in size. Remove towel and plastic then knead 15 to 20 times. Turn dough over and cover as before. Let rise again until double, then repeat. The third time it rises, knead down again and let it rest for just 10 minutes. Shape into desired shapes and forms and place in, or on, greased baking pans. (If making dinner rolls, I like to form the balls a little smaller than golf balls, then place in pan about 1 inch apart so they will rise together.) Cover and allow to rise to double the size. Place pans of formed dough into preheated 375 degree oven. Bake until nicely browned (about 18 to 20 minutes depending on the size of the loaves). Thump the bottom of the loaf. If it sounds hollow, it is done. Remove from pans onto a cooling rack. Allow to cool completely before covering or placing in bags.

When I was a child, my father always made bread. This was one of his recipes and oh, how we loved it! Sometimes he would put raisins in it also. It's a very heavy bread but so tasty.

❋

Regular Nut or Poppy Seed Rolls

10 cups Flour	½ cup Lukewarm Water
1 cup Sugar	½ cups Milk
2 tsp Salt	2 cups Sour Cream
6 Eggs, YOLKS ONLY	½ lb Butter or Margarine
2 tsp Sugar	3 pkgs Dry Yeast or 2 oz cake yeast

Dissolve 2 tsp. sugar and yeast in lukewarm water. Allow to set until it rises.

Measure flour, then sift. Add 1 cup sugar, salt and butter and work as for pie dough until it's the consistency of course corn meal. Beat egg yolks. Add sour cream and milk to egg yolk, then add this to dry ingredients. Mix very well, then place onto a floured worktable and knead until dough is very smooth and totally incorporated. Divide dough into 6 equal balls. They should weigh about 13 oz. each. Lightly oil each ball and place onto a lightly oiled pan. Cover and chill overnight, or 5 hours, in the refrigerator.

Nut Filling

⅔ cup Boiling Water   1 lb Walnuts, ground fine
1½ cup Sugar   1 tsp Butter

Mix all ingredients together, then cool enough to spread onto prepared dough.

After dough has chilled, remove from fridge. Working with one ball at a time, place onto a floured work surface and roll out to a ⅓-inch-thick into a rectangular shape. Spread dough with the nut filling. Starting with edge closest to you, roll as a jellyroll, away from you. Don't roll too tight as the filling will come out and the roll itself will bake curved. Slash diagonally across the top of each roll about ⅓ to ½-inch deep. This allows the steam to release and give a more even baking. Repeat with all the dough balls. Place them at least 4 to 5 inches apart onto a baking sheet. Place into preheated 375 degree oven for about 20 minutes. When they are golden brown and sound hollow when tapped on bottom, remove from oven. Brush the top of each roll with melted butter and place the rolls onto a cooling rack.

You may also fill these with a Poppy, Apricot, Cheese or Prune filling.

Cheese Filling

1½ lb Cream Cheese   1 Orange, Grated rind of
2 tsp Vanilla   ¼ cup Sugar

Blend all together for small Danish. This wouldn't work in the larger rolls.

Poppy Seed Filling

½ cup Poppy Seeds, ground   2 Egg Yolks
¼ cup Milk   2 tsp Lemon Juice
⅓ cup Brown Sugar   1 tsp Vanilla
2 tbs Butter

Place the poppy seeds in top of double boiler. Add the milk and bring mixture to a boil. Remove pan from heat. Add brown sugar and butter. Mix well. Place the pan OVER, not in, the hot water. Add the egg yolks, stirring constantly until the mixture thickens. Remove from heat. Add the lemon juice and vanilla. Mix thoroughly. Allow to cool slightly before using on the pastry. This can be used in small pastries or the larger rolls.

Prune or Apricot Filling

1 cup Prunes or Apricots, cooked   4 to 6 tbs Butter
   according to package directions   4 tsps Orange Rind, grated

Combine all together for use in small pastries or larger rolls.

To make small pastry type treats, after rolling the dough out, cut into 2½-inch squares. Place a teaspoon of your favorite filling on the center of each square. Bring opposite corners into the center and push down to close. Bake for 10 or 12 minutes. Remove from oven and brush with butter.

These are great for special breakfasts or brunches

Some thirty years ago, we lived on a farm in Saltsburg, PA. We certainly were not farmers; we just occupied the house and loved it. The country is such a great place to raise a family except the children had to walk quite a distance to catch the school bus. At the end of the lane, lived The Duncan family. They had 5 or 6 sons who were the same age as some of our children. They all worked hard on that farm but Mrs. Duncan had a second job at a local supermarket as a baker. One holiday she gave us a Nut Roll, which I thought, was just about the best thing I had ever tasted. I asked her for the recipe and this is what I got. I have used it many times, especially on holidays. I used to sell them at Beverly's Specialty Foods, at Easter and Christmas. What is it about those two holidays that makes a person want all these wonderfully rich foods? If you try this, you will love it!

Orange Walnut Bread

2½ cups Flour
1¼ cups Sugar
1 tsp Baking Powder
½ tsp Baking Soda
½ tsp Salt
2 Eggs

1½ sticks Butter or Margarine, melted
½ cup Orange Juice
2 tbs Orange Peel, grated fine
2 tbs Water
1 cup Walnuts, chopped medium

Mix dry ingredients together in a bowl that is large enough to hold all ingredients. Combine eggs, melted butter, orange juice, orange peel and water in a separate bowl, then add all at once to flour mixture. Stir quickly until dry ingredients are moistened. Stir in walnuts. Turn into prepared 9×5×3-inch loaf pan that has been brushed with **Pan Grease** (recipe in the Misc. Chapter). Bake in preheated 350 degree oven for 45 minutes to 1 hour or until a toothpick comes out clean when inserted into the center of loaf. Remove from oven and cool on rack for 10 minutes. Remove from pan and cool on wire rack, or serve warm.

Plain Ole White Bread

10 to 12 cups White Flour
2 tbs Salt
¼ cup Sugar

4 cups Warm Water, about 120
   degrees
2 tbs Dry Yeast
½ cup Vegetable Oil

Dissolve yeast and sugar in warm water. The sugar and warm water activates the yeast, however if the water is too hot, it will kill the yeast. Add salt and oil.

Place flour in large mixing bowl. Make a well in center, large enough to hold the liquid. Gently pour the liquid mixture into the well. With a wooden spoon, gently mix in the liquid, taking small amounts of flour from sides of well as you go. Mix until you can't mix with spoon any longer. Knead with hands until the dough is not sticky but still soft, adding a little flour as you go, (probably about 20 minutes). The dough should be very elastic and smooth. Remove dough from bowl. Scrape out any bits of dough. Lightly oil the bowl. Place the dough into bowl and turn once so the top is oiled. Cover with plastic wrap and a clean kitchen towel. Place in a warm spot to rise. When doubled in size, knead down 15 or 20 times until smooth again. Turn with smooth side up. Cover and allow to double in size again. Knead down, then let rest for 10 minutes. Form into whatever shape loaf you desire. Place loaves into or on greased pans. At this point, my mother would always pierce the loaves with a fork to break any air bubbles that may be inside. Let rise until double in size. Place pans into preheated 350 degree oven for 20 to 30 minutes depending on the size of the loaf. They should be golden brown and sound hollow when thumped on bottom.

Bread Sticks

Use the above dough recipe. Work with about ¼ of it at a time. Place dough onto floured surface. Roll out to about ½ inch thick. Don't work the dough too much or the breadsticks will be tough. With a sharp knife cut the dough into strips 3 or 4-inches long by 1-inch wide. (Place the knife on the dough and press down—do not use a sawing motion.) Place sticks onto a greased baking sheet, just barely touching each other. Allow to rise until they are not quite double in size. *Gently* brush them with a good quality Olive Oil. Sprinkle with Kosher Salt, Garlic Powder and Parmesan Cheese. Bake in a preheated 350 degree oven for 15 minutes. They are delicious and freeze very well. Reheat in oven, NOT the microwave, before serving. As a matter of fact DON'T MICROWAVE *ANY* OF MY DOUGH PRODUCTS.

Dinner Rolls

Using recipe for "Plain Ole White Bread," shape the dough into golf ball size pieces. Place onto prepared baking sheet. Allow to rise until double in size. *Gently* brush the surface with a mixture of equal parts scrambled egg and cream. Sprinkle with Kosher Salt, Poppy Seeds or Sesame Seeds. They will be soft in the center and crusty on the outside, especially if you heat them just before serving.

Onion Rolls

Using the recipe for "Plain Ole White Bread", pinch off a golf ball size piece of dough. While forming the roll, enclose a tsp. of diced raw onions into the center. Make sure the onions are completely enclosed. If you want a larger roll than a dinner roll, use more dough. Place on greased baking pans about 2 inches apart. Allow to rise until double in size. Brush the top with egg mixture. Sprinkle top with dried onion flakes and bake in 350 degree oven for about 15 to 20 minutes.

This dough can also be used for pizza.

❋

Melissa and pizza, a natural combo

Scones

2 lbs Flour	1 lb Unsalted Butter, very cold
⅔ cup Sugar	1 tbs Orange Peel, grated fine
3 tbs Baking Powder	2 cups Buttermilk
1 tsp Baking Soda	2 cups Raisins, Currants or Frozen
½ tsp Salt	Blueberries

Place the dry ingredients into a large bowl. Stir just to mix. With the large side of a grater, shred the ice cold butter into the flour mixture a little at a time while continually covering the butter with flour to prevent it from sticking together. Work with hands until butter is in small pieces. If using currants or raisins add them with the orange rind and toss to coat the fruit with the dry mixture. Add the buttermilk and mix with a rubber scraper, just until the flour is absorbed. Turn out onto a lightly floured work table. Press dough out, with hands, to about 1½-inches-thick, then fold over into thirds. Press out again. Do this 3 times. Divide the dough into 3 equal parts. At this point, if you are making blueberry scones, you will want to press the dough out and place the frozen blueberries in one layer on the top of dough. Fold dough over to enclose the blueberries. Work as quickly as possible before the berries have a chance to defrost and discolor the dough. The blueberry version is a little more tricky than the others. Take one piece at a time and form it gently and quickly into a round. Place the round onto the lightly floured surface and pat out to 1-inch-thick. Cut into 8 equal wedges. Repeat with the remaining 2 balls. Place the wedges onto a baking sheet about 2 inches apart. Brush the top with cream, sprinkle with sugar and place pan into the preheated 425 degree oven for 10 minutes. Like the muffins, you'll want to give them a hot shot in the beginning and then reduce the heat to 375 degrees and continue to bake for another 10 to 15 minutes or until springy in the center.

Beverly making scones

Serve hot from the oven with homemade **Orange Marmalade** and **Raspberry Butter**.

I worked on this for years until I finally perfected my scones. They are light and fluffy inside and crisp on the outside. If you can't master it just keep trying or call me and I'll sell you some.

❋

Streusel Coffee Cake

¾ cup Sugar
½ cup Crisco® or Butter, softened
1 Egg
1½ cups Flour

2 tsp Baking Powder
½ tsp Salt
½ cup Milk

Prepare 8-inch pan by brushing with **Pan Grease**. Sift the flour, baking powder and salt together and set aside. Cream the sugar, egg and butter together until very light in color. Add the dry ingredients alternately with the milk. Combine well after each addition. Pour half of the batter into prepared pan. Top with half of the streusel mixture, then the remaining batter and then the remaining streusel mixture. You can also add fresh blueberries or apple slices between the layers. Bake in preheated 350 degree oven for 20 to 25 minutes.

Streusel Mixture

1 cup Brown Sugar
½ cup White Flour

¼ cup Butter, softened
1 tsp Cinnamon

Place all ingredients into bowl and mix with hands to combine making sure the butter is totally mixed in. You could mix in processor for a few seconds instead.

When I was expecting my second child, many years ago, we lived in a little apartment in a duplex in Baton Rouge, LA. I can still picture my next door neighbors, who were newlyweds. I don't remember their names, but I do remember this recipe came from her. I've used it all these years and it has been one of our family favorites and a favorite at Beverly's also.

❁

Sweet Potato Biscuits

1½ cups Sweet Potatoes, peeled,
   cooked and mashed
⅓ cup Sugar
1 tsp Salt

1 tbs Baking Powder
⅓ cup Crisco®
2¼ cup Flour
½ tsp White Pepper

Prepare sweet potatoes and set aside to cool. Lightly grease baking pan and set aside. In a separate bowl, mix the dry ingredients. Add the Crisco® and cut in with pastry cutter or 2 knives. Add the cooled sweet potatoes and mix with wooden spoon until all is incorporated. Turn dough out onto floured work surface and pat out. Then fold into thirds and pat out again. Pat or roll out to ½ to 1-inch thickness. Cut into rounds with a floured biscuit cutter. Place rounds onto prepared baking pan. Place in 375 degree preheated oven. Bake for 25 to 30 minutes.

   The moisture in the sweet potatoes substitutes for milk. These biscuits are a little heavy but very tasty. Serve them for breakfast, brunch or with a Roast Pork dinner.

❁

Walton's Mountain Coffee Bread

½ cup Pecans, halves or pieces

2, 15-oz pkgs Frozen White Dinner Rolls 18 to 24 (I like to cut the roll in half)

1 pkg Instant Butterscotch Pudding

1 cup Brown Sugar

½ cup Butter

½ tsp Cinnamon

Generously Grease a 10-inch bundt or tube pan with **Pan Grease**. Sprinkle pecans on bottom of pan. Arrange frozen dough balls on top of pecans. Sprinkle the pudding mix over balls. In saucepan, place the butter, brown sugar and cinnamon. Heat until the butter is melted. Mix well and pour over the dough balls. Cover and refrigerate 12 to 24 hours. Remove from refrigerator and allow to rise about an hour before baking. Uncover and bake in preheated 350 degree oven for about 30 minutes. Immediately invert the pan onto a large serving plate. Wait a few minutes before removing pan.

Serve warm with more butter. This is a beautiful bread and fairly easy to make.

My friend, Marlene McGrath, from Baltimore, MD gave me this recipe. Marlene and I have known each other for many years. We were friends when we lived in the Saltsburg, PA farmhouse. Our husbands were partners in a small newspaper in Blairsville, PA, *The Blairsville Dispatch*.

❉

Zucchini Bread

3 Eggs

1 cup Vegetable Oil

2 Sugar

1 Lemon, zest only

2 cups Zucchini, shredded course

2 tsp Cinnamon

1 tsp Salt

1 tsp Baking Soda

¼ tsp Baking Powder

3 cups Flour (white or ½ white and ½ whole wheat)

1 cup Walnuts, chopped med

Brush a 9×5×3-inch loaf pan with **Pan Grease**. In a bowl of mixer, beat the eggs until foamy. Gradually beat in oil and sugar. Beat until creamy. Add zucchini, lemon zest, cinnamon, salt, baking soda, baking powder and mix well. Gradually blend in flour, mixing well after each addition. Fold in chopped nuts. Turn into prepared pan. Bake in preheated 350 degree oven for 45 minutes to 1 hour.

This recipe came from the *Daily News*, (I'm not sure which one), many years ago. I've used it and used it and used it.

❉

Appetizers

Baby Red Potatoes filled with
Sour Cream and Caviar

Red Potatoes

Olive Oil

Aunt Jane's Crazy Salt®

Sour Cream

Caviar OR Chives

Use Red Potatoes no larger than a half dollar. Scrub to clean. Dry with paper towel. Place into bowl large enough for tossing. Drizzle ¼ cup good olive oil over all and toss to coat. Place onto baking pan large enough to accommodate the potatoes in a single layer. Sprinkle with Aunt Jane's Crazy Salt®, turn once and coat the other side. Bake in 400 degree oven about 45 minutes until cooked. Remove from oven and cool. Split in half lengthwise allowing them to set flat on tray. Scoop out center with melon baller. Pipe or spoon in sour cream. At this point you can either place a small amount of caviar on the sour cream or sprinkle with thinly sliced chives. Serve cold. A good dish to pass or can be placed on a buffet table.

This is an original and has proven to be a very popular item at cocktail parties. You should plan on 3 or 4 halves per person.

Boiled Shrimp

3 lbs Shrimp, Deveined and Peeled

3 tbs Crab Boil®

1 tbs Aunt Jane's Crazy Salt®

1 tsp Black Pepper Corns

1 Bay Leaf

1 Lemon

4 to 6 qts Water

To devein and shell shrimp you will need a pair of kitchen scissors. I have found this to be the quickest and easiest way for me. Hold the shrimp in your left hand with the legs facing down and the front of the shrimp facing you. Insert the scissors into the top vein and cut towards the tail of the shrimp to the last joint in shell, leaving that and the tail intact. Skin will peal right off along with the vein and legs. When the shrimp is cooked, the back will fan out just like in a restaurant

Cut lemon into quarters. Squeeze juice into large pot along with the rinds and the remainder of the ingredients, except the shrimp. Bring to a boil and place shrimp into the boiling liquid. Stir often so the shrimp are evenly exposed to the hot water no longer than 4 to 5 minutes for jumbo U 20 shrimp [under 20 count shrimp per pound]. If you use smaller ones, of course, it will take less time. You want to cook shrimp JUST until the transparency is gone. Drain immediately into sink [or strain and reserve the liquid for a gumbo or chowder.] Spray a little cold water over shrimp just to remove some of the seasoning and to stop the cooking process. I don't like to totally submerge them in cold water because it seems to take away some of the flavor.

To serve as shrimp cocktail I like to use a stem martini or dessert glass, or a flat champagne glass. Place a nice piece of red leaf lettuce in glass (it doesn't have to cover the entire bowl), then Add a layer of large diced celery. Hang the peeled cooked shrimp off the rim of the glass with the tails down. 4 or 5 per serving is plenty. Place cocktail sauce in center of shrimp. Garnish with a wedge of lemon on rim also. What a great presentation and the flavor and texture of the shrimp is delightful. Your guests will think you ordered them from your favorite restaurant.

If you are going to serve boiled shrimp in the rough just boil as above except forget about the peeling and deveining. Serve them chilled in a large bowl with a side container for shells, a bowl of *Cocktail Sauce*, a bowl of lemon wedges, your favorite crackers and a lot of napkins.

❋

Bourbon Pork Tenderloin

2 Pork Tenderloins [there are usually 2 in 1 package]	1 or 2 tsp Fresh Garlic, minced
1 cup Bourbon	¼ cup Kikkoman® Soy Sauce
¼ cup Brown Sugar, or to taste	¼ tsp Fresh Ground Pepper
1 tsp Fresh Ginger, grated	½ cup Toasted Sesame Seeds
	1 cup Hot Sweet Mustard

To make marinade combine all ingredients together, except the pork, sesame seeds and mustard. You may adjust the soy and brown sugar to your own taste.

Trim all fat and silver skin from tenderloin. Score tenderloin in a criss-cross pattern to allow marinade to penetrate a little more. Place pork into marinade for at least 2 hours, turning every 15 minutes or so. You could either grill on an outdoor grill for 20 to 25 minutes, turning every 10 minutes, or roast in a preheated 400 degree oven. Inside meat temperature should reach 130 degrees in about 35 to 45 minutes. Remove from heat and allow to rest for 15 minutes before slicing. Diagonally slice about ⅓-inch-thick.

Thin the mustard with a little water to bring it to a dipping consistency. Dip each slice of pork into the mustard, covering about ¼ of one side of the slice and then dip it into the sesame seeds. Cover a round tray with your favorite edible greenery. Starting at the outside of tray arrange pork slices in a circular pattern with the undipped side facing out, overlapping as you go until you reach the center. In the center, you could place 2 or 3 nice day lilies or a tomato rose with sprigs of fresh parsley around it. This should be served room temperature. You could also just slice the meat, arrange on the tray with small dishes of the sesame seeds and mustard on the side for your guests to help themselves. This works okay on a buffet table but is rather messy to pass in this fashion.

The credit for this tasty dish goes to my daughter Tammy. She has always served this at her parties with great success. I did make a few changes with the ingredients to give it a little teriyaki twist. Thank you Tammy for this tasty treat.

Daughter Tammy

Chopped Chicken Livers

2½ lbs Chicken livers
1½ sticks Butter
1 lg Spanish Onion, diced
2 tbs Fresh Garlic, minced

¼ cup Fresh Parsley, minced
8 Hard-boiled Eggs
¼ cup Cognac, sherry or Marsala
1 tsp Fresh thyme

Clean and devein the livers cutting out all fat and gristle. Set aside. In a hot skillet melt butter, add onion and garlic, sauté until transparent. Add livers, sprinkle with salt, pepper and thyme and continue to sauté until very brown. Place all ingredients into processor bowl. Deglaze skillet with liquor, add to livers and process with on and off button to desired consistency. Add chopped hard-boiled eggs and adjust seasoning.

Serve in a crock or press into a mold that has been sprayed with a non-stick spray. Cover with plastic wrap and chill for several hours. To remove from mold, place container in hot water, for just a few minutes. If mold is plastic, it will take a few minutes longer. Be careful not to get water into livers. Place serving platter upside down onto mold, turn right side up and tap mold gently. If need be, you can twist mold to dislodge onto platter.

Serve with your favorite crackers or a crusty French bread.

I created this version after serving chopped livers at Sanginitis, where I worked in Akron. I always make this for holidays and am expected to do so.

Cocktail Sandwich Suggestions

When I make cocktail or tea sandwiches, I use a variety of breads, cut off the crusts, [unless I'm using slices of baguette] and butter or mayonnaise each slice. This keeps the bread from getting too dry.

*Roast Beef with a little *Cole Slaw* and a dab of Dijon mustard.

*Cucumber with Watercress butter

> To make watercress butter, wash the fresh watercress very well to remove all the sand. Place into processor bowl with butter and process until very smooth. The proportions of butter to watercress would be to your own liking. Add salt and pepper to taste. This mixture goes very well on a light bread. Just spread it on the bread and top it with thin slices of cucumber.
> Garnish with sprigs of watercress.

*Mini Reuben's

> For this I always use dark cocktail bread and I do not cut off the crust. Spread a layer of *Russian Dressing* on the bread. Then a layer of very thinly sliced corned beef, a tablespoon of well drained sauerkraut, then top that with shredded swiss cheese. When ready to serve, place under broiler for 6 to 8 minutes or until all the cheese is melted and the sandwich is hot.

*Cream Cheese, Date and Walnuts

> Place cream cheese and chopped dates into processor bowl; pulse on and off until blended and soft. Spread on bread, sprinkle with chopped walnuts or top with a walnut half.

*Cream Cheese and Olives

> Same method as above but use either black or green olives, or a combination.
> Garnish with a sliver of pimento.

*Ham Salad

> Place into bowl of processor
>> ½ lb. Baked Ham, leftover baked ham is really good for this
>> 1 tbs Grated Sweet Onion
>> 1 Rib Celery, chopped course
>> 1 tsp Mustard of your choice, I prefer Dijon
>> 2 tsp Relish, I use my homemade which has a wonderful flavor. Check for recipe in *Canned Goods*.
>
> Fresh ground pepper and just enough Hellmann's® to hold it together. Place all ingredients into processor bowl, pulse on and off until it reaches the consistency you desire.

Chicken Salad

> You can use the *Chicken Curry Salad* mixture but process it a little just to make it smaller textured. Garnish with a thin slice of apple that has been rubbed with lemon juice to prevent it from turning brown.

*Roast Turkey and Brie with Honey Mustard

Spread the bread of your choice with honey mustard. Place thinly sliced roast turkey onto bread and top with a small piece of brie. Serve warmed or at room temp.

* *Tuna Salad* topped with a slice of sweet pickle.

*Smoked Salmon Roll-ups

Use a spinach tortilla. Spread with a mixture of equal parts Hellmann's® and Dijon mustard. Place a layer of thinly sliced smoked salmon in the middle of the tortilla. Below the salmon, place 2 or 3 very thin slices of tomato, and some very thin slices of onion. You could also add some very crisp bacon. Starting at the edge of the tortilla closest to you, roll it away from you until completely rolled up. Slice about 1 inch thick diagonally across the roll-up. Place spiral side up on platter. A toothpick inserted through it will hold it together. This also makes a great lunch sandwich. Just use 1 whole tortilla per person and arrange on plate spiral side up in a circle around the outside of plate with a salad of choice in center. The presentation of this is eye-catching and the combination of flavors is tantalizing.

*Sliced *Roasted Filet of Beef*

I like to serve this on a slice of baguette. Spread the baguette slices with butter. Place several thinly sliced pieces of the beef filet on the bread and top with a little Dijon mustard or *Sour Cream Horseradish*.

*Asparagus Rolls

Use Wonder bread [believe it or not]! Cut off crust and spread each slice with cream cheese that has been softened to a spreadable consistency and mixed with a little Aunt Jane's Crazy Salt®. At the edge of the slice of bread lay one asparagus. You can either use fresh that has been lightly cooked, or canned. I prefer the fresh cooked because it has more texture. Now roll the asparagus up with the bread. Slice into 1 inch pieces and place onto serving tray cut side up.

Cocktail Sauce

2 cups Heinz® Catsup	¼ tsp each Onion and Garlic Powder
2 to 4 tbs Horseradish	Course or Freshly Ground Black Pepper

Mix all ingredients together and adjust to your own taste. I like to add a little fresh lemon juice also. This can be kept refrigerated almost indefinitely. If it congeals don't be alarmed, just stir it up and it will go back to its original consistency.

Cream Cheese and Crab Spread

16 oz Cream cheese
16 oz Crabmeat
16 oz *Cocktail Sauce*

Work cream cheese until it is soft, add crabmeat, mix until blended.

Place onto serving platter and shape it into a round flat form. Pour cocktail sauce over all and serve with your favorite cracker. I like Triscuits.

I prefer using fresh vacuum-packed crabmeat as opposed to the canned found on the grocery shelves.

What an easy dish to make and everyone will love it.

Curried Eggs

1 doz Hard Boiled Eggs, this will
   give you 24 halves or 48 quarters
¼ tsp Onion Powder
⅛ tsp Garlic Powder
1 tsp Curry Powder
⅛ tsp White Pepper
¼ tsp Dry Mustard

½ to 1 tsp Worcestershire Sauce
2 or 3 drops Hot Sauce OR a
   sprinkling of Cayenne Pepper
Salt to taste
Hellmann's® Mayonnaise to reach a
   consistency for piping

Cook eggs. [look for complete directions on how to get the *Perfect Hard Boiled Egg*.] Cut the boiled egg in half lengthwise. Remove yolk carefully so as not to break the white.

Place all the ingredients, except the egg whites and mayonnaise, into bowl of processor; pulse on and off until yolks are completely pulverized. Add mayonnaise, a little at a time. Remember you can always add more but once it's in there, you can't take it out.

Place a large star tip in a pastry bag and fill with the egg yolk mixture. If you don't have a pastry bag, you could use a spoon but a much nicer appearance is achieved by using a pastry bag. Place egg whites on a tray that has been lined with your favorite greenery. Pipe the holes full of the yolk mixture and garnish with a sprinkling of paprika, a slice of olive or a sliver of red pepper.

You could substitute the curry with dill weed to make dilled eggs.

Believe it or not deviled eggs are still a popular number at parties.

Dates, Cointreau, Cream Cheese and Walnuts

1, 8-oz pkg Pitted Dates

1, 8-oz pkg Cream Cheese

½ cup Cointreau

1 cup Walnuts, finely ground

You will need a pastry bag for this and a tip large enough to allow cream cheese to be piped through it.

Be sure to purchase pitted dates.

Soak dates in cointreau for 30 minutes or so, tossing every so often. Soften cream cheese until it is of piping consistency. Place cream cheese into pastry bag and pipe into dates on one end until the dates are full then roll in nuts. These are sweet but delicious, good and people love them.

Eggplant Caviar

4 Large Eggplant

¾ cup Good olive oil

1 cup Sweet onion, minced

1 tbs Fresh garlic, minced

½ cup Parsley, chopped fine

4 Tomatoes, medium in size and
   very ripe

Salt & Pepper to taste

Split eggplant lengthwise and brush all sides with olive oil. Place cut side down onto baking sheet that has been sprayed with a non-stick spray. Roast until it collapses (about 45 minutes). Peel tomatoes cut in half, crossways, squeeze out seeds and chop fine. Scrape eggplant from skin and chop fine. Mix everything together except parsley, and chop all fine. This can be done in processor but be careful not to over process. You want to keep some texture but not large chunks. Add remaining oil and chopped parsley, season to taste with salt and pepper. Chill thoroughly. I like to serve this with **Crustinis.**

I have served this at many parties, and it is loved by all who enjoy eggplant.

Grilled Shrimp with
Orange Marmalade Cocktail Sauce

2 lbs Shrimp, 16 to 20 size or larger
1 cup Orange Juice
1 tsp Fresh Garlic, minced
1 tbs Fresh Ginger, grated

1 tsp Salt
½ tsp Fresh Ground Pepper
1 tsp Curry Powder
½ cup Vegetable Oil

Peel and devein shrimp. [Look under **Boiled Shrimp** for easy directions].

Mix remaining ingredients in a container large enough to also hold shrimp. Marinate shrimp for about 30 minutes, mixing every 15 minutes to expose all sides of the shrimp to the marinade. Do not marinate longer as the shrimp may get tough when exposed to citrus juice too long. Place onto a very hot grill. Cook for 3 to 4 minutes on each side *no longer*. Remove from heat and place in a flat container large enough for the shrimp to be in 1 layer. This allows them to cool quickly therefore stopping the cooking process faster. Chill completely.

Orange Marmalade Cocktail Sauce

1 cup Orange Marmalade, I use my
    homemade but store-bought will
    work

1 to 3 tbs Horseradish, according to
    your taste
¼ tsp Fresh Ground Pepper
¼ tsp Salt

Mix all ingredients together.

Put into a small bowl. Cover the surface of a round tray with your favorite edible greenery. Place the bowl of cocktail sauce in the center. Starting from the outside edge arrange the shrimp overlapping, with the tails pointing up, in a spiral pattern until you reach bowl in center.

This will be a big hit at your summer function; it always is at mine.

I claim credit for the shrimp but the cocktail sauce idea goes to Walter Keller who owns Binnekill Square Restaurant in Margaretville, NY.

Herbed Cheese

4 oz Cream Cheese, soft
1 lb Sharp Cheddar, shredded
4 oz Danish Blue Cheese
2 tbs Worcestershire Sauce
2 tbs Hellmann's® Mayonnaise
2 tbs Sweet Onion, grated

1 tsp Fresh Garlic, finely minced
1 tbs Fresh Parsley, minced
1 tsp Fresh Ground Black Pepper
A little hot sauce or cayenne if you like a little spice.

Place cream cheese and mayonnaise into bowl of mixer and blend together. Add remaining ingredients and mix well. Remove from bowl and chill.

Form into the shape you desire.

Roll in coarsely ground walnuts. Serve at room temperature with Stoned Wheat Thins.

I started to make this cheese mixture a very long time ago. It has evolved into this. People seem to enjoy it and I'm sure you will too. Serve it anytime, anywhere, but it is especially nice at Christmas time. I have divided the mixture into two parts and formed them into logs. Roll one in chopped parsley and the other in paprika for that red and green theme.

This past Christmas I was invited to a house party with everyone taking a dish. I had 6 or 7 small pieces of cheese in my fridge so I used them all in this dish. I shaped it into a standing up snowman, using celery for the arms, celery leaves for hair, a small carrot for the nose and raisins for the eyes. It was a big hit, especially with the children.

✳

Hummus

3, 13-oz cans Chick peas
1 large tbs Fresh garlic, minced
½ cup Good olive oil
2 oz Tahini

2 or 3 Lemons, juiced
pinch Cumin
to taste Cheyenne pepper
and salt

Place all ingredients into bowl of processor and process until smooth.
Taste for seasoning. You may want it a little more tart or a little more spicy. This is wonderful served with wedges of pita or as a dip for fresh vegetables. I like to serve it at room temp.

Several years ago there was a girl who worked at Beverly's with the most beautiful long blonde hair and a face and body to match, but her most endearing attribute was the beauty she had inside and her love for her family, life and music. She is now a recording star. Her name is Terri Cantz.

Also, being a vegetarian, she made a mean hummus and this is it.

Terri Cantz and Michael

70

Éclairs with Savory Filling

Prepare *Éclairs* according to recipe but omit the sugar. Make éclairs 2-inches long.

After baking, they can be stored in an airtight container in the freezer for 2 or 3 weeks. Thaw. To freshen up, place on a baking sheet, in a 350 degree oven for 5 minutes.

Cut a thin slice off top and remove any membrane looking stuff from the inside. Reserve tops as you may want to replace them after filling the éclairs.

Suggestions for filling:
Chicken salad
Ham Salad
Shrimp Salad
Crab Salad

Seasoned Oyster Crackers

1 lg box Oyster Crackers
1 pkg Hidden Valley® Original
   Ranch Dressing Mix
½ tsp Garlic Salt

½ tsp Dill Weed
½ tsp Lemon Pepper
¾ cup Vegetable Oil

Place all ingredients, except oil, into a plastic bag and shake well.

Add oil and shake well again. Close bag and let stand 1 hour or overnight.

This gem came from my Aunt Emma who, at this writing, is 96.

The recipe card is dated 2/14/88. I'm not sure where she got the recipe but I'm guessing from the Hidden Valley® package. In any case, it is a great snack.

Shrimp or Crab Dip

1 lb Cream Cheese, room
    temperature
½ cup Hellmann's® Mayonnaise
½ cup Sour Cream
2 tbs Sweet Onion, grated

¾ lb Cooked Shrimp, chopped, or
    Crabmeat, excess liquid squeezed
    out
3 tbs Barbecue Sauce, Chile Sauce,
    or Catsup
Salt and Pepper to taste.

Place cream cheese in mixer bowl and add remaining ingredients, except the seafood.

Mix very well. Add the seafood, stir just to blend. Adjust seasoning to your taste. If it seems to be too stiff for a dip add a little milk or more sour cream. If you want to use this as a spread, reduce the amount of sour cream.

Serve this mounded on a greenery-lined serving tray with your favorite crackers, veggies or both. A big hit at any party.

An original from Beverly's Kitchen by Beverly.

Shrimp or Salmon Mousse

¼ oz or 1 tbs Knox® Gelatin
¼ cup Cold Water
1, 13-oz can Tomato Soup
1 cup Hellmann's® Mayonnaise
3, 8-oz cans Shrimp OR

24 oz *Pouched Salmon*
¾ cup Celery, small diced
¾ cup Onion, diced
1, 8-oz Cream Cheese, room
    temperature

First of all, if you use canned shrimp, drain it very well. If you use fresh salmon, you can place it into a microwave proof dish that has been sprayed with a non-stick spray. Pour ½ cup white wine over it or you could use water. Sprinkle with a little seasoning salt and dill weed. Cover with plastic wrap and place into microwave on high temp for 6 to 8 minutes, depending on the thickness of the salmon. Remove and let cool to room temperature. Or, you could use the recipe in the *Seafood Chapter* for *Oven Pouched Salmon*.

While this is cooking and cooling, or if you are using the canned shrimp, proceed from here.

Sprinkle gelatin on the cold water and stir well. Let sit to soften.

In a mixing bowl mash up the shrimp or salmon. Add cream cheese, stirring well to mix completely. Add remaining ingredients and mix thoroughly. Place into a fish mold that has been sprayed with a non-stick spray. Cover with plastic wrap and chill at least 6 hours, or overnight is even better, to allow the flavors to blend. Unmold onto your favorite platter and garnish with greens, halved cherry tomatoes and small lemon wedges. This is great served with Stoned Wheat Thins®.

Thank you to Susie Marcus for this tasty treat.

Smoked Gouda and Sun dried Tomato Dip

¾ lb Smoked Gouda, shredded
1 lb Cream Cheese, room
    temperature
½ cup Hellmann's® Mayonnaise

½ tsp Fresh Garlic, minced
½ tsp Black Pepper, course ground
1 cup Sour Cream
¼ cup Sun dried Tomatoes, minced

In bowl of mixer, place cream cheese, mayonnaise, garlic and black pepper. Mix until very well blended. When cream cheese is blended with the other ingredients add sour cream and mix again, scraping the sides of the bowl. Add smoked gouda and the sun dried tomatoes. Mix well. Place the dip into a small bowl, or a bowl made of red cabbage leaves. Place on a serving tray with your favorite raw vegetables. You want this dip to be room temperature. If it is too stiff, add a little more sour cream. Adjust seasoning with salt and pepper.

Another original from Beverly's kitchen. I have always been one to just put things together, tasting as I go along and imagining what else would taste good in the dish. Well this was one of those creations.

    I'm sure you will love this and so will your guests. It's particularly tasty with carrots and cauliflower.

Smoked Salmon Tartare

2 lbs Smoked Salmon, coarsely
    chopped
4 tbs Egg Whites, boiled and
    chopped fine
4 tbs Fresh Parsley, chopped fine
2 Lemons, juiced

4 tbs Sweet Onion, minced fine
2 tbs Capers, chopped fine
2 tsp olive oil
8 drops Tabasco®, or to taste
4 oz Cream Cheese

Soften cream cheese. Mix all ingredients together until very well blended but not mashed. Place on a flat serving tray and garnish with fresh dill or chives or both. Small lemon wedges look nice with this and taste good too. This can also be served on pumpernickel rounds or toast. On the other hand, serve on a buffet table with crusty bread or crackers.

This recipe came from a wonderful cookbook of the Greenbriar in West VA. What a beautiful place, especially in the fall, and the food is awesome, too.

Spinach Dip—one more time

1 cup Hellmann's® Mayonnaise
24 oz Cream Cheese
12 oz Sour Cream
24 oz Frozen Chopped Spinach
½ cup Fresh Chopped Parsley

1 pkg French Onion Soup® Mix
½ cup Sweet Onion, chopped fine
1 tsp Salt and Black Pepper, or to
  taste

Place spinach in colander until completely thawed. By hand, squeeze out as much liquid as possible. Place cream cheese into bowl of mixer, mix until soft. Add mayo and sour cream. Scrape sides of bowl to release all the cream cheese. Mix well. Add parsley, onion, soup mix, salt and pepper. Mix well again, add spinach and blend until totally incorporated. Serve in a hollowed out loaf of bread as a dip for vegetables and/or chunks of bread. One can also make a bowl from leaves of red cabbage for the center of the veggie tray.

If you remember when the French's Onion Soup® Mix first came out, there was a recipe for a dip using it. Well I just basically used that idea to make this great spinach dip. When I had the gourmet food stores, I packaged this for retail sales and it was a big hit.

Tapenade

2 cups Kalamata Olives, pitted OR
  you could use a combination
  adding green
1 tsp Fresh Garlic, minced
¼ tsp Fresh Ground Pepper

3 tbs Capers
4 Anchovy Filets OR
1 tsp Anchovy Paste
¼ cup Olive Oil, use a very good
  grade

Place all into bowl of processor and process until it reaches a course consistency. You want to be able to spread this onto crustinis or bruschetta. If the consistency is too dry add a little more olive oil.

Place the mixture into a serving dish on a tray. Arrange crustinis, crackers, crispy bread or vegetables on the same tray.

This is one of my favorites and was served at Eartha's, when I worked there. It was delicious. However, as any recipe I've borrowed from other restaurants, I change it a little so I can claim it as mine. Thank you, Carolyn . . .

Baked Artichoke Dip

1, 14-oz Can Artichoke Hearts,
  drained
1 tbs Fresh Garlic, minced
½ cup Parmesan

1 tbs Lemon Juice
¼ cup Hellmann's® Mayonnaise
¼ cup Cream Cheese, soft
2 tbs Breadcrumbs

Mix breadcrumbs and 2 tbs. of the parmesan together and set aside. Place remaining ingredients into processor bowl and process on and off to reach a chunky consistency. Place mixture into a 1-qt. size casserole dish that has been sprayed with non-stick spray. Sprinkle top with breadcrumb mixture. Bake in 375 degree oven for 20 minutes or until bubbly. Serve warm with crusty bread, crostini, crackers or vegetables.

Baked Brie with Caramelized Almonds

1 cup Sliced Almonds
1 stick Butter

½ cup Brown Sugar
2 lb Wheel of Brie [or 2, 15-oz ones]

Unwrap the brie. With a sharp pointed small knife, score around the perimeter, on the top, about ½ inch in from the outside edge. Scrape off the rind that's inside the circle. Keep the outside edge intact to hold the melted brie together.

In a hot skillet, melt the butter. Add brown sugar and the almonds.

Toss just enough for the three ingredients to mix completely. If this is cooked too long, the sugar will melt and turn into a candy. What you want is a sugary consistency, so don't overcook it. When totally mixed, place on the top of the brie. You can prepare this up to this point and finish it off at a later time.

To finish off place on a flat cardboard cake circle that has been wrapped in foil or on a flat tin, keeping in mind it will have to be transferred to a serving tray. If using the cake circle, place it onto a baking sheet. Bake in 375 degree oven for about 20 minutes. Push on the sides of the brie. If it has a lot of give, it has baked long enough. Remove from oven, place spatula under cardboard and transfer to serving plate. The reason for the cardboard is for easy moving after it has been heated.

Serve with grapes, strawberries, crusty bread or crackers.

This is another original and a very popular item at parties, but it has to be served as soon as it comes from the oven.

Baked Crab Dip

1 lb Lump Crab Meat	1½ tbs Worcestershire sauce
¼ lb Butter	½ Red sweet pepper, diced
3 tbs Flour	½ cup Sweet onion, minced
1 cup Half and half	1 cup Dried bread crumbs
2 tbs Hellmann's® Mayonnaise	1 cup Mushrooms, finely chopped
1 tsp Dry Mustard	

Melt butter in medium size saucepan. Add flour and stir over medium heat until flour just begins to change colors, then add half and half while whisking. Continue to whisk over medium heat until it thickens and begins to bubble. Remove from heat, add Hellmann's®, dry mustard and Worcestershire sauce. Mix well.

Sauté onions and mushrooms in a little butter until they are just transparent. Add to above mixture along with diced red pepper and crab meat. Mix until all is blended. Place into ovenproof baking dish.

Top with bread crumbs and bake for 30 minutes at 375 degrees. Serve with a cracker that is fairly bland, not to overpower the dip. Serve hot.

Magda Mahoney and I became acquainted in Orlando, FL. where we were moved by the Tribune Company, and we have her to thank for this one.

Bruschetta

I try to use homemade baguettes for this but store-bought ones will work also.

Slice diagonally across the bread into slices no more than ½-inch-thick. Brush with a good quality olive oil, bake in a 375 degree oven until crisp and slightly brown. Remove from oven, cool and store in airtight container.

From here, you can make several kinds. One of my favorites is brie with **Caramelized Red Onions**. To prepare this type, place a slice of brie on the toasts and top it with the onions, then bake in 375 degree oven for 10 to 12 minutes or until brie is slightly melted.

Another delicious topping is
Tomatoes with Goat Cheese.

3 Ripe Tomatoes, dice medium	2 tbs Olive Oil
1 tsp Minced Garlic	3 oz Goat Cheese or Mozzarella
2 tbs Fresh Basil, chopped	Fresh ground pepper and salt to taste.

Toss to mix, top the toasts with this mixture and bake in oven for 10 to 12 minutes.

Eggplant Caviar may also be used. Serve hot or cold.

Bruschetta has become a very popular party food and your guests won't mind making their own.

Potato Pancakes with Chevre

2½ lbs Idaho Potatoes, shredded
  course
3 tbs Lime Juice
½ cup Spanish Onion, shredded
2 tbs Fresh Parsley, minced fine
6 oz Chevre [goat cheese]

⅓ cup Flour
¼ tsp White Pepper
Several gratings of Nutmeg
Salt and Fresh Ground Pepper to
  taste

Place grated potatoes on a kitchen towel and wring out as dry as possible. Pour lime juice over potatoes and stir to coat. This prevents the potatoes from turning brown and also adds flavor. Add everything but the chevre. Mix well then crumble the goat cheese into the mixture and stir just until it is mixed. Drop by tablespoons into hot oil that is about ½ inch deep in frying pan. Again, I like an iron skillet for this. It gives even heat but it gets much hotter than the normal fry pan so be careful. Brown on one side, turn over and brown on the other. Serve warm.

Can be passed or placed on buffet table on warmer. Serve with an herbed sour cream.

Chicken Teriyaki Kabobs

2 lbs Chicken Breast, boneless
¾ cup Kikkoman® Soy Sauce
¼ cup Brown Sugar
1 tsp Fresh Garlic, minced
1 tbs Fresh Ginger, shredded
2 tbs Vegetable Oil

¼ tsp Fresh Ground Pepper
2 tbs Cider Vinegar
2 lg Red Pepper
1 Pineapple
5-inch skewers

To prepare pineapple, cut off both ends. [Save the top for garnishing the platter.] Using a very sharp knife, slice skin off all around, turning it as you go. Cut the pineapple off the core. You should have 4 pieces. [You could purchase one already peeled and cored or you could use canned chunks.] Cut the pepper and pineapple into 1½-inch cubes.

Rinse chicken breasts and remove all the skin and fat. Cut into 1½-inch cubes. Mix the remaining ingredients together in a container that is large enough to hold the chicken also. Place the chicken in the marinade, stir to coat and let sit for 1 hour. Don't marinate too long as it will make the chicken tough. Place chicken cubes on skewers alternately with the pepper and pineapple. Brush with marinade and bake in 375 degree oven for 12 to 15 minutes. Serve hot immediately or at least warm.

This can also be served as a main dish by using larger skewers and adding onions and mushrooms. Serve on a bed of gingered rice.

An original recipe but the idea has been around for a long time.

Mussels or Clams Casino

4 or 5 doz Fresh Mussels or Fresh
    Clams
2 Lemons
¼ lb Butter, melted
2 Bay Leaf

1 tbs Fresh Garlic, minced
1 tsp Black Pepper Corns
1 cup White Wine
¼ cup Fresh Parsley, chopped
Herb Butter

Soak clams, or mussels, in cold water for an hour or two. This helps them to discharge the salt water, and clean the inside of sand. Drain and replace with fresh water, which will keep your broth from getting to salty.

With a stiff brush, clean the outside of the mussels and clams really well to prevent the broth from getting sandy. Place the clams or mussels into a very large flat pan. I like to use the bottom of my lobster steamer. Add the remaining ingredients. Cut lemons in half, squeeze in juice and then place lemon rinds right into the water. Pour the butter on top of everything. I suggest a large flat pan so the shellfish have room to open their shells and also absorb the wonderful flavors of the broth.

From here you can do several things. Serve them as steamed shellfish in individual bowls with lots of hot crusty bread for dunking. Or, you can remove each one from the shell, saving 1 half of the shell to place the body of the shellfish on it. After doing that, pipe on about ½ tsp. *Herb Butter*, then top with a small piece of lean bacon. Bake in 400 degree oven for about 12 minutes or until the butter is bubbly and the bacon is crisp. Serve immediately. This can be served at cocktail parties or as an appetizer before dinner. Serve with lemon wedges, a cocktail fork and hot crusty bread.

Walter Keller gets the credit for this one also. I do hope he doesn't mind being published.

Cocktail Quiche

Mini Cupcake Pans
Several Recipes of my *Pie Dough*, recipe in *Dessert* chapter
Imported Swiss Cheese, finely shredded
Recipe for my *Quiche Filling*
Tasty suggested combinations; Broccoli, Zucchini, Bacon, Ham, Onion,
    Mushroom, Spinach, Tomato/Basil, Smoked Salmon/Scallion,
    Crabmeat, Shrimp/Tarragon and the list could go on.
Just use your imagination or a combination of any of the above.

Spray the muffin pan with nonstick spray. This will allow for easier removal after baking. From the pie dough, make balls about as big around as a quarter. Place 1 ball into each muffin cup. With a tart tamper [one of those gadgets you will hardly ever use but it's a great tool for this], dip the smaller end into flour and then press it down onto the dough. The dough will squeeze up around the tamper. Press the top of the dough around the top of the muffin cup to cover the entire cup. If it is above the top of the cup, just trim it off with a small sharp knife. Save the excess dough for the next one.

If you want to do a dozen little quiche. Take about a cup of the cheese and chop it up fine. To this add approximately 3 to 4 tbs. of the ingredient or ingredients of your choice also chopped fine. Mix together and fill each little cup with the cheese mixture. Then very carefully add the liquid quiche mixture with a spoon. [If you figure out a better way, let me know, please].

Fill to about ⅛ inch from top. Don't pack the cheese mixture in too tightly; you have to allow room for the liquid to seep down through the cheese. Place filled muffin tin onto a baking sheet and bake in 375 degree oven for 15 to 18 minutes. Remove from oven and cool on a cooling rack to slightly warm. With a small thin blade go around the quiche between the pan and the crust to loosen. Carefully remove to cooling rack. They can be prepared much in advance. Keep chilled or frozen in a airtight container. When ready to serve just reheat in the oven until hot.

This recipe is an original. It's very tedious but well worth it. Have fun!

Crabmeat Stuffed Red Potatoes

3 lbs Red Potatoes, medium in size
4 oz Cream Cheese
½ cup Sour Cream
4 to 6 oz Crabmeat
¼ tsp White Pepper
¼ tsp Dried Tarragon OR

1 tsp. Fresh Tarragon
3 tbs Butter
½ lb Mild Cheddar, shredded
Salt and Black Pepper to taste
Olive Oil
Aunt Jane's Crazy Salt®

Clean the potatoes thoroughly, pat dry. Rub with olive oil and coat with Aunt Jane's®. Place onto a baking sheet and bake at 400 degrees for 45 minutes or until cooked through. Remove from oven and let sit until cool enough to handle. Cut into quarters. Leaving ½ inch of the potato on the skin, scoop centers out into a bowl large enough to hold the remaining ingredients. Have cream cheese warm enough to mix. Mash potato centers and add the remaining ingredients, except cheddar. Mix very well. Fill potato skins with the mashed potato mixture. Spray tops of filled potatoes with a vegetable oil spray to prevent drying. At this point, you can stop and finish off when ready to serve. Place in an airtight container and refrigerate up to 3 days.

When time to serve, place the filled potato quarters on a baking sheet [I sometimes line the baking sheet with foil to make for easy cleanup], top with the shredded cheddar, place in oven that has been preheated to 375 degrees for 12 to 15 minutes or until hot. Serve immediately.

Another popular original from Beverly's kitchen.

Mushroom Caps with Escargot

White Button Mushrooms, size of half dollars
Canned Escargot, plan on 4 or 5 person
Herb Butter

Clean mushrooms with damp paper towel. Remove stems and hollow out the mushroom with a melon baller. Be careful not to break the mushroom or the herb butter will leak out. Open, drain and rinse the escargot. Place 1 escargot in each mushroom cap. Top it with 1 tsp. herb butter. Bake for 20 minutes in a 400 degree oven. Serve immediately with a lemon wedge and hot crusty bread. Usually 4 or 5 per person is sufficient.

You can also serve the escargot without the mushroom cap, using an escargot dish that has the little compartments or you could just use a baking dish. Prepare the escargot the same way but place each snail into a compartment and fill completely with herb butter. Bake for 15 or 20 minutes in a 400 degree oven. This dish is so delicious you will use the hot crusty bread to get every drop and morsel.

Again, the credit for this goes to Walter Keller from Binnekill Square Restaurant in Margaretville, NY.

❀

Hot Refried Bean Dip

2, 16-oz cans Pinto or Red Beans
2 cups Spanish Onion, chopped
3 or 4 tsp Garlic, Minced
¼ cup Vegetable Oil

1 or 2 cups Chile OR Salsa
1 cup Cheddar Cheese, large grated
Salt and Pepper to taste

Process beans until a little chunky. Heat iron skillet and vegetable oil until hot. Add onion and garlic and sweat until transparent. Add beans, salt and pepper. Cook until it is very thick, stirring often. At some point you will have to use a metal spatula to keep it scraped off the bottom of the skillet. Place bean mixture into a baking/serving dish that has been sprayed with oil spray. Top with chili or salsa, then the cheese. Bake in 400 degree oven until cheese is melted and bubbly. Serve with large Frito Dippers.

This recipe was created at some point with leftover pinto beans and leftover chili that I had in the refrigerator. I was going to a party and didn't really have too much in the house to be creative with, so I put this together, picked up a bag of chips on the way and baked it off there—everyone loved it.

❀

Potato Pancakes

4 cups Raw Potatoes, grated
Lemon Juice only
6 Eggs
3 tbs Flour
2 tsp Salt

2 tbs Onion, grated
¼ tsp Nutmeg
¼ tsp Black Pepper
½ cup Parmesan, grated (optional)

Squeeze lemon juice over potatoes, mix thoroughly; drain well, place grated potatoes on heavy kitchen towel then squeeze liquid out.

Mix remaining ingredients together, add potatoes and mix just to combine.

Heat a heavy skillet with enough olive oil or vegetable oil to cover the bottom. Drop the potato mixture by tablespoons full into the hot skillet. They will flatten out. Brown very well on one side then turn over and brown the other. Repeat this until all the batter is used. Keep warm by placing them onto a platter that has been lined with a paper towel and hold in a warm oven until ready to be served.

They can be made ahead of time and re-heated in a 400 degree oven until hot.

These are great for a cocktail party; just make them smaller than dinner size.

I serve these with *Applesauce* and **Roast Pork.**

Sesame Chicken Fingers with Lemon Dipping Sauce

2 lbs Chicken Breasts
1 cup Sesame Seeds, Toasted
2 cups Flour
1 tsp Salt
1 tsp Pepper
¼ tsp Curry Powder
1 tsp each Garlic and Onion Powder

1 cup Milk
As needed Sesame Oil
1 cup Chicken Broth
1½ tbs Corn Starch
3 tbs White Wine
1 Lemon, juiced

Rinse chicken breast and remove skin. Cut into finger size pieces. Place into a container large enough to hold chicken and the milk. Pour milk over chicken and mix just to coat chicken.

In another bowl, mix the dry ingredients [except the cornstarch] together. Place the chicken, one piece at a time in the dry mixture, and pressing it to coat. Brown in a hot skillet that has about ½ inch of oil and butter mixed and 1 tbs. sesame oil. Sesame oil is very strong so you only want enough to give the chicken a little more sesame flavor. Brown the pieces on one side, then the other. Remove from skillet, to paper towels. Keep warm. Repeat until all pieces are browned.

Lemon Dipping Sauce:

Pour off as much of the fat as you can, reserving the tasty particles on the bottom of the skillet. To the skillet add 1 cup chicken stock, the juice of 1 lemon, salt and white pepper to taste and heat. Thicken the broth with 1½ tbs. cornstarch that has been dissolved in 3 tbs. white wine. Add this to the hot broth mixture while whisking. Pour into a small dish that can be placed with the chicken pieces for dipping. This may be passed or placed on a buffet table. This dish can be made ahead of time and reheated. If doing so, undercook the chicken a little just to allow for reheating. Reheat by placing chicken pieces on a sheet pan and heating in a 350 degree oven for 15 minutes. The sauce can certainly be reheated in the microwave.

✳

Shrimp wrapped in Bacon

2 lbs Shrimp, size 16 to 20 is a good size
1 lb Bacon

Peel and devein shrimp as suggested in the **Boiled Shrimp** recipe. Have bacon at room temperature or warm in microwave slightly. Cut each slice in half. Wrap each shrimp with a half slice of bacon and secure with tooth pick .Place on a baking pan with sides or place on a rack on a baking pan, to take the fat away from the shrimp. Bake in 375 degree oven until bacon is cooked, about 15 minutes.

✳

Spicy Meatballs

3 lb Ground Chuck
1½ cup Dried Bread Crumbs
1 cup Milk
6 Eggs
6 tbs Worcestershire Sauce
½ cup Chile Sauce
1 tbs Chile Powder

1 tbs Fresh Garlic, minced
½ cup Fresh Parsley, chopped fine
2 tbs Fresh Lemon Juice
2 cups Spanish Onions, diced fine
1, 16-oz Jar Chutney of your choice
Salt and Pepper to taste

Pour milk over breadcrumbs and let stand until the milk is absorbed. Mix all ingredients, except chutney, until well blended. Form into balls the size of a quarter. Place onto a baking pan that has been sprayed with non-stick spray. Bake in 375 degree oven for 20 minutes. Remove from oven and place pan onto a cooling rack. Raise one side of pan to allow grease to drain away from meatballs. When well drained, transfer to a chafing dish. [These meatballs could also be browned in skillet on top of stove, but I find it much quicker to do them in the oven.] Dilute chutney with a little water or chicken stock to a pouring consistency. Pour over meatballs and allow to set for at least ½ hour for the meatballs to absorb the flavor of the sauce. This can be made well ahead and even frozen if desired. To reheat after being frozen just thaw in refrigerator remove to a microwavable dish, place in microwave, heat to desired temperature, or may be reheated on the stove in a skillet. Do not stir as it will break the meatballs; just shake the skillet gently. These should be served hot in a chafing dish on a buffet table with small plates or toothpicks.

✳

Spinach—Ricotta Pie

1 Recipe *Pie Dough*
2 lb. Spinach, finely chopped
½ cup Butter or Olive Oil
¾ cup Onion, chopped med
1 tsp Fresh Garlic, minced
16 oz Ricotta
¼ cup Parsley, finely chopped

4 Eggs
¼ tsp Nutmeg
¼ tsp White Pepper
½ cup Dried Bread Crumbs
¼ cup Parmesan
Salt to taste

Roll dough out to cover bottom and sides of a half sheet pan or a sheet pan that measures 12-inches by 15-inches. Set aside.

Sauté onions and garlic in butter/oil, cool. Place all ingredients [except the breadcrumbs and parmesan cheese] into a mixing bowl and mix thoroughly. Adjust seasoning. Put into prepared pie shell, with a spatula push filling to cover the entire shell and uniform in thickness. Combine bread crumbs with parmesan sprinkle on top of the pie. Place into preheated 375 degree oven for 45 minutes to 1 hour or until slightly browned and firm in the middle. Cool slightly and cut into desired size and shapes. This can be made ahead of time, reheated in the oven and makes a very good dish for cocktail parties. Or cut into bigger pieces and serve with a green salad, for lunch or a light dinner.

Please don't reheat MY pie crust in the microwave, it will make it very soft.

Stuffed Mushrooms

2 lbs Mushrooms, white ½ dollar
   size
2 ribs Celery
½ cup Spanish Onion, diced
¼ cup Fresh Parsley, chopped fine
1 stick Butter

1 tsp Fresh Garlic, minced
1 cup Bread Crumbs
3 tbs Parmesan
¼ tsp Oregano
½ lb Italian Sausage (optional) OR
½ lb Crabmeat (optional)

Wipe mushrooms with damp paper towel to remove any loose dirt. Carefully break off stems and hollow out mushroom with a melon baller. Place stems, celery, onion and garlic into processor bowl and process on pulse to a fine to medium consistency. Melt butter in skillet; add the processed mixture and sauté until all are opaque. Remove from heat; add parmesan, oregano, salt and pepper and fresh parsley. Mix thoroughly. Add just enough bread crumbs to absorb the butter. You don't want it to be dry. At this point you can add Italian sausage that has been sautéed and drained **or** crab meat that has been squeezed as dry as possible. Fill mushroom caps with filling. Sprinkle top with a little more parmesan and bake in 400 degree oven for 15 to 20 minutes.

Swedish Meatballs

3 lb Ground Chuck
2 Large Potatoes, peeled
½ cup Fresh Parsley, chopped fine
2 tbs Lemon Zest
2 cups Dried Bread Crumbs
1½ cup Milk
2 tbs Lemon Juice
2 tsp Salt

3 Eggs
1 tsp Pepper
½ tsp Nutmeg
1 tsp Paprika
1 Large Spanish Onion, diced small
10 cups Water
2 pkg Vegetable soup mix or 3 tbs
    vegetable base

Make vegetable stock with water and soup mix or base. Let simmer for 20 minutes. Strain and reserve liquid to cook meat balls in. Place liquid into large flat skillet or pan. Keep hot.

Pour milk over bread crumbs, let stand while preparing other ingredients. Sauté onion in 2 tbs. butter or oil. Either small shred the raw potatoes or process finely. Press as much liquid from the potatoes as possible. Place everything in large bowl, except the vegetable stock, and mix completely. Roll into quarter-sized meatballs and drop into boiling stock. Simmer about 15 minutes. Remove balls from stock with slotted spoon and place onto a flat sheet pan to cool. Do not stack in bowl; they will collapse. Continue this process until all the meatballs are cooked. Thicken the stock with a little flour that has been dissolved in water. Serve hot in a chafing dish on a buffet table. These meatballs are soft so be careful not to stir, they will break up. This dish can also be served on a bed of hot egg noodles as a main course.

❈

Soups & Sauces

Soups

Autumn Bisque

1 lg Spanish Onion, cubed
2 tbs Butter
1 lg Butternut Squash, split in half
    lengthwise, seeds removed
3 McIntosh Apples, peeled, seeded
    and quartered

3 cups Chicken Stock
1 cup Cider
½ cup Heavy Cream
Salt, Black and White Pepper to
    taste.

Place the prepared squash, cut side down, onto a greased baking sheet. Bake in a 350 degree oven until fork tender (about 45 minutes). When cool enough to handle, remove and discard the skin. Sauté the onion in the butter in a large soup pot then add the chicken stock, apples, cider and the squash. Bring to a boil, reduce heat to a simmer and cook until the apples are tender. Remove from heat and process until smooth. Add the heavy cream, mixing well, then season with salt and pepper to taste.

Serve piping hot. You can double or triple or even 10 times, (which is what we did at Beverly's) the recipe and it will not hurt the flavor.

This recipe was given to me by one of my customers in Stepney, CT.

Carrot Bisque

4 lbs Carrots, peeled
2 cups Onions, peeled
6 ribs Celery
4 cloves Fresh Garlic
2 Bay Leaf

¼ tsp Whole Black Peppercorns
6 Whole Cloves
2 qts Chicken Broth
1 pint Half and Half
Salt and white pepper to taste

Cut all the vegetables into chunks and place into a large soup pot, along with the remaining ingredients *except* the half-and-half. Bring to a boil, lower heat and continue to simmer covered until all the vegetables are tender. Remove bay leaves. Puree in processor to a very smooth consistency. Do not remove the whole peppercorns and cloves, as they will give it a nice spicy flavor. Add half-and-half, adjust seasoning and reheat to the boiling point.

    If you want thicker bisque, you may add **Roux** to thicken it to your liking before you add the cream.

What a wonderful fall soup! It makes a great addition to Thanksgiving or Christmas dinner.

Another great item from the kitchen of Walter Keller, but, of course, it has some of my touches also.

Chilled Cucumber and Yogurt Soup

3 cups Plain Yogurt
½ cup Milk
1 Cucumber, peeled, seeded and finely chopped
1 Egg, hardboiled and finely chopped

¼ cup Scallions, finely chopped
1 tsp Salt
1 tsp Pepper
1 tbs Fresh Parsley, finely chopped
1 tbs Fresh Dill, finely chopped

Combine all ingredients except dill and parsley. Stir to mix well.

Refrigerate for several hours. Serve in chilled individual bowls. Garnish with parsley and dill.

❈

French Onion Soup

2 lbs Spanish Onions, julienned medium thin
2 tbs Butter
1 tbs Sugar
2 tbs Flour

2 qts Water or Beef Stock
¼ cup Worcestershire Sauce
1 tsp Salt
1 tsp Pepper
Beef Base to Taste

Melt the butter in a heavy soup pot, over high heat. Sauté onions until opaque in color. Sprinkle with sugar, to induce browning and continue to cook until golden brown. Add the flour and stir to combine. Add remaining ingredients, mixing well. Add beef base to taste. If beef base is not available, you can use beef bouillon. Remember both of these are very salty, so add a small amount at a time. You can always add more, but you cannot take it out. Simmer over medium low heat for 45 minutes or until it reaches the richness and consistency you desire.

Place into individual crock bowls. Place a piece of toasted dry French bread on top and then mound shredded Swiss cheese on top of the bread. Place onto baking sheet, place under broiler and broil until crispy and dark golden brown.

An old stand-by, but one of the best standard soups to have.

When I rewrote my menu for the last time, one of my chefs said to me, "why don't you take the onion soup off, it is so out?" Well I didn't because onion soup will never be "OUT".

❈

Gaines' Carrot and Orange Soup

1¼ lbs Carrots, peeled and sliced
1 medium Spanish Onion, diced
3½ cups Orange Juice
1½ cups Strong Chicken Stock
¼ tsp Cinnamon

¼ tsp Mace
¼ tsp Nutmeg
Salt and Black and White Pepper to
   taste
1 cup Sour Cream

Combine carrots, onion, orange juice and chicken stock in a saucepan. Simmer until vegetables are tender. Add cinnamon, mace, nutmeg, salt and pepper. With a slotted spoon, place the vegetables into the processor and puree until very smooth. Then add back to the stock and adjust seasoning. Chill well. Fold in sour cream and serve in individual chilled bowls. Garnish with a dollop of sour cream and orange zest.

Quite a few years ago, I catered a party for the Gaines family. Yes, it is the Gaines Dog Food Family. They had a beautiful old house on North Broadway. They owned horses and came to Saratoga every summer. When Mrs. Gaines booked me as their caterer, she requested this soup and even gave me the recipe. It's a great soup, it was a great party, and they were great to work for!

✳

Gazpacho

9 Large Fresh Tomatoes, very ripe
3 Red Peppers, seeded
½ medium Spanish Onion
3 tbs Shallot, minced
3 Cucumbers, peeled and seeded
¾ cup Red Wine Vinegar

¾ cup Olive Oil
4 small cans V-8 Juice®
¼ cup Dill Weed
Pinch of cayenne or to taste
Salt to taste

Cut all the veggies into large chunks and process to the consistency you desire. Adjust the seasoning. Serve ice cold with a dollop of sour cream on top and a sprig of fresh dill.

You can ripen your tomatoes to a nice bright red just by keeping them out of the cold for a week or two. This is a great recipe!

I always took pride in trying to be the first in town, in the spring or early summer to put gazpacho on the specials board.

✳

Potato Cheddar Soup

1 lb Potatoes, peeled and cut into cubes
2 cups Chicken Stock
½ cup Carrot, peeled and cut into cubes
½ cup Celery, diced

½ cup Onion, diced
2 tsp Chicken bouillon granules (optional)
Salt and pepper to taste
1 cup Sharp Cheddar, shredded
Minced Fresh Parsley

In a large saucepan, place potatoes, chicken stock, onions, carrot, celery and bouillon. Over medium-high heat, bring to a boil, reduce heat to simmer and continue to cook for 25 minutes or until vegetables are tender. Process, half at a time, to a smooth consistency. Return mixture to saucepan. Add cheese, then cook and stir over medium heat until cheese melts. Adjust seasoning.

Ladle into individual serving bowls and sprinkle with fresh parsley.

Roasted Pumpkin Bisque

1 med size Pumpkin, peeled and cut into 1-inch cubes (reserve seeds)
½ head Celery, sliced in 1-inch chunks
4 Carrots, peeled and cut into 1-inch chunks
1 lg Onion, peeled and cut into 1-inch chunks
6 cloves Fresh Garlic, peeled and chopped course

2 Shallots, peeled and chopped course
1 Bunch Scallions, cleaned and cut into 1-inch chunks
2 cups Chicken Stock or canned broth
2 cups Heavy Cream
¼ cup Butter
½ cup Olive Oil
Salt, Fresh Ground Nutmeg, Black and White Pepper to taste.

Be careful with the white pepper as it has a very strong flavor (a little is enough). Toss all the vegetables with the olive oil, season with salt and pepper, and place all in a large shallow roasting pan that has been sprayed with pan spray. Put into a preheated 375 degree oven and roast until all is tender and edges are beginning to brown. Process in processor until very smooth. Combine the processed vegetables with half of the chicken stock and half of the heavy cream. You can add more if needed. Adjust the seasoning, add the fresh ground nutmeg and white pepper, a little at a time. Pour into a hollowed out pumpkin that has been warmed in the oven for 10 minutes. Serve soup piping hot and sprinkle top of each individual bowl with roasted shelled pumpkin seeds.

I usually serve the **_Carrot Bisque_** for Thanksgiving dinner, but one Thanksgiving I had an abundance of pumpkins so I created this soup. When I was finished, my mother asked how I knew what would taste good in it. I guess I just trust my intuition and love to experiment with food, flavors and seasonings. We were having a large dinner at Beverly's with a lot of family members, friends and some employees. (Somehow, the employees were most always friends or family, with few exceptions.) Everyone contributed a side dish. Michael and I were responsible for the turkey, which I located one through Polacsek Farms (one of my meat suppliers). It weighed approximately 35 pounds. Surprisingly enough, it was very tender and delicious. That was a fun day and everyone left with a full tummy and a doggy bag. After dinner, we moved the tables and chairs aside and danced a little. Thanks to the dance teacher from Skidmore by the name of Debra Fernandez and our wonderful, life-loving friend "V", we had great fun! Can't wait to do it again.

Michael and Beverly with 35 lb turkey at Beverly's Thanksgiving dinner.

Smoked Cod and Corn Chowder

1½ lbs Smoked Cod, soaked in
    water for 1 hour then diced
1 cup Onion, diced
1 cup Celery, diced
¼ cup Red Pepper, minced
2 cloves Fresh Garlic, minced
¼ cup Butter

1 cup Potatoes, cooked and diced
2 cup Whole Kernel Corn
1 qt Chicken Stock
1 qt Half and Half
Salt and White Pepper to taste (be
    careful with the pepper)
Roux if needed.

Rinse the cod very well and set aside. Melt the butter in a large pot. Add and sauté the onion, celery, red pepper and garlic until transparent. Add the chicken stock and the cod. Simmer for 10 to 15 minutes then add the corn and cream. Bring to a boil and add some *Roux* if you desire a thicker chowder. Adjust the seasoning.

Serve in individual bowls garnished with sprigs of chives and a chive blossom.

I visited Rob in Nantucket, during his internship at the White Elephant.

    I went to the American Grill for dinner one evening and this chowder was served. It was so delicious, I came back to Beverly's and did my rendition of it which came pretty close.

❀

Tortellini in Chicken Stock

2 qts Fresh Chicken Stock
1 Carrot, Peeled and thinly sliced
1 cup Broccoli Florets
2 Scallions, sliced including the
    green

2 cup Tortellini
Fresh ground pepper
Fresh shredded
    parmesan

Heat chicken stock. Add carrots, broccoli and tortellini. Simmer for 5 to 7 minutes or until carrots and broccoli are al dente. Ladle into individual serving bowls then top with scallions, fresh ground pepper and parmesan.

    This is a very simple and delicious soup.

One lunchtime, my friend, Ralph Petruzzo, came into the kitchen at Beverly's, pulled a stool up to the counter and asked, "what's for lunch?" I had some fresh chicken stock on hand so I whipped this up. Being Italian, he loved it.

❀

Turkey, Mushroom and Wild Rice Soup

3, 10-oz cans Chicken Broth, or the
    equivalent of chicken stock
2 cups Water
½ cup Wild rice
3 tbs Dry Sherry
1½ cups Turkey, chopped
1 tbs Pimento, chopped

½ cup Green Onion, finely chopped
½ lb Mushrooms, sliced
½ cup Butter
¾ cup Flour
¼ tsp Poultry Seasoning
2 cups Half and Half
Salt and Pepper to taste

In half the butter, sauté onions and mushrooms until the onions are opaque. Add the chicken broth, water and rice. Simmer 35 to 40 minutes or until rice is just tender. Remove from heat. Meanwhile, in a medium pan, melt remaining butter then add flour and seasonings. Cook on low heat, stirring constantly, until smooth and bubbly. Add the half-and-half and heat 2 minutes until thickened slightly, stirring constantly. Add remaining ingredients and heat thoroughly. Serve immediately in hot bowls with crusty bread.

This recipe came from my daughter Tammy. I'm not sure of the story behind it, but it's written in her hand writing and it's a great way to use up some leftover turkey.

❉

Sauces

Barbecue Sauce

1, #10 can or 104 oz Chile Sauce
1, #10 can or 104 oz Heinz® Catsup
1½ lb Brown Sugar
7 oz Yellow Mustard
1 lb Butter or Margarine
4 cups Spanish Onions, diced
1 bulb Fresh Garlic, minced

3 cups Worcestershire Sauce
2 cups Cider Vinegar
2 cups Dark Beer (optional to
    replace vinegar)
Salt, Red Pepper, White Pepper and
    Black Pepper to taste.

In a 10-quart, heavy pot, place the butter, onions and garlic. Sauté until they are opaque.

Add remaining ingredients; stir to combine. Bring to a boil while stirring often; reduce heat to a simmer and continue to cook over low heat for 2 to 3 hours or until it reaches the consistency you desire.

This can be jarred up to preserve, used immediately or stored in the refrigerator indefinitely.

My father used to make this sauce in a more moderate quantity, but when I opened Beverly's I wanted to sell it as part of the shelf goods, hence the large quantity. I think you will find this to be the best homemade barbecue sauce recipe.

Black Bean Sauce

1, 15-oz can Black Beans
1 Fresh Tomato, diced
½ cup Spanish Onion, minced
2 cloves Fresh Garlic, minced
2 tbs Vegetable Oil

1 tsp Cumin
1 Lemon, juiced
2 tsp Fresh Cilantro, minced
    (optional)

Salt and Pepper to taste.

Sauté onions and garlic in oil until they are transparent then add tomatoes and cook until juice is evaporated to half. Add beans, lemon juice and seasoning. Cook for 5 minutes. Puree to a fine consistency.

Serve with poached sea bass, baked chicken or Mexican food.

Hollandaise

1 lb Butter
2½ ozs ea Knorr® Hollandaise and
   Béarnaise Sauce Mixes

1 qt Milk
4 Egg Yolks
3 Lemons, juiced

Mix egg yolks with lemon juice and set aside. Over medium heat melt butter in heavy pan then add sauce mixes and stir to incorporate. Add milk whisking frequently. When mixture is thick and on the verge of boiling, pour ⅓ of the hot mixture into the egg mixture, while whisking, (this is called tempering). Continue to whisk while pouring the egg mixture back into the sauce mixture and return to heat. Bring just to the boiling point and remove from heat immediately. Be careful not to overcook as it will separate. This sauce will hold at a moderate temperature for some time before separating and clumping up and will work well on a buffet.

Long before I opened Beverly's, one of my friends, Faye Griffin, gave me the tip of adding egg yolks and lemon juice to the Knorr Hollandaise mix. I happen to like the flavor of that little bit of tarragon in the Béarnaise Sauce mix, hence, the combination of the mixes. Hundreds of people have told me that Beverly's has the absolute best hollandaise sauce they have ever tasted, so there you have it; the secret is out.

Horseradish Sour Cream Pecan

1 cup Sour Cream or Yogurt
4 tbs Horseradish
2 tbs White Wine Vinegar
1 tbs Creole or Whole Grain
   Mustard

1 tsp Salt
1 cup Heavy Cream, whipped
6 tbs Chopped Toasted Pecans
White Pepper to taste.

Mix all ingredients together, then serve with roast beef, corned beef, ham or whatever you like.

Hot Dog Chili Sauce

2 lbs Ground Beef
3 lg Onions, chopped medium
2 tbs Fresh Garlic, minced
1 tbs Salt
1½ oz Chile Powder
1½ oz Paprika
1 tsp Cloves, ground

1 tsp Nutmeg
1 tbs Sugar
1 tbs Black Pepper
1 cup Flour
5 cups Water
14 oz Catsup

Sauté onions, garlic and ground beef until meat is cooked, stirring while cooking to break up meat. Mix spices and flour together then add to meat mixture, stirring to combine. Add water and cook over medium heat. Bring to a boil, reduce heat and simmer for about 1½ hours, stirring often to prevent sticking. If mixture is too thick, you may add some water, a little at a time.

You may jar this and process it, freeze it or just refrigerate it. It should last several days in the refrigerator.

As a child, when we needed to do any kind of shopping, we had to drive 20 miles to the city of Butler, PA. One of the best things about those trips was a visit to the Hot Dog Shoppe on Jefferson St. I remember in the beginning it was a shoe repair on one side and a counter on the other where you could buy the absolute best hot dog in the world. Eventually the shoe repair went out and the Hot Dog Shoppe enlarged. When I go back to visit my mother, a trip to the Hot Dog Shoppe is always a must-several times. They still taste the same, but the dog has gotten smaller and the price has gotten larger!

This recipe has been passed around a lot in Western PA, and I'm not sure of the accuracy, but it tastes pretty close to the real thing. I hope you enjoy it as much as our family has.

Marinara

2 lbs Spanish Onion, diced medium
1 lg Bulb Garlic, minced
1 cup Olive Oil
2, #10 cans or 208 oz, Crushed or Chopped Tomatoes
1, #10 can or 104 oz, Spaghetti Sauce

1 bunch Fresh Parsley, washed and minced
½ lb Fresh Basil, washed and minced
¼ cup Fresh Oregano (optional), washed and minced

Sauté onions and garlic in olive oil in a large heavy pot until opaque. Add the parsley and half of the basil to sizzle. Add tomatoes, sauce, salt and pepper. Mix well and bring to a boil, stirring often. Reduce heat and simmer for 1 to 1½ hours. Add the remainder of basil at the end to have the fresh taste of basil.

This can be jarred up to preserve, freeze or refrigerate up to 1 week. If jarring, after filling jars, place in a hot water bath and process for 1 hour.

Mushroom Demi Glaze

2 lbs Mushrooms of your choice
3 tbs Fresh Shallots, minced
2 tbs Fresh Garlic, minced
¼ lb Butter

¾ cup Dry Red Wine
2 cups Stock
Salt and Pepper to taste.
Cornstarch or **Roux** if needed.

Clean mushrooms by wiping with a damp paper towel then slice medium thick. If using portabellas, discard stems.

Melt the butter in a large heavy skillet then add the shallots and garlic,. Sauté until transparent and then add the mushrooms. Cook until the liquid evaporates. Remove with a slotted spoon into a small bowl. Set aside. Reserve any remaining liquid. Add the wine to the skillet, deglaze and reduce the wine by about half. Add the stock and juice from the mushrooms, simmering on medium heat until reduced by about one quarter. At this point if the sauce is too thin, mix 1 tbs. cornstarch with a little water and stir into sauce or add **Roux**, a little at a time, until the sauce reaches the thickness you desire. Correct the seasoning. Add the mushrooms back into the sauce and heat well. Serve immediately with your favorite beef dish or with whatever your imagination desires.

Sour Cream and Cucumber

2 large Cucumbers, peeled, seeded
and diced very fine
1 tsp Aunt Jane's Salt®

¼ tsp Black Pepper
1 tbs Onion, grated
1 pint Sour Cream

Mix the salt with the cucumber and onion and then place the mixture into a colander. Cover it with plastic wrap right on the mixture. Force out the liquid by placing something heavy (like a heavy bowl) on it. Drain it for at least an hour. Put the mixture into a bowl and stir in the sour cream and black pepper. Adjust the seasoning.

Serve this with chilled *Poached Salmon* and *Orzo Salad*.

Teriyaki Sauce or Marinade

1½ cups Brown Sugar
1 cup Red Wine Vinegar
½ cup Vegetable Oil
1 cup Kikkoman® Soy Sauce

1 tbs Fresh Garlic, minced
2 inches Fresh Ginger, grated
1 tsp Black Pepper

Mix in glass or plastic container that is large enough to hold the meat and the marinade to cover it.

This is an excellent marinade for pork, chicken or beef.

White Sauce

1 cup Butter
1½ cup Flour
3 qts Milk

¼ tsp each Nutmeg, Black Pepper,
White Pepper, Paprika, Dry
Mustard
Salt to taste

Combine butter and flour in saucepan. Cook on medium heat while stirring for 5 minutes. Whisk in milk. Add remaining ingredients. Continue to whisk until mixture has boiled and is thick. Taste for needed salt.

Salads & Dressings

Salads

Arugala, Pear and Stilton

3 oz Arugula, washed and drained
¼ Pear, washed and quartered (I like to use Red Pears)
3 stems Asparagus

2 oz English Stilton ("The King of Cheeses"), crumbled
1 tsp Almonds, sliced, toasted and sugared

Arrange the cleaned and well-drained Arugula on individual salad plates. Slice each pear quarter into three slices and arrange in a fan manner on the Arugula. Next, arrange the asparagus. Place the crumbled stilton on top of arranged salad. Refrigerate until ready to serve. Drizzle with *Raspberry Vinaigrette* and sprinkle the almonds on last.

This recipe is per person. A wonderful salad to serve either before or after the main course.

❋

Black Bean and Mango

1 lb Dry Black Beans, pick through, wash, soak overnight and cook until tender OR use
3, 15-oz. cans Black Beans
2 ripe Mangoes, peel and cut into 1 inch cubes
½ tsp Fresh Garlic, minced

2 Limes, juiced
¼ cup Vegetable Oil
¼ cup Fresh Cilantro, chopped
1 inch Fresh Ginger, grated
¼ cup Red Onion, diced medium
Cayenne Pepper, Salt and Black Pepper to taste.

Cook the black beans without salt. If dried beans are cooked with salt, it is difficult to get them to soften. Depending on the size and the juiciness of the limes, you may have to use more limes to acquire the flavor and sweetness you desire. Combine all the ingredients. Correct the seasoning to your liking. Allow flavors to blend for at least ½ hour in the refrigerator. Serve chilled or at room temperature.

If you want to serve a great little salad plate or buffet on a hot summer day try these 4 salads; *Black Bean, Snow Pea, Sweet Potato* and *Chicken Curry*. The eye appeal is catching and the combination of tastes is incredible.

This recipe came from my oldest son Mark. As did the *Sweet Potato* and *Snow Pea*.

❋

Caesar Salad—Tableside

5 cloves Fresh Garlic
1½ tsp Dry Mustard
2 tbs Worcestershire Sauce
4 or 5 Anchovy Filets
½ cup Red Wine Vinegar
2 cups Olive Oil
¾ cup Parmesan

½ tsp Salt
1 tsp Fresh Ground Pepper
1 Lemon, juiced
2 Egg Yolks, from coddled egg, (optional)
1 head Romaine, washed, drained, torn and chilled

You will need a large wooden bowl and a wooden paddle for hand use in muddling.

Place garlic into bowl and muddle with the paddle until it is a paste. Add anchovies and do the same until they are completely paste. Add mustard, fresh ground pepper and Worcestershire sauce. Blend until combined. Add vinegar and lemon juice. Mix again until well blended. Finally, add olive oil slowly as you mix until completely blended. Put the prepared greens into the same bowl and toss until totally coated. Add egg yolks from the *coddled eggs and half of the parmesan cheese. Toss until the yolks have totally disappeared. Add the *Croutons* (recipe in the Misc. Chapter) and toss some more. Place the salad onto 4 chilled dinner plates. Sprinkle with the remaining cheese and serve with more fresh ground pepper and a lemon wedge. It is so delicious, your guests will want to skip dinner and go for another round of salad.

*To coddle eggs, place the eggs into boiling water while you are preparing the salad, (about 10 minutes). The salad is good without them but they do add a certain creaminess.

I learned to make a Caesar Salad tableside at Sanginitis Restaurant in Akron, Ohio. I haven't seen it done this way for many years, but I'm sure there are restaurants, somewhere, that still prepare it this way.

Chicken Curry With Apples and Walnuts

1, 5-lb Roaster Chicken, stewed
1 tbs Onion flakes
½ tsp Garlic Powder
1 bunch Stems from Fresh Parsley
Salt and Pepper
1 Red Delicious Apple
½ bunch Celery, sliced thin

2 tbs Spanish Onion, grated
½ to 1 tsp Curry Powder
1 tsp Tarragon
Salt and Black Pepper to taste
3 cups Hellmann's® Mayonnaise, approximately
¼ cup Walnuts, diced

To cook chicken, place it into a pot large enough to cover the chicken with water. Add the onion flakes, garlic powder, parsley stems, salt and pepper. Bring to a boil, reduce heat, cover and simmer until chicken is tender. If it has a pop out gauge that will tell you when it is done. Remove from stock, reserving stock for soup. Allow to cool to room temperature. Pick chicken from bones removing all skin, gristle and veins. By picking the chicken at room temperature, it is much easier than if it were ice cold. Tear into bite-size pieces and place into a large mixing bowl. Wash apple, quarter it and remove core. Cut into bite-size pieces. Leaving the skin on adds color to the salad. Add remaining ingredients except mayonnaise and walnuts. Gently toss together with a rubber scraper. Add 2 cups of the mayonnaise and mix just to coat. If you need more, add it. Remember you can always add more, but you can't take it out. Correct seasoning to your liking. The curry will turn brighter yellow as it ages so don't be alarmed if you don't see it immediately, because you can certainly taste it. If you like a little stronger curry flavor, add more.

Serve chilled on a bed of lettuce with your favorite garnishes or on a heated croissant. Sprinkle walnuts on top just before serving, as they will discolor the salad if mixed in. This is great on a salad buffet with the *Snow Pea, Sweet Potato/Ginger and Black Bean Salads.* Great eye appeal!

Another original from Beverly's kitchen.

❋

Chicken Teriyaki

Handful per person Mixed Salad Greens, of your choice.
1 Fresh Orange per person, peeled and separated or cut into bite-size pieces. Red Onion, peeled. sliced and pulled apart to make rings.

2–3 Cherry Tomatoes per person, sliced in half
1 Grilled Boneless Chicken Breasts per person, marinated in *Teriyaki Marinade* and grilled *Orange Curry Salad Dressing* (in Salad Dressing Chapter)

Marinate the chicken breasts for no more than 2 hours. Grill the breasts for 3 to 4 minutes on each side. Do not over cook as they will get tough. As long as they are not pink in the center, they are cooked.

Arrange salad greens onto a serving plate. Can be prepared on individual plates or on a large serving platter. Slice grilled chicken breasts across the grain diagonally. Arrange the sliced chicken breasts on top of the greens. Garnish with the orange slices, red onion rings and cherry tomatoes.

Mix the salad dressing thoroughly and pour over the salad. Serve immediately. This salad is best served with the chicken right off the grill and the salad greens cold.

Another original from Beverly's Kitchen that has stayed on the most popular list since its creation, many years ago.

❋

Father Toms Bean Salad

2, 15-oz cans Green Beans
2, 15-oz cans Yellow Wax Beans
1, 15-oz can Each: Kidney Beans, Hominy and Chick Peas
1 can Whole Baby Corn, cut into bite size pieces
4 Carrots, peeled, sliced and blanched

1 large Sweet Onion, cut into 1 inch cubes
1 each Red and Green Pepper, cut into 1 inch cubes
1½ cup each Cider Vinegar, Sugar and Vegetable Oil
Salt and Pepper to taste

Drain all the canned veggies very well. Place into a large mixing bowl. Add remaining vegetables. Toss to mix. In another bowl mix the sugar, oil, vinegar, salt and pepper together. Stir until the sugar is dissolved. Pour over the vegetables and toss gently to coat. This should marinate for several hours for the flavors to blend.

Serve chilled. Can be stored for several days or up to a week in airtight glass containers in the refrigerator. It's a great dish to take to a picnic.

This is a wonderful salad that my father made when we were all still at home. Of course he used all of our home-canned veggies, which made it even better. He always made plenty so we had it for snacks, lunch and dinner for days. Every once in awhile I have to make it for old times sake.

❋

Fresh Tuna, Bowties and Pesto

1 lb Fresh Tuna, in one piece, rubbed and roasted Jane's Crazy Mixed Up Salt®
1 lb Bowtie Pasta, cooked according to package directions. Toss with
2 tbs Olive Oil

8 oz Frozen Peas, right out of package
2 cups *Pesto*
Salt and Black Pepper to taste.

To roast fresh tuna, rub tuna with olive oil and season with Aunt Jane's Crazy Mixed Up Salt®. Place in shallow baking pan and roast in 400 degree oven just until done, (depending on the cut, about 15 minutes). It will become tough if roasted too long. If it is a thin piece, cut down on the roasting time. Remove from oven and allow to cool.

Place the pasta into a large mixing bowl. Break up the tuna into flakes, putting it in bowl with the pasta. Add remaining ingredients and mix gently with rubber spatula. Correct seasoning to you liking.

Serve chilled or hot. Great on a summer buffet or as the main course for lunch or a light dinner.

One more original from Beverly's kitchen.

❋

Fresh Green Bean and Tomato

2 lb Fresh Green Beans, stemmed
and broken into 1-inch pieces
2 lb Cherry Tomatoes, cut in half
1 small Red Onion, julienned

Parmesan, if desired
Italian Dressing, (recipe found in
the *Salad Dressing Chapter*.)

Blanch the green beans for 3 minutes or until bright green. Chill immediately in ice water. Drain well. Place into a mixing bowl. Add the cherry tomatoes and red onion. Pour salad dressing over all and toss gently until all is coated. Allow to marinate for 30 minutes. Sprinkle with parmesan, if desired.

Can be served chilled or at room temperature. This is a beautiful dish for a Christmas Party buffet or for any time at all.

This recipe was created, by me, out of boredom from serving the same salads for so many years, and it has been a great addition.

Macaroni—Elbows

1 lb Elbow Macaroni
1 Green Pepper, diced
½ head Celery, sliced thin
2 tbs Spanish Onion, grated
1 Carrot, peeled and coarsely grated
2 tbs Fresh Parsley, finely minced
2 tbs Fresh Dill, finely minced OR

1 tsp Dry Dill Weed
2 cups Hellmann's® Mayonnaise
¼ cup Cider Vinegar, I prefer
Heinz®
¼ cup Sugar
1 tsp Dry Mustard
Salt and Pepper to taste.

Cook elbows according to package directions. Cool with cold water and drain immediately and very, very well. You want all the liquid out of the elbows so the salad won't be too wet. Mix the mayonnaise, vinegar, sugar, mustard, salt and pepper together in a small bowl. Place well-drained elbows into a large mixing bowl. Add the prepared vegetables along with the mayonnaise mixture, then mix until all is blended. Place into a serving container and garnish with shredded carrots and minced parsley or sprigs of fresh dill.

Michaels Antipasto Salad

½ Small Head Cauliflower, broken into small florets
½ cup Artichoke Hearts, cut into quarters
1 large Sweet Onion, sliced
½ cup Baby Corn, cut into bite-size pieces
½ cup Hot Green Chiles
½ cup Sliced Carrots
½ cup Sliced Celery
½ cup Ripe Olives
2 tsp Capers
½ cup Green Olives, chopped
¼ cup Red Wine Vinegar
¾ cup Olive Oil
1 tsp Fresh Garlic, minced
¼ tsp Fresh Ground Black Pepper

Drain all the canned veggies very well. Combine all ingredients, except last 4, in a mixing bowl. In a smaller bowl combine last four ingredients, mixing well to blend. Pour over vegetable mixture. Place into a glass container. Cover and refrigerate for 48 hours allowing the ingredients to marinate and absorb the flavors.

Serve cold or at room temperature. Great for picnics, buffet tables and any time.

This is a wonderful refreshing salad. Thank you, Michael.

✳

Oriental Chicken Salad

1 per person Chicken Breast, skinned, boned and marinated in *Teriyaki Marinade* at least 2 hours
½ cup Oriental Rice Noodles per person that have been fried according to package directions
2 cups Mixed Salad Greens per person
1 tsp Toasted Sesame Seeds per person
8–10 Cashews per person
¼ cup *Oriental Salad Dressing,* per person

Grill the chicken breasts by placing the marinated chicken on a preheated grill. Cook for 4 minutes on each side. Do not overcook, as they will get tough. I think one tends to overcook chicken breasts. As long as they are not pink in the middle, they are cooked. While doing so, place the greens into a large mixing bowl, pour dressing over and toss to cover the greens with dressing. Arrange greens on individual plates or on one large serving platter. Mound the fried noodles on top of the greens. Slice chicken breast diagonally across the grain, arrange decoratively on top of noodles. Sprinkle with the sesame seeds and cashews. If you want a little color you could add some cherry tomato halves, red onion rings or red pepper spears, but this is not necessary.

The flavors of this salad are incredible. It was brought to Beverly's by my son Michael and it is right up there as one of the most popular menu items. Thank you, Michael. As you all know Michael now owns and operates Beverly's.

✳

Orzo and Lemon

1 lb Orzo, cooked as directed on
package, chilled
2 tbs Olive Oil
1 Red Pepper, sliced thin into
1-inch long slivers
½ head Celery, thinly sliced

1 bunch Scallions, cleaned and sliced
diagonally ⅛-inch thick
4 Lemons, juiced
½ cup Olive Oil
3 tbs Fresh Parsley, chopped
2 tbs Fresh Mint, chopped
Salt and Pepper to taste.

Toss the first 2 tbs. of olive oil with the orzo immediately after cooking, to prevent the orzo from sticking together.

Toss all ingredients together. Correct seasoning for lemon, salt and oil.
Serve chilled.

This is an original recipe. I've had great response serving this dish with chilled *Poached Salmon* and *Cucumber Dill Sauce.*

❋

Shrimp Salad

1 lb Shrimp, cooked
1 tbs Sweet Onion, grated
¼ Sweet Red Pepper, finely diced
1 rib Celery, finely diced
½ tsp Old Bay® Seasoning
¼ tsp White Pepper or to taste

½ Lemon, juiced
A sprinkling of thyme
Salt to taste
Just enough Hellmann's® to hold it
together.

I'm really not a mayonnaise lover so I don't use it freely, but the lemon juice will give some moisture. You can use frozen cooked shrimp for this recipe, but if you do, squeeze out all the excess moisture, otherwise this salad will be too wet.

Place everything into a bowl except the mayonnaise, toss together then add the mayonnaise a little at a time to prevent using too much. One of my favorite expressions is," you can add more, but you can't take it out".

This can be used in several different ways:
In a Croissant
Fill a nice ripe Tomato for a luncheon
Place into small *Éclairs* for an appetizer
Cocktail Sandwiches
As a spread for Crackers
Filling for Cherry Tomatoes

❋

Smoked Duck Breast—Raspberry

1 Smoked Duck Breast per person
Mixed Greens of your choice
Grilled Red Onion Rings

Raspberry Vinaigrette
Fresh Raspberries as garnish
(optional)

In a mixing bowl place chilled greens and enough **Raspberry Vinaigrette** to totally coat the greens when tossed thoroughly. Place on chilled individual plates or a large serving platter. Slice duck breast into ¼-inch slices, cut diagonally across the grain of the breast. Arrange slices in a fan design on top of the greens. Garnish with the grilled red onions rings and the raspberries.

This was one of the first salad platters to appear on Beverly's menu. I think the blend of flavors are incredible. You have sweet, sour, smoky, salty and crisp flavor. Try this: you will love it.

Snow Pea and Water Chestnut

1 lb Fresh Snow Peas, washed, stem
end and string removed
1, 6-oz can Water Chestnuts, sliced
and drained

1 tbs Sesame Seeds, toasted
1 small Red Onion, julienned
¼ cup Sesame Oil
½ cup Kikkoman® Soy Sauce

Toss all ingredients together and serve. This is best if chilled and served within an hour. The Kikkoman will discolor the snow peas if allowed to set too long and they will also loose their crispness.

Suggested salad combinations would be: **Sweet Potato, Black Bean and Mango, and Chicken Curry**. 4 Great salads that go very well together.

The credit for this one goes to my oldest son, Mark.

Potato and Sour Cream

5 lbs Russet Potatoes, boiled whole
   in salted water
3 tbs Spanish Onion, grated
½ bunch Fresh Parsley, washed
   drained and chopped fine
¾ head Celery, sliced thin
¼ cup Heinz® Cider Vinegar

½ tsp Garlic Powder
2½ lbs Sour Cream
¾ cup Hellmann's® Mayonnaise
Salt and Pepper to taste. This will
   require a lot of salt but add it as
   you test it.

Slice celery across the rib ⅛-inch-thick, chop parsley and grate onion. Set aside. As soon as the potatoes are cool enough to handle, peel and cube them into 1-inch cubes. You want to make this salad while the potatoes are still fairly warm as the flavors will blend better and the potatoes will be more flavorful. Cut potatoes into a mixing bowl large enough to hold everything and still have room for mixing. Sprinkle potatoes with garlic powder, salt and pepper, parsley, onion, celery and vinegar. Toss gently and allow to stand together for 15 minutes. This time allows the flavors to be absorbed into the potatoes instead of in the dressing. Add sour cream and mayonnaise. Mix well. It may seem a little wet but as it cools the moisture will disappear.

   Serve chilled or at room temperature. Best if served very fresh. Garnish with fresh parsley.

Another original from Beverly's Kitchen. Not liking mayonnaise much, I decided to try sour cream instead. I created this recipe quite a few years ago and it has been a huge success.

Seafood and Shells

1 lb Pasta Shells, cooked as directed
   on package. I prefer the medium
   size shell so the bits of seafood
   can get trapped in them.
¼ cup Olive Oil
1 lb Shrimp, cooked. Either cook
   them yourself (if you do cook,
   drain and chill thoroughly) or
   you can use the frozen cooked
   ones. If you use frozen, make
   sure all the excess water has been
   squeezed out. The little baby
   shrimp are kind of fun for this. I
   just prefer to cook them myself. I
   like the texture better.

1 lb Bay Scallops, poached. To poach
   scallops use the same method as for
   boiling shrimp (look in the
   Appetizer Chapter) only on a much
   smaller scale. Cook the scallops
   ONLY 3 or 4 minutes as they will
   get too tough. Drain and chill.
4 Scallions, cleaned and sliced
   diagonally across
1 Red Pepper, cut into 1-inch slivers
1½ cup Hellmann's® Mayonnaise
½ cup Heinz® Catsup
1 Lemon, juiced
Salt, Black Pepper and Cayenne
   Pepper to taste.

Cook pasta. Chill down with cold running water, drain thoroughly and toss with olive oil. Place into large mixing bowl. In a small bowl combine mayonnaise, lemon juice and catsup. Add all ingredients to pasta and mix until everything is coated with the dressing. Correct seasoning to your taste. I like it a little spicy.

This is one of my originals. Serve this on a buffet table or as the main course for lunch or a light supper.

❋

Spinach, Mandarin Orange and Red Onion

Fresh Spinach, cleaned and deveined
Mandarin Orange Sections,
   drained
Red Onion, sliced and separated
   into rings

Orange Curry Salad Dressing
   (found in the *Salad Dressing Chapter*)

The amounts you would use depend on your individual taste and the number of guests that you have.

Arrange spinach on plate. Top with orange sections and red onion rings. At this point you could place it into the refrigerator until serving time. Pour salad dressing over all and serve immediately. This is a nice salad to serve either before or after the main course and quite tasty also.

One day, when there used to be a Grand Union in town, I overheard a woman talking about this salad combination. The mandarin oranges were on sale so I bought some, tried it and loved it. A great combo!

❋

Spinach with Hot Bacon Dressing

Fresh Spinach, stemmed, washed,
   drained and chilled
Fresh Mushrooms, wiped with damp
   paper towel and sliced
Crisp Bacon, crumbled

Hard Boiled Eggs (to make the
   perfect hard boiled egg look in
   the *Misc. Chapter*)
Red onion rings or sliced scallions
   for garnish
Hot Bacon Dressing, found in the
   Salad Dressing Chapter

The amounts depend on your individual tastes and the number of guests you are serving.

Place chilled spinach onto chilled individual salad plates or a large chilled platter.
   Heat dressing in microwave on low, or use as soon as dressing is prepared. If reheating in the microwave, be careful not to overheat it as it will over cook the eggs and cause

it to separate. Spoon the heated dressing over the top of the spinach. Add the sliced mushrooms and top it with the bacon crumbles. Arrange the hard boiled egg in the center and serve immediately while the dressing is still hot. If desired, garnish with red onion rings or sliced scallions.

What a great salad! This dressing may also be served on a dandelion salad, which, as a child was a family favorite in late spring or early summer.

Sweet Potato and Ginger

4 lbs Sweet Potatoes, cooked whole with the skins left on(This allows the sugar to be contained in the potato) chilled, peeled and cut into 1-inch cubes.
¼ cup Red Onion, diced
1 cup Green Pepper, diced
¼ cup Fresh Parsley, minced
2 Limes, juiced

1 tsp Beef Base OR 2 Beef Bouillon Cubes, dissolved in
¼ cup Hot Water
1 tbs Curry Powder
2 inches Fresh Ginger, grated
¼ cup Olive Oil
Salt, Black Pepper and Cayenne Pepper to taste.

Be careful not to overcook the potatoes, as they will turn to mashed potatoes.

Place the prepared sweet potatoes in a large mixing bowl. Mix the olive oil, lime juice and the beef bouillon together, pour over sweet potatoes, and mix gently.

Combine all ingredients together and toss lightly but completely, being careful not to break up potato cubes. Chill at least an hour, for flavors to blend.

For an eye-catching menu, serve this with the **Snow Pea**, the **Chicken Curry**, and the **Black Bean Salads**. You will be the hit of summer picnics.

This is another one from my son, Mark. He was a great cook and a wonderful person.

Sweet and Sour Cole Slaw

1 med head Green Cabbage, sliced very thin or cut on a slaw cutter
1 large Carrot, peeled and shredded
1 med Green Pepper, seeded and shredded
2 ribs Celery, shredded

2 tbs Spanish Onion, grated
1 cup Sugar
1 cup Heinz® Cider Vinegar
1 cup Vegetable Oil
Salt and Pepper to taste

Place all the prepared vegetables into a mixing bowl. Mix vinegar, sugar and oil together and toss with vegetables. Mix well then season with the salt and pepper. Allow to marinate about 30 minutes.

For a different taste treat, you can add some raisins, apples or crushed pineapple.

This is a wonderful deviation from the mayonnaise dressed slaw that we are all accustomed to. I created this because of my lack of love for mayonnaise and it has been accepted very well because it has less fat and the flavor of the vegetables will not be overwhelmed by the mayonnaise.

❋

Tuna with Fresh Herbs

2, 6-oz cans Water Packed White
    Tuna, well drained
2 ribs Celery, sliced thin
4 leaves Fresh Sage, chopped or ½
    tsp dried
4 leaves Fresh Mint, chopped or ½
    tsp dried

¼ tsp Dill Weed, chopped
1 tbs Spanish Onion,grated
1 Lemon, juiced
Hellmann's® Mayonnaise
Salt and Pepper to taste.

Combine all the ingredients together. Add mayonnaise a little at a time to suit your own taste.

    This is a great combination. The fresh sage, mint and lemon juice add so much to a normally ho hum tuna salad.

This is another great idea from my son, Mark.

❋

Salad Dressings

Blue Cheese Dressing or Dip

1 lb Danish Blue Cheese or Roquefort, half crumbled very finely and half broken into larger chunks. I prefer the imported as it seem to be milder.

1 pint Sour Cream

1 pint Hellmann's® Mayonnaise

½ cup Cider Vinegar

1 tsp each Salt, Pepper, Dry Mustard

1 tsp Fresh Garlic, minced

2 or 3 tbs Worcestershire Sauce

Combine all of the ingredients in a large mixing bowl by using a whisk. Adjust seasoning to your liking. If it is a little to thick you can thin it some with either buttermilk or a little half and half.

When I worked at Sanginitis in Akron, Ohio, they had the absolute best Blue Cheese dressing ever. I have tried over the years to make it and keep it just that.

I hope you enjoy this as much as we have.

Caesar Salad Dressing

5 cloves Fresh Garlic

1½ tsp Dry Mustard

2 tbs Worcestershire Sauce

4 or 5 Anchovy Filets

½ cup Red Wine Vinegar

2 cups Olive Oil

¾ cup Parmesan

½ tsp Salt

1 tsp Fresh Ground Pepper

1 Lemon, juiced

2 Egg Yolks, from coddled egg (optional)

1 head Romaine, washed, drained, torn and chilled

Place all ingredients, except oil, into processor bowl using the steel blade. With processor running, very slowly pour the olive oil through hole in lid. This should get fairly thick. Adjust the seasoning. The anchovies and the parmesan are both salty so you may want to add the salt last. Use immediately or store in fridge in an airtight container until ready to be served. At this point you can toss the greens with the prepared dressing along with *Croutons* and more parmesan. Place on chilled plates, sprinkle a little parmesan on top and serve.

Creamy Garlic

2 tsp Fresh Garlic, minced
½ Carrot, chopped
¼ cup Cider Vinegar
½ cup Hellmans Mayonnaise
½ cup Sour Cream
1 tsp each Fresh Parsley, Basil,
    Thyme, chopped fine

1 tsp Dill Weed (optional)
1 tbs Salt
½ tsp Black Pepper
2 cups Blended Oil, half olive and
    half vegetable oil

Except the oils, place all the remaining ingredients into bowl of processor with the steel blade. Process until all the ingredients are finely chopped. Gradually add the oils through hole in lid, with processor running. This mixture should be nice and thick. Adjust seasoning to your taste.

This is also good as a dip for those vegetables. That is when the dill comes in play.

I think you will really enjoy this dressing.

When I opened Cheese Etc. in Connecticut, I was trying to think of anything I could make to bring in more revenue. That's when this line of salad dressings came to fruition. And, by the way everyone of them is my own creation.

Creamy Cole Slaw Dressing

1 pint Sour Cream
1 pint Hellmann's® Mayonnaise
½ cup Sugar

½ cup Cider Vinegar
½ tsp Dry Mustard
Salt and Pepper to taste

Mix all ingredients together and pour over prepared slaw ingredients.

This recipe came from my mother. Instead of using sour cream, she would add vinegar to milk or cream, causing the milk to curdle and thicken. She also used salad dressing instead of mayonnaise. She would make this dressing for fresh-from-the-garden leaf lettuce and green onion salad. Usually we would have just plain boiled potatoes with this and homemade bread, of course. I can still taste it.

Honey Balsamic Vinaigrette

1 tsp Fresh Garlic, minced
½ cup Honey
¼ cup Water
½ tsp Black Pepper

2 tsp Salt
½ cup Balsamic Vinegar
Olive oil

Place all ingredients, except olive oil, into processor bowl with the steel blade.

With processor running, very slowly pour olive oil through the hole in lid until it gets to the consistency of your liking. This is a great all-around dressing.

I created this dressing for a fundraiser at the Canfield Casino, in Saratoga Springs, NY, a few years ago. The food was donated by local restaurants and food suppliers. My donation was gallons of this dressing and sheets of carrot cake.

Hot Bacon Dressing

¼ cup Bacon Drippings
1 cup Spanish Onion, minced
1 tsp Fresh Garlic, minced
1 cup Cider Vinegar
1 cup Brown Sugar

1 cup Water
¼ cup Worcestershire Sauce
6 Eggs
Salt and Pepper to taste.

Sauté onions and garlic in the bacon drippings until they are transparent. Add the remaining ingredients, except the eggs, and simmer for 15 minutes. In a separate bowl, whisk the eggs until the yolks and whites are totally combined. Temper the eggs by very slowly pouring in half of the hot liquid, whisking all the while. (If you add it too fast, it will cook the eggs and cause a curdled appearance which is not appealing to the eye.) Then very slowly, while continuing to whisk, add the egg mixture into the remaining hot liquid. (You have just learned the procedure of tempering.) Return the mixture to the heat, whisking as you go, and continue to heat just until it comes to a boil. This dressing has to be served hot. Adjust the seasoning to your liking.

This is a take-off from a dressing my mother used to make for wild dandelion salad, which she served hot over new, boiled potatoes with homemade bread of course. It was a spring thing. The dandelions should be picked only in the spring when they are small and before they flower. A little bitter, but oh so delicious. Now you can buy dandelions in the produce department of your grocer, but somehow it's not the same. Try using those weeds, that you dig up in the spring with this dressing. . . . You'll love it!

Italian Vinaigrette

2 tsp Dry Mustard
12 cloves Fresh Garlic, crushed with skins on
1 cup Red Wine Vinegar
½ cup Water
1½ tbs Salt

1 tsp Black Pepper
1 tsp Dried Oregano
1 tsp Dried Basil
2 cups Blended Oil, half olive and half vegetable

Place all ingredients into a glass 4-cup container and shake to mix. Allow to set for at least 2 hours for the flavors to combine. If you use a bottle, punch holes in the top to allow the dressing to be shaken onto the salad.

This is delicious topped with crumbled blue cheese.

This recipe came from Sanginitis Italian Restaurant in Akron, Ohio, where I worked for a few years. I can still see the salad woman shaking the gallon jug of dressing onto each individual salad. Her name was Tiny. What a great place!

❋

Orange Curry and Ginger Dressing

1 Orange, zested and cut into small dice
1 tbs Fresh Garlic, minced fine
2 tsp Fresh Ginger, grated
1½ cup Orange Juice
1 cup Cider Vinegar, Heinz® only

1½ tbs Curry Powder
1½ tsp Salt
1 tsp Black Pepper
4 tbs Sugar
4 cups Blended Oil, ½ Vegetable and ½ Olive

You will need a full size processor for this recipe or you'll need to cut the recipe in half. In the bowl of the processor, using the steel blade, place all the ingredients except the orange zest, diced orange and the oils. With processor running, slowly pour oil through hole in lid. The dressing should thicken some. Remove from processor, stir in zest and diced oranges. Correct seasoning to your liking.

I created this recipe years ago at Cheese, etc. my second gourmet shop. I bottled and sold my home-made dressings for retail consumption. This was one of the most popular ones. Most recently, at Beverly's Specialty Foods as it was called in the beginning, it really gained notoriety when the *Chicken Teriyaki Salad* was created and put on the menu. If you like orange, curry and ginger, you will love this recipe.

❋

Oriental Dressing

1 cup Honey
½ cup Sesame Oil
2½ cups Vegetable Oil
2 cups Rice Wine Vinegar

1 tsp Dry Mustard
2 tsp Black Pepper
2 tsp Salt

Place all ingredients into mixing bowl and whisk to blend. This dressing will keep for a long time in the refrigerator in an airtight container.

Michael came up with this recipe to go along with the **Oriental Chicken Salad.**
 It has been one of the two most popular ones since the day it went on the menu. Thank you, Michael.

Pepper Parmesan Dressing

½ cup Red Wine Vinegar
1 tsp Fresh Garlic, minced
1 tsp Black Pepper, course ground
1 tsp Dry Mustard

1 tsp Salt
¼ lb Parmesan
3 cups Olive Oil

Place all ingredients, except the oil and salt, into bowl of processor with steel blade. With processor running, slowly pour oil through hole in lid. Dressing should thicken up quite well. The parmesan is quite salty, so you may want to taste the finished product before adding the salt.

Years ago at one of my shops, someone asked me to make a pepper parmesan dressing. I did and this is it! If you want it more peppery, just add more pepper.

Poppy Seed Dressing

1½ cup Sugar
1 tsp Dry Mustard
2 tsp Salt
⅔ cup Cider Vinegar

3 tbs Spanish Onion, grated
2 cups Olive Oil or Vegetable Oil
3 tbs Poppy Seeds

Dissolve sugar in vinegar. Add remaining ingredients and whisk until blended.
 This is a wonderful dressing, but it is sweet. It will keep forever, but it won't stay in your refrigerator long enough for you to find out!

I got this recipe from one of my best friends, Marie Ruhe. We were partners in the Cheese Barrel in Margaretville, NY, twenty something years ago. Marie and her husband Skip are retired and have moved to southern California, where they have a beautiful mini-ranch on top of a hill from which you can see forever. It's a beautiful place for retirement.

❋

Raspberry Vinaigrette

1 cup Raspberry Vinegar
½ cup Water
½ cup Raspberry Jam
2 tsp Salt

1 tsp Pepper
2 tsp Fresh Shallots, minced
3 cups Blended Oil, half vegetable
  and half olive

Place all ingredients, except the oils, into processor bowl using the steel blade. With processor running, slowly pour oils through hole in lid. The dressing should thicken quite well.

Another original from Beverly's kitchen. I created this recipe to go with the **Smoked Duck Salad**. What a wonderful blend of flavors. Also use this dressing for: **Arugula, Pear and Stilton Salad** or use your own imagination.

❋

Russian

2 cups Hellmann's®
2 cups Heinz® Catsup
4 tbs Relish, I use my home-made
  (you can find the recipe in the
  Family Pantry). Store-bought

can be used, but it's a little
  stronger.
2 tbs Cider Vinegar
1 tbs Spanish Onion, grated
Salt and Pepper to taste.

Whisk all ingredients together in a mixing bowl, until the mayonnaise is incorporated and there are no white lumps. Store in an airtight container.

When I added reuben sandwiches to the menu at Beverly's, I created this recipe. I think the store-bought dressing is much too tart and strong, so I'm sure you will enjoy this one.

Thousand Island can be made from the above by adding chopped hard boiled eggs and chopped stuffed green olives. This alone can be used as a sandwich spread too.

❋

Sweet and Sour Dressing

2 cups Cider Vinegar
2 cups Vegetable Oil
2 cups Sugar
¼ cup Spanish Onion, finely minced

1 small Tomato, seeded and
   chopped fine
2 slices Bacon, crisp and crumbled
Salt and Pepper to taste

You can cut this recipe in half without any problem, but it keeps well and is great to have available. Mix all the ingredients together and place in an airtight container. Chill for at least an hour to blend flavors. The bacon may be omitted but the smoky flavor adds a lot.

This dressing is great on a spinach salad. You can use this recipe without the bacon and tomato for coleslaw. Enjoy it as is or experiment with it.

Tomato and Basil Dressing

2 cups Canned Crushed Tomatoes
2 tsp Fresh Garlic, minced
¼ cup Fresh Basil, chopped
½ cup Water
¾ cup Balsamic Vinegar

4 cups Blended Oil, half olive and
   half vegetable
1½ tbs Salt
1 tsp Black Pepper
1 cup Fresh Tomato, seeded and
   diced fine

In bowl of processor place all the ingredients, except oil, basil and fresh tomatoes.

With the processor running, steel blade in place, slowly pour oil through the hole in lid. It should thicken up quite nicely, if you pour the oil in slowly enough.Remove to a mixing bowl and add the fresh chopped tomatoes and fresh basil. Adjust the seasoning to your taste.

Meats & Seafoods

Great Uncle Will

Apple Stuffed Pork Chops

4 Double thick cut pork chops
2 cups Stale Bread, cut into ½ inch
   cubes
¼ cup Spanish Onion, diced
1 rib Celery, diced
3 tbs Butter

1 Apple, washed, cored and cut into
   ½-inch cubes
3 or 4 Fresh Sage Leaves, minced
   fine
Salt and Pepper to taste

Don't use a Macintosh apple as they cook up too much; use any kind but.

Make a deep cut into the pork chop from the fatty side towards the bone, making as much of an opening as you possibly can. Rinse and pat dry with paper towel. Sprinkle inside and out with a little salt and pepper. Set aside. In a heavy skillet, melt butter, then add onions, celery and apple and sauté until transparent. Place the bread cubes into a mixing bowl along with the sage and sautéed vegetables.

Mix well. Add just enough chicken broth or water to hold it together. Taste for salt and pepper. You don't want the stuffing to moist as it will be doughy and soggy. Place as much of the stuffing in each chop as you can. Stand the chops on the bone end with the stuffing filled opening up. Place onto a sprayed baking pan. Put about ¼-inch chicken broth or water in bottom of the pan. Place into a preheated 375 degree oven for about 45 minutes. Use the drippings to make a gravy or sauce.

B.J.'S Chicken

1, 3 or 4 lb Fryer, cut into serving
   size pieces
1 cup Onion, chopped medium
3 cloves Garlic, minced
1 Green Pepper, chopped medium
3 Fresh Tomatoes, chopped medium
8 oz Fresh mushrooms, sliced
1 small can Sliced Black Olives,
   drained

1 tsp Dried Basil
1 tbs Dried Parsley
¾ cup Dry White Wine
2 cups Chicken Broth
Olive Oil
Flour for dredging (about 2 cups)
1 tsp each Salt and Pepper

Mix flour, salt and pepper together to use for dredging the chicken.

Heat a heavy skillet with ¼ cup olive oil. When hot, add a layer of chicken, skin side down. Brown very well on both sides. Remove from skillet to a large baking pan or large roaster. When all chicken pieces have been browned and removed from skillet, add onions, garlic, peppers and mushrooms using a little more olive oil, if needed. With heat on medium high, sauté until opaque. Add tomatoes and mix. Remove with slotted spoon and place over chicken.

Deglaze the skillet with the wine. Add basil and parsley then pour over chicken along with the chicken broth. Sprinkle with a little more salt and pepper. Cover loosely and place into a 375 degree oven for 45 minutes to 1 hour.

Quite a few years ago while visiting my mother and being the C.O.D. (Chef on Duty) I decided to be a little creative with chicken. This dish is what I came up with and it has been called B. J.'s Chicken ever since. (J is for Jean.) I have used canned mushrooms and no wine. It is good either way and quite easy to prepare. Enjoy!

Beef Chili with Beans

2½ lbs Ground Chuck
2, 28-oz Cans Chopped Tomatoes
1 lg Spanish Onion, chopped
4 ribs Celery, cubed small
2 tsp Fresh Garlic, minced

2, 15-oz Cans Beans of your choice.
½ cup *Chili Seasoning*, recipe found in **Misc Chapter**
1, 13-oz Can Tomato Soup (optional)

Sauté ground meat in a hot, heavy pan, stirring regularly to break up meat. When all is browned, add onions, garlic and celery. Continue to brown until the onions are transparent. Add seasoning, tomatoes and beans. I use any kind of canned beans—even a mixture of several. It gives the chili an interesting appearance, texture and taste. I have also used cooked dried beans that have been prepared separately.

Reduce flame and simmer until the onions and celery are tender. Stir often.

If the chili has a harsh acid taste, add the tomato soup. It really mellows it out.

Beef Stroganoff

1½ lbs Sirloin or Filet Ends, sliced
   almost paper-thin
1 stick Butter
1 lb White Mushrooms, sliced
½ cup Onions, chopped fine
1 tsp Fresh Garlic, minced

½ cup White Wine
2 cups Sour Cream
1 tbs Fresh Parsley, chopped
1 tbs Flour
Several gratings of fresh nutmeg.
Salt and pepper to taste

Partially freeze the meat. This makes for easier slicing. Drain on paper towels for 20 minutes to dry. Melt ½ of the butter in a large, very hot skillet. Add the meat and sprinkle with salt and pepper. Sauté, stirring constantly for uniform cooking. When meat is almost cooked through, transfer it to a warm platter with a slotted spoon. Drain any juice back into the skillet that may have been transferred with the meat. Cover meat and place in a slightly warm oven to retain the heat. Continue to cook the liquid in skillet until it has reduced to almost nothing but the remaining butter. Add other half of the butter, onions and garlic. Sauté until transparent, then add mushrooms and continue to cook, stirring often, until the mushrooms have lost their whiteness and have turned a light brown and are limp. With your fingers, sprinkle flour over the mixture. Don't put it all in one spot. Stir to mix in the flour. Add the wine and continue to cook until the liquid has reduced to a small amount in the bottom of the skillet. Add the meat back into the skillet along with the sour cream. Grate nutmeg over the top. Stir very well and continue to cook until heated through. Adjust the seasoning to your taste.

Serve with egg noodles or *Spaetzle, Braised Red Cabbage* and *Homemade Applesauce*.

My friend Annie bugged me for months to teach her how to make Beef Stroganoff, I agreed. So I thought as long as I'm cooking for one let's just have a little cooking class/party. I decided to invite other friends and make it a girls gathering: much wine, many laughs, lots of fun and wonderful food.

Try this menu, you will be delighted and so will your guests.

Beef Wellington

1 Filet of Beef
3 Puff Pastry Sheets, you can find
   this in the frozen food
   department of the grocery store.

½ lb Country Pâté, sliced very thin
   OR
½ lb Baked Ham, sliced thin OR
   Mushroom Paste

Preheat oven to 375 degrees. Prepare the filet according to the *Roast Filet of Beef* recipe. Be sure it is roasted rare (110 degrees) to allow for baking in the puff pastry. Chill thoroughly. Place two sheets of puff pastry onto a work surface overlapping a little. Dampen the edges with a wet pastry brush. Press down on the overlap to seal the seam. In the center of the dough, place one layer of pâté the size of the meat, then a layer of ham or the mushroom paste. Place the meat on top of the pâté and ham or mushroom paste. Cover the top of the meat with pâté and ham or mushroom paste totally covering the meat. Bring the sides of pastry dough up to totally enclose the pâté-covered meat. Fold the ends under. You want only enough extra dough to seal it, so trim off any excess. Place seam side and folded ends on the bottom so the weight of the meat seals the dough. Place onto a baking pan that has been sprayed with vegetable spray.

Brush the entire surface with an egg wash made from 2 egg yolks and 2 tbs. water beaten together. Use the extra sheet of puff pastry dough to make cut out decorations for the top. You can make stars, holly leaves, Christmas trees or whatever you like. Brush decorations with egg wash. Place into 375 degree preheated oven. Bake until the pastry is golden brown (about 30 minutes). You have to allow time for the center of the meat to reheat. Remove from oven. Allow to stand for 10 minutes before slicing. Slice into 1½ to 2-inch slices per person. Serve hot with Hollandaise, Béarnaise Sauce or Mushroom Demi.

Chicken-Lemon Sesame

This dish can be served as hors d'oeuvres or an entrée

3 Whole Chicken Breasts	½ cup Vegetable Oil
6 Lemons, juiced	½ cup Sesame Oil
2 tsp Fresh Garlic, minced	¼ cup Soy Sauce
¾ cup Sesame Seeds, toasted	1 cup Brown Sugar
¾ cup Tahini Paste	

Cut the chicken into the desired size. If using for hors d'oeuvres, use 1½-inch squares. If for entrée, slice the breasts into 1-inch-thick slices.

Into a non-aluminum container mix the lemon juice, garlic, tahini, oils and soy sauce whisk to mix. Place the chicken pieces into the marinade. Refrigerate overnight. Just before serving, sauté the chicken pieces in a little of the marinade and the brown sugar until brown. Remove the chicken pieces and roll each piece in sesame seeds.

If serving as hors d'oeuvres, spear each piece with a toothpick, arrange on a platter with dipping sauce.

Dipping sauce:

⅓ cup Sesame Oil	½ cup Tahini
1 or 2 Lemons, juiced	3 tsp Soy Sauce
1 tsp Minced garlic	Salt and Fresh Ground Pepper

Whisk all ingredients together. Place in a small bowl to be served with the above chicken.

Serve hot or at least room temperature.

❋

Chicken and Spaghetti

1 Large Chicken, either a roaster or a stewer	1 lb Fresh Mushrooms, sliced
1 lb Spaghetti, medium thickness	1½ cups Celery, sliced thin
1 Green Pepper, diced	1 lb Sharp Cheddar, grated course
1 Red Pepper, diced	1 stick Butter
3 Large Onions, dice two, leave one whole	Salt and Pepper

Rinse chicken and place it into a stockpot. Add 2 quarts water. Sprinkle with salt and pepper, add the whole onion and bring to a boil. Reduce heat and simmer until the chicken is very tender. Remove from the pot onto a shallow pan or bowl and cool. Strain and reserve the stock, then return it to the pot. Continue to simmer until the quantity reduces to about 1 quart, then add the spaghetti and cook to not quite done or el dente. Don't overcook as it will be baked for 30 minutes. Pull the chicken from the bones into bite sized pieces, discarding the skin, bones and veins. Set aside. Meanwhile sauté the vegetables in butter, sprinkle with a little salt and pepper mix, add 1 cup water, and cook until the vegetables are tender. When spaghetti is cooked and the vegetables are sautéed, place all the ingredients, including the cheese, into a large mixing bowl. Mix well. Place mixture into a greased baking pan, bake in a preheated 350 degree oven for 30 minutes or until cheese is melted and all is bubbly.

Another tasty recipe from my sister in law, Dot McCollister, she is an excellent southern cook. I wish I had retained more of her recipes. I do have a few more in other chapters. This dish became a real treat for the customers at Beverly's and also a great dish for a buffet table any time of the year. Thank you, Dot!

❈

Chicken Breast Stuffed with Carrots, Ginger and Raisins

4 Whole Chicken Breasts, cut into halves
3 Carrots, peeled and shredded fine
2 inches Fresh Ginger, grated
¼ cup Raisins
2 tbs Orange Marmalade
3 tbs Butter

2 tbs Shallots, minced
¼ tsp White Pepper
½ tsp Salt
¼ cup Butter
¼ cup Dry White Wine
¼ cup Orange Juice

Pound out the chicken breasts to about ⅓-inch-thick. Put aside. Sauté the shallots and carrots in the butter until the carrots are turning limp but not cooked through. Remove from heat and add remaining ingredients, except the orange juice and wine.

Mix very well. Adjust seasoning. Lay the pounded-out breasts onto a work surface. Divide the carrot mixture between them. Close, by tying with string in 2 places. Lightly dredge the breasts in seasoned flour. Sauté in a hot skillet with butter, browning and turning until all sides are seared. Place into a baking dish. Pour wine and orange juice over all. Sprinkle lightly with a little salt and pepper mix. Cover loosely with foil or cut holes in top to allow the steam to escape. Bake in a preheated 375 degree oven for 45 minutes or until the inside temperature of the stuffed breasts reaches 140 degrees. Remove breasts onto a heated platter. Cover loosely with the foil to retain heat.

In the meantime, thicken the drippings with a cornstarch—water mixture, pouring it in slowly as it will thicken quickly. Adjust the seasoning. Drizzle over the breasts. Garnish with orange zest and fresh chopped parsley. Serve immediately.

❈

Chicken Florentine

2 lbs Chicken Breasts, skinless and
   boneless
1 lb Fresh Spinach, stemmed and
   chopped
¼ lb Gruyere, shredded
2 tbs Fresh Parsley, chopped
1 tbs Fresh Shallots, minced
¼ lb White Mushrooms, chopped

2 tbs Butter
⅓ cup Hellmann's® Mayonnaise
¼ tsp Nutmeg
½ tsp Fresh Ground Black Pepper
½ cup Dry White Wine
Salt to taste
Flour

Cut the chicken breasts into two sides. Place the halves between plastic, pound out to ⅓-inch-thick. Put aside. Sauté shallots and mushrooms in the butter for 5 minutes. Add spinach, parsley, gruyere and mayonnaise. Add seasonings. Mix thoroughly. Lay the pounded chicken breasts out onto a work surface. Place the spinach mixture on the chicken breast dividing as equally as possible. Close the breasts by tying with string in two places. Lightly coat the breasts with a little flour. Sauté in hot butter on all sides. Place into a baking dish. Bake in a preheated 375 degree oven for about 35 minutes, or, until the inside temperature reaches 140 degrees. Remove from oven. Place the breasts onto a warm platter covering with foil to retain heat.

To the drippings add ½ cup dry white wine. Simmer for 10 minutes, to reduce the strong flavor of alcohol. Thicken with a cornstarch—water mixture to your desired thickness. Adjust seasoning. Drizzle the sauce over the breasts. Garnish with fresh chopped parsley.

❈

Chicken Pot Pie

1 Roasting Chicken
10 Parsley Stems, reserve leaves for
   other dishes or garnish OR
1 tbs Dried Parsley
1 tsp Fresh Garlic, minced
½ cup Onion, chopped large

Salt and Pepper
5 med Potatoes, peeled and cubed
5 Carrots, peeled and cubed
½ head Celery, cubed or sliced med
1 large Spanish Onion, cubed
½ tsp Sage

Rinse chicken. Place into a large pot with salt, pepper, parsley stems, garlic and chopped onions. Bring to a boil. Reduce heat and simmer with lid on until chicken is well done. In the meantime, prepare potatoes, carrots, celery and the onion. Set aside. Remove chicken to a cooling pan, strain and reserve broth. Discard vegetables. Skim off as much fat as possible. (I use this to make a **Roux** for thickening.) Return to burner continuing to simmer until broth is reduced to the strength you desire. You will need 2 quarts of liquid. Taste and if needed add more salt and pepper, chicken base or chicken bouillon.

Place the remaining prepared vegetables into the stock. Continue to simmer until vegetables are almost cooked. Add sage. Thicken with chicken roux (this gives the pot pie a stronger chicken flavor).

To make a roux, place the reserved fat into a thick skillet or pan. With heat on medium, allow the fat to heat until all the liquid has evaporated, leaving just the fat. Add just enough flour to absorb the fat. Continue to cook until the flour starts to turn light brown. Add to the stock a little at a time to prevent over thickening. In the meantime, while the vegetables are cooking, pick the chicken from the bones, removing all the skin and veins. Break the meat into bite sized pieces. After the stock is thickened and the flavor has been adjusted, add the chicken. Stir gently just to combine, being careful not to break up the chicken pieces.

At this point, you can either make pot pie or serve the mixture over hot *Biscuits*.

To make pot pies; line a large pie tin with *Pie Dough*. Fill with the above mixture. Top it with another sheet of pie dough, sealing the edges in a crimped fashion. Slash the top crust in a decorative manner to allow the steam to escape. Brush top with milk to enhance browning. Place pie on a larger baking pan, which has been lined with foil, to catch the drips that may occur. Place the entire arrangement into a preheated 400 degree oven for 45 minutes or until the top is golden brown. Remove from oven and serve immediately.

What great "Comfort Food"! And it makes your house smell sooooo delicious, too. I always serve this with homemade cranberry sauce. Don and Jean Richards love this dish and kept several in reserve when I made them.

Chili—Cincinnati Style

1 lb Ground Beef	½ tsp Allspice
2 med Onions, diced medium	½ tsp Cinnamon
4 cloves Garlic	¼ tsp Ground Cloves
1 cup Thick Bar B Cue Sauce	¼ tsp Coriander
½ cup Water	1 tsp Salt
1 tbs Chile Powder	1, 16-oz Can Kidney Beans
1 tsp Black Pepper	Tomato juice as needed
½ oz Unsweetened Chocolate, grated	9 oz Spaghetti, cooked and lightly buttered
½ tsp Cumin	1 lb Cheddar Cheese, grated
¼ tsp Turmeric	Oyster crackers for garnish

Brown meat with ½ the onion and garlic, stirring to keep it loose. Set balance of onion aside for garnish before serving. Drain fat from meat, then add barbecue sauce, salt, pepper, spices and water and bring to a boil. Reduce heat and simmer for 30 minutes, stirring occasionally. Chili will thicken as it cooks. Add tomato juice, as needed, to create a mixture that will ladle up easily. Allow to rest at room temperature for at least 30 minutes in loosely-covered pot. This can be prepared ahead of time, refrigerated and reheated just before serving.

When it's time to serve, cook spaghetti, then drain and lightly butter.

Heat kidney beans and drain. Place a serving of spaghetti in individual pasta bowls, top with a large spoonful of kidney beans and a ladle of chili, then top with a handful of grated cheddar and a sprinkling of onions. Serve with bowls of oyster crackers and hot sauce.

When I was in Cincinnati, Ohio attending God's Bible School way back in 1956–57, one of my favorite things to do was go to a place called Skyline Chili to eat large quantities of this wonderful chili. I craved it for years and dabbled with the recipe but just couldn't get it quite right. Just a few years ago, I was excited to find the recipe in Sky Magazine, in the article *Doing Dishes* by Jane and Michael Stern. I don't know the exact date, but I'm pleased to finally have the right ingredients list. Thank you Jane and Michael. After seeing so many ingredients involved, I can understand why I couldn't get the recipe quite right.

I hope you enjoy this as much as my family has. It's a nice dish to serve on a cold winter night after skiing or sledding, or just any old time.

❋

Cordon Bleu

2, 1×3-inch pieces Chicken, Veal or
    Pork Tenderloin, per person
1 slice Swiss Cheese, per person
1 slice Baked Ham, per person

¼ cup Flour, seasoned with salt and
    pepper for dredging
¼ cup Milk
½ cup Bread Crumbs
¼ cup Butter

You can use chicken, veal or pork for this recipe. Trim any fat, gristle or skin from meat. Cut the meat into 1×3-inch pieces. You will need 2 pieces per serving.

Place each piece between sheets of plastic and pound out to a thickness of about ½-inch. You will also need 1 slice of imported Swiss cheese and 1 slice of good baked ham for each serving, and they should be sliced about ⅛-inch-thick. Place one slice of the pounded meat on the work surface, top with cheese and baked ham and then another slice of pounded meat. Dredge the sandwich-like meat in the seasoned flour. Then gently dip it into milk moistening all the flour but not washing it off. Coat the whole thing with breadcrumbs. Pressing them somewhat to secure. Melt the butter in a large heavy skillet. When melted and hot, place a single layer of the prepared meat into it and brown on one side for about 10 to 12 minutes. Turn over and brown on the other. Remove from skillet onto a warm platter. Repeat the process, keeping the browned cordon bleu in a warm oven until all are completed. Do not cover, as you want them to remain as crisp as possible. Serve immediately with wedges of lemon.

This dish requires a little prepping, but it is well worth it. I learned to make this from my friend, Walter Keller, of Binnekill Square Restaurant, in Margaretville, NY. Thank you again, Walter. He makes the best Veal Cordon Bleu you will ever have the privilege of eating.

❋

Dijon Encrusted Rack of Lamb

1 Rack Lamb per person
1 tsp Dijon Mustard per rack
1 cup Bread Crumbs

½ tsp Salt
¼ tsp Fresh Ground Black Pepper
pinch Garlic Powder

Trim the rack of some of the fat then rinse and pat dry.

Mix dry ingredients together. Coat the topside (meaty side) of the rack with mustard. Press it into the bread crumb mixture to create a coating affect. Place on a baking pan, rib side down. Place into 400 degree preheated oven. Roast for about 15 minutes, or until it reaches the degree of doneness you desire. Remove from oven. Allow to rest for 5 minutes. Place onto a cutting surface. Using a very sharp knife, cut down through the meat between every, or every other, rib. Place onto warmed plates crisscrossing the rib bone end. Serve with your *Homemade Mint Jelly*.

Another big "thank you" goes to Walter Keller from Binnekill Square Restaurant in Margaretville, NY. This has been one of my favorites and I'm sure it will be yours also.

❋

Garlic Stuffed Roast Pork with Thyme

You can use any cut you want, even a fresh ham. I prefer a bone-in loin, because in my opinion, it has better flavor. However if you're looking for easy slicing, boneless is the way to go.

4 lbs Pork
3 or 4 Cloves Fresh Garlic, slice thin
  lengthwise
1 tbs Aunt Jane's Crazy Salt®

Pepper
2 tbs Fresh Thyme, minced fine
½ cup Dry Vermouth
2–3 tbs Cornstarch

Have the meat at room temperature. Rinse very well and pat dry with paper towel. With a small, sharp paring knife, make cuts 1½ to 2 inches apart and 1 inch deep into the meat. Insert the garlic slivers into each cut. Coat with Aunt Jane's and pepper.

Place a little oil in a hot roasting pan. Sear the meat on one side. Sprinkle the top with ½ of the thyme. When the bottom is browned, turn it over and sear the other side.

Sprinkle the remaining thyme on the top. If you are using a bone-in roast be sure to have the bones on the bottom while roasting, and the fatty side up. This allows for a more juicy meat. Cover and place into a 400 degree oven for 15 minutes. Reduce heat to 325 degrees and continue to roast until the pork is falling off the bone (about 2 hours or to the temperature you desire).

During the roasting time, check every 30 minutes to make sure there is at least a ½ inch of liquid on the bottom of roaster. You don't want it to go dry. It should create it's own juice, if not add a little water. When roast reaches your desired degree of doneness, remove from roaster onto a serving platter. Cover to retain heat.

Deglaze the roaster with vermouth. Put lid back on roaster and place the roaster on a top burner. Allow to simmer for a few minutes to allow the splatters on the sides to loosen and go into the juice. At this point I always scrape the sides down with a rubber scraper not to loose a bit of that wonderful flavor. The drippings will be strong. Taste and adjust seasoning to your liking. If too strong, dilute with some hot water, if not strong enough, you could add a chicken bouillon cube or two. Thicken with cornstarch that has been brought to a pouring consistency, by mixing with either water or white wine. Depending on the amount of drippings you have, you will probably need 2 or 3 tbs cornstarch.

With the drippings simmering, whisking constantly, pour the cornstarch mixture in very slowly until it gets to the thickness you desire. Don't pour it in all at once, you may not need it and it can thicken up quite quickly.

Serve this with *Spaetzle, Braised Red Cabbage, Homemade Applesauce* and *Honey Baked Squash*. It makes a wonderful fall dinner, fit for the most educated palates.

Quite a few years ago, while living in Roxbury, NY, and working at Roxbury Run Restaurant, I invited Walter and Jackie Keller, the owners, for dinner. This was the menu I chose. As I was offering Walter seconds on what I called "gravy", he said to me," that's not gravy, that's sauce". What a compliment. He is a great chef.

Grilled Leg of Lamb

1 Boneless Leg of Lamb, butterflied
2 tsp Fresh Garlic, minced
2 inches Fresh Ginger, grated
1 cup Red Currant Jelly

¼ cup Red Wine or Balsamic
   Vinegar
1 tbs Vegetable Oil
1 tsp Salt
1 tsp Fresh Pepper (course ground)

Trim as much fat and silver skin from meat as possible then rinse and pat dry.

Melt jelly with the wine to loosen it. Add remaining ingredients stirring until well blended. Place meat into a non-aluminum container, pour the marinade over the meat, turn once to coat the surfaces and cover with a lid or plastic wrap. Marinate for two hours at room temperature, turning every 15 minutes.

Place onto a very hot grill. Grill for 10 minutes on each side. You want this to be rare or at least medium.

If your cookout guests enjoy lamb, they will love this! I served it with grilled yellow and red cherry tomatoes and a Couscous Salad.

Lamb Curry and Coconut Stew

4 lbs Stewing Lamb, trimmed of any
    fat and gristle, cut into 1½ inch
    cubes
½ lb Butter
4 med Onions, diced medium
3 tbs Fresh Ginger, chopped fine or
    grated
3 tbs Curry Powder

1 tbs Fresh Mint, chopped fine
1½ cups Coconut
4 cups Milk
½ cup Fresh Lime Juice
1 cup Heavy Cream
Salt and pepper mix
Sugar

Melt butter in a large heavy skillet, then add the onion and cook until transparent.

Remove onions and brown the meat in batches, sprinkling each batch with the salt and pepper mix and a sprinkle of sugar to enhance the browning process. Return all the meat and onions to the pan along with the ginger, curry powder, mint, ½ cup of the coconut and 3 cups of milk.

Heat the remaining cup of milk and just before it boils, add the remaining cup of coconut. Remove from heat and allow to stand for 30 minutes. Strain, reserving the milk. Press out as much milk as possible and discard the coconut. You just want to flavor the milk. Add the milk to the meat. Cover and simmer for one hour. Stir in the lime juice and then the cream and heat without boiling until ready to serve.

Adjust the taste by adding more lime juice and sugar if desired. Serve with steamed brown rice.

You will never taste a better and more eloquent lamb stew. Years ago when I first started catering out of my home kitchen, I bought a book entitled "Cash From Your Kitchen". This recipe was in it. Of course, I changed it here and there, but it is a tasty dish that you and your guests will enjoy.

Beverly's Meatballs

1 lb Ground Beef
1 lb Ground Turkey
1 lb Hot Italian Sausage
½ cup Onions, diced
1 tbs Fresh Garlic, minced
2 tbs Dried Basil or ¼ cup Fresh

2 tbs Dried Parsley or ¼ cup Fresh
4 or 5 Eggs
1½ cups Bread Crumbs
2 tsp Fresh Ground Pepper
Salt to taste

Mix all ingredients together and form into desired size. Brown in olive oil and place into sauce. Simmer for 45 min to 1 hour.

A nice variation!

❋

Meatballs by Mary Fiecich

2 lbs Ground Beef
1 lb Ground Pork
1 Egg per lb of meat
½ cup Bread crumbs per lb of meat

1 tbs Dried Parsley Flakes per lb of meat
1 tsp Fresh Chopped Garlic per lb of meat
Salt and Pepper to taste.

Mix all ingredients together. Form into balls the size you prefer and drop into simmering sauce. You can also brown meatballs on all sides in olive oil and then add to sauce, or place uncooked balls on sprayed baking sheet and bake in 350 degree oven for15 to 20 minutes, then add to sauce.

Simmer for ½ hour or so, to allow the flavor of the sauce to incorporate into the meatballs.

Mary Fiecich was a long time neighbor of my sister Louise back in Pennsylvania. This recipe has always been a family favorite.

❋

Meatloaf—Stuffed

Prepare *Meatloaf with a Twist* recipe.
Prepare *Bread Stuffing* recipe or use your favorite.

It is good to use ground sirloin for this because it has less fat. Place meatloaf mixture onto a worktable that is covered with plastic wrap. Press meat mixture out into a rectangular shape about 1-inch-thick. Place stuffing in center of rectangle, all the way to the end in a roll form. Enclose the stuffing with the meat mixture. This can be made easy be picking up the sides of the plastic wrap to lift the meat mixture into place. Place the meat roll seam side down onto a baking pan that has been sprayed with vegetable spray or lined with foil and then sprayed. Bake 1 to 1½ hours, or until juice runs clear when knife is inserted and removed.

Remove from oven. Allow to rest for 10 minutes before slicing. Slice into desired thickness. Arrange onto platter and serve immediately.

Another interesting dish from my sister, Louise.

Meatloaf with a Twist

2 lbs Ground Chuck	1 cup Dried Breadcrumbs
1 medium Potato, peeled	¾ cup Milk
1 small Carrot, peeled	4 Eggs
½ cup Onion, diced	1 tsp Salt
1 tbs Fresh Parsley, minced	½ tsp Black Pepper
1 tsp Fresh Garlic, minced	¼ cup Catsup

Pour milk over breadcrumbs, stir and set aside. Cut potato and carrot into chunks. Place into processor bowl with metal blade inserted. Add eggs and process until vegetables are very fine. Place all ingredients into a large mixing bowl. Mix by hand until well mixed. Shape into a loaf. Place into a sprayed baking pan. The meatloaf may be topped with a little catsup, onion rings or pepper slices. Cover with foil. Bake in 350 degree oven for 45 minutes. Remove foil and continue to bake until liquid comes out clear when a knife is inserted in the center.

When my children were younger, I always made a heart shaped meatloaf on Valentines Day. When it was cooked, I would transfer it to a large serving platter. With a large pastry bag and a large star tip, I piped mashed potatoes around the outside, to make it look ruffled. Using catsup and a squeeze bottle, I wrote, "I Love You" on the top. Works great for your Sweetheart, too.

Osso Bucco

Call the local butcher to inquire about the availability of veal shanks. If they don't have them on hand, they can order them for you. Have the butcher cut them into 3-inch pieces. You will need 2 per person.

8 pieces Veal Shank
2 cloves Fresh Garlic
3 tbs Olive Oil
1 Large Onion, large cubes
2 ribs Celery, ½-inch slices
2 Carrots, peeled and sliced into
    ½-inch pieces
1 tbs Fresh Garlic, minced
6 Whole Cloves

8 Parsley Stems [save the leaves for
    something else like garnishing]
¼ tsp Hot Pepper Flakes (optional)
3 Bay Leaves
1, 14½-oz Canned Diced Tomatoes
    OR
3 large Fresh Tomatoes, cubed large
¾ cup Dry Red Wine
Salt and Pepper

Season the meat with a little salt and fresh ground pepper. Braise all sides in a hot dutch oven with a little oil. Remove and repeat until all are braised. Place the meat into another pan while preparing the vegetables.

Place the celery, onions, carrots and minced garlic into the hot pan. Sauté and stir for 5 minutes. Add the remaining ingredients, stirring to combine all. Place the meat back into the pan. Add water to bring the liquid level half way up the meat. Sprinkle again with a little salt and pepper. Cover and place the dutch oven into a 325 degree oven. Roast until the meat is fork-tender and almost ready to fall off the bone. Remove the meat onto a platter. Cover with foil to retain heat. Place meat back into oven that has been turned off, just to keep warm. Strain the stock, reserving every drop. Pressing as much stock out of the vegetables as you possibly can, then discard them. Thicken the stock with *Roux* or a cornstarch and water mixture.

If using the cornstarch method, bring 4 tbs. corn starch to a liquid by adding just enough water to reach a pouring consistency. Very slowly add the cornstarch mixture to the boiling stock, whisking all the while, until it gets to the degree of thickness you desire.

If using the roux method, add roux a tbs. at a time, whisking until the sauce reaches the consistency you desire.

I have two German Chef friends to thank for this dish. One, of course, is Walter Keller and the other is my friend Rinehart whom I met in Key West during the winter of 2000. I had served Walter Keller's many times, while in his employ, but I never had the privilege of participating in the preparation of it. However, I did get to assist Rinehart with this dish as he was preparing it for another friend, David Dressey, in Key West. What fun we had working together and correcting his English at the same time. His girlfriend Gerti insisted that I try.

❋

Piccata

5 oz Per Person of Pork Tenderloin,
   Veal or Boneless, Skinless
   Chicken Breast
1 cup Flour for Dredging

2 oz Per Person Swiss Cheese,
   shredded
to taste Salt and Black Pepper
Butter for sautéing

For this dish, you can use pork tenderloin, veal or boneless, skinless chicken breast.

Trim meat of all fat, silver skin and gristle. Cut meat into slices 1-inch-thick and 3×3-inch square. Place pieces between sheets of plastic. Pound out to ¼-inch-thick, then season with a little salt and pepper mix. Dredge each pounded slice with flour.

Gently coat the entire slice with egg wash (eggs that have been whisked with a little water). Cover the slice completely with shredded swiss cheese, gently pressing to adhere cheese to meat. Place one layer of the prepared meat into a hot, heavy skillet with ½ inch melted butter. Brown for 4 minutes on one side and then the other. Remove onto a warm serving platter or onto individual plates. Serve with lemon wedges.

At Roxbury Run Restaurant, Walter Keller made this with veal. I have gone a little further to use chicken or pork tenderloin. Thank you, Walter for this great dish.

You can probably find this at Bennekill Square Restaurant in Margaretville, NY. Tell Walter, Beverly sent you.

❈

Pork Tenderloin Scaloppini

2 Pork Tenderloins
1 lb White Firm Mushrooms, sliced
1 stick Butter
1 tsp Fresh Garlic, minced
1 tsp Fresh Shallots, minced

½ cup Sherry
1 cup Flour
1 cup Heavy Cream
2 tsp Salt
1 tsp Fresh Ground Pepper

Mix salt and pepper in small bowl. Trim the tenderloins of any silver skin or fat. Rinse and pat dry. Cut into 1-inch slices across the grain of the meat. Place each slice between two sheets of plastic. With a meat pounder, pound out each piece of meat to ½-inch-thick. Sprinkle lightly with the salt and pepper mix. Dredge each piece of meat in flour. In a large heavy skillet, melt 2 tbs. butter. When it is very hot, add one layer of the prepared meat slices. Brown quickly on one side and then the other. Transfer to a large warm platter as you go. Add butter as needed. Repeat until all is sautéed.

Add the remaining butter, mushrooms, garlic and shallots and sauté, stirring until almost all of the liquid has evaporated (about 15 minutes). Add the sherry to deglaze the pan. Heat to reduce the sherry and burn off the alcohol. Add heavy cream and stir to mix. Continue to simmer to reduce the cream to the consistency you desire for the sauce. Place the meat back into the sauce, just to heat. Arrange the meat onto a serving platter or individual plates and top with remaining sauce.

This is a great alternative to veal, less expensive and very hard to tell the difference. You could also use chicken.

❈

Pot Roast of Beef

4 lbs Top or Bottom Round or
    Rump of Beef
3 cloves Garlic, sliced lengthwise
3 tbs Olive Oil
1 large Onion, cubed
2 ribs Celery, sliced thick
2 Carrots, peeled and sliced about 1
    inch thick
1 tbs Garlic, minced
6 Whole Cloves
8 or 10 Large Parsley stems
¼ tsp Hot Pepper Flakes (optional)

3 Bay Leaves
1, 14½-oz Canned Tomatoes OR
3 Fresh Tomatoes, Peeled and
    seeded
¾ cup Red Wine
2 lbs Additional Carrots, peeled and
    sliced diagonally ½ inch thick
1 lb Small Boiling Onions, peeled
2 lbs Potatoes, peeled and cut into
    serving piece size
To taste Salt and Black Pepper

Have meat at room temperature, rinse and pat dry. With a paring knife, make cuts in the meat 1 inch deep and 2 inches apart. Insert the garlic slices into the cuts. Season the meat with salt and fresh ground pepper. Braise all sides in a hot dutch oven with a little oil. Remove meat from pan onto a platter. Place the sliced vegetables, except the additional carrots, boiling onions and potatoes, into the pot. Sauté and stir for 5 minutes. Place the meat back into the pot with the vegetables. Add the whole cloves, bay leaves, parsley stems, pepper flakes, red wine and the tomatoes. Add water to bring the level halfway up the meat. Sprinkle with a little more salt and pepper. Cover and place into 400 degree, preheated oven for 20 minutes. Reduce heat to 325 degrees and continue to roast until meat is fork-tender (about 2 hours). Remove meat from roasting pan onto platter and cover to keep warm. Drain, reserving the liquid. Press as much liquid from the vegetables as you can, reserving every drop. Place the additional carrots, small onions and the potatoes into the stock. Cover and return to oven until the vegetables are fork tender.

In the mean time, slice roast to desired thickness. Arrange on the center of an oval platter, overlapping the slices. Cover to keep warm. When the vegetables are cooked, remove them with a slotted spoon and place around the sliced meat. Cover to maintain warmth. Skim off as much fat as possible. Reserve to make a roux or for Yorkshire Pudding.

To make roux to thicken the stock, place skimmed-off fat into a small pot. You'll want ½ cup, so if you need to, add butter to make up the difference. Add enough flour to absorb the fat. Brown flour slightly, to avoid the gravy tasting floury. Whisking constantly, add the hot stock to the flour, stirring and cooking until thick. Or you can thicken it with cornstarch that has been made into a pouring consistency with water. The cornstarch method certainly cuts down on fat calories.

※

Roasted Filet of Beef

One Filet of Beef
Olive Oil

Aunt Jane's Crazy Salt®

Preheat oven to 500 degrees. Trim all fat and silver skin from meat. Remove the chain, reserving for **Stew**, trimming as much of the tendons, silver skin and fat off as possible. If you use it for **Stock**, you won't need to trim it at all. If you want to cut off the ends to make it uniform, you may. The ends work great for **Beef Stroganoff**. I leave them on tucking the tapered end under to make it more uniform in size. Also, by having it not uniform in size, it will give you different degrees of doneness. Rub entire surface of meat with olive oil. Sprinkle generously with salt. Place on rack that has been placed in a baking pan. Place pan into a 500 degree preheated oven and immediately reduce the oven temperature setting to 350 degrees. Bake until the inside temperature of meat reaches 120 degrees. Filet is always served rare. By having the filet not uniform in size, it allows for those well done meat eaters. Allow to stand for 10 minutes before slicing.

Arrange decoratively in an overlapping manner around the serving platter. Serve with **Sour Cream Horseradish Sauce**, **Hollandaise Sauce**, **Portobello Demi** or nothing at all.

Roasted Leg of Lamb with Garlic and Rosemary

1 Leg of Lamb, boneless or bone-in
3 cloves Fresh Garlic, sliced
   lengthwise into 5 slices each
2 tbs Fresh Rosemary, chopped fine
   OR

1 tbs Dried Rosemary, chopped fine
2 tbs Vegetable Oil
1 tsp Salt
1 tsp Fresh Ground Pepper
¼ cup Red Wine

Have meat at room temperature for a more even roasting. Trim as much fat and silver skin off leg as possible. Rinse and pat dry with paper towels. With a sharp paring knife, make 1-inch deep cuts into meat, just the width of the knife, about 2 inches apart. Insert a slice of garlic into each cut. In a heavy dutch oven or roaster, sear the meat on all sides.

Mix rosemary, salt and pepper together. Sprinkle the mixture on all sides of meat. Add about ½ cup water to help create its own juice. Cover and place into a preheated 500 degree oven. Immediately lower the oven temperature dial to 350 degrees. Check periodically for liquid. If it seems to be low and getting dry, add a little more water. Roast until it reaches the degree of doneness that you prefer. I like this to be fork tender and falling from the bone.

Transfer from roaster to a warm serving platter. Cover with foil to retain heat. To the roaster add ¼ cup red wine and enough water to reach about 2 cups liquid. Replace the lid on the roaster and place on a top burner. Simmer for 10 minutes to allow all the flavors to be steamed from the sides. Remove lid and scrape sides with a rubber scraper, returning flavors back into the stock. Adjust seasoning to your taste. If it is not quite strong enough in flavor you could reduce it either to a lesser amount or you could add a little beef base or beef bouillon.

To make sauce, thicken with **Roux** by adding a little at a time until the thickness you desire has been reached or use a cornstarch and water mixture by mixing 2 tbs cornstarch and enough water to bring it to a pouring consistency. Drizzle slowly into stock, whisking all the while to prevent lumps. You may not need the entire mixture so be sure to add it very slowly until the sauce reaches the thickness you desire.

I like to serve this dish for Easter Dinner along with fresh Steamed Asparagus, **Roasted New Red Potatoes**, **Homemade Mint Jelly** and **Coffeed Carrots**

Mother's Baked Beans

2 lbs Dried Navy Beans
3 cups Spanish Onions, diced
4 cloves Fresh Garlic, minced
½ lb Brown Sugar

2 to 3 cups Catsup
½ lb Bacon
Salt and Black Pepper to taste

Pick through the beans to make sure there are no stones or dirt then wash very well, cover with cold water and soak overnight. Be sure there is enough water for the beans to soak up. Place the beans into a heavy pan, cover with water, and add half of the onions and garlic. Do not add salt at this time or the beans will not become soft. Bring to a boil, reduce heat to a slow cook and continue to cook until beans are tender but still whole. Add the remaining ingredients, except the bacon, mix very well and adjust seasoning to your liking (I happen to like a lot of pepper). Pour into a baking pan that has been sprayed with a non-stick spray. Bake in a 350 degree oven. Stir every half hour, continuing to bake for 2 hours adding more liquid as needed. During the last 45 minutes, place the bacon on top in a decorative manner.

Can you imagine eating this with thick slices of homemade bread. Well that is the way we had it as kids. This recipe makes the tastiest baked beans ever.

Louise's Calico Baked Beans

2 lbs Ground Beef
½ lb Bacon
½ lb Sausage (optional)
1 med Onion, diced
3 cloves Fresh Garlic, minced
1 cup Catsup
½ cup White Sugar

½ cup Brown Sugar
1 tsp Vinegar
1, 15-oz can Lima Beans
1, 15-oz can Pork and Beans
1, 15-oz can Kidney Beans
Salt and pepper to taste

In a large heavy dutch oven, cook the ground meat, bacon and sausage until very well done. Drain into a colander until all the fat is gone. Add the meat back into the pan along with the remaining ingredients. Mix well, check the seasoning and pour into a baking dish that was sprayed with a nonstick spray.

Bake for 45 minutes in a 350 degree oven. Serve hot or at room temperature.

My sister Louise gets the credit for this recipe and what a great change from the usual baked beans.

❋

Top: Michael and
Mark
Middle: Rob
Bottom: Grandson
Jonathan

Seafood

Baked Scallops with Garliced Bread Crumbs

1 lb Scallops, either bay or sea
½ cup Butter
1 cup Bread Crumbs
1 tsp Fresh Garlic, minced

¼ cup Dry White Wine
1 Lemon, juiced
1 tsp Fresh Parsley, minced
Salt and Fresh Ground Pepper

Rinse scallops and place into a sprayed baking dish that is just large enough to have the scallops in one layer. Pour the wine and lemon juice over the top. Sprinkle with a little salt and pepper.

In the meantime, melt the butter in a skillet and add the garlic. Sauté for 2 minutes over medium to low heat, then add the breadcrumbs a little at a time to absorb the butter. You may not need quite all of them. Stir to combine and to let the crumbs absorb all the butter and get crisp. Spoon the crumbs over the scallops. Place into a preheated 400 degree oven for about 15 minutes or until the crumbs are lightly browned, bubbling around the edges and hot in the center. Be careful not to overcook them or the scallops will get tough. If using bay scallops, it won't take as long as with sea scallops.

This idea came from a hotel in Quincy, MA, some 25 years ago. It's a tasty and easy dish.

Brett's Pan Seared Chilean Sea Bass with Champagne Caviar Nage and Zucchini Spaghetti

4, 8-oz. Fresh Sea Bass Filets, skin on and rubbed with olive oil, black pepper and parsley
1 tbs Shallot, chopped
1 cup Dry Champagne
1½ cup Fish Stock
½ cup Heavy Cream
4 tbs Butter, cold

2 tbs Fresh Basil, chopped
1 tbs Fresh Parsley, chopped
2 tbs Caviar, (salmon roe preferably)
4 whole Green Zucchini Squash
1 clove Garlic, chopped
1 tbs Canola oil
Salt & Pepper to taste

Shred Zucchini lengthwise on mandolin (outside meat without seeds) spaghetti size and set aside. In hot skillet with canola oil and pinch of kosher salt, add sea bass with flesh side down until golden brown and then turn over. Add ¾ cup fish stock and finish in 425 degree oven for approx. 10 min. In another medium hot skillet place 1 tsp. Canola oil and shallots and stir for 30 seconds. Add champagne and remaining fish stock and continue to cook to reduce the liquid by ½. Add heavy cream, caviar and 1 tbs. basil and reduce again until desired consistency is reached. Remove from heat and stir in 2 tbs. cold butter until completely incorporated. Add salt & pepper to taste. In third hot skillet, place 2 tbs. butter, shredded zucchini, 1 tbs. basil, garlic and salt & pepper. Stir and sauté until the zucchini is bright green.

Twirl up spaghetti in center of plate. Place sea bass skin side down, atop zucchini, topping with sauce over all. Garnish with basil chiffonade and a dollop of caviar.

Chef Brett and Tammy

Couscous Crusted Tuna with Tomato Fennel Broth

6, 6-oz Fresh Tuna, steaks
1 box Plain Couscous, prepared
    according to directions on box
1 cup Flour
Salt and Pepper, for seasoning flour
Olive Oil for frying

2 Eggs, beaten
16 oz Stewed Roma Tomatoes
3 Fresh Fennel Bulbs, julienned
½ cup Kalamata Olives, pitted and
    halved
3 cloves Fresh Garlic, minced

Dredge tuna steaks in flour on the flat sides, not around the edges. Then dip into the beaten eggs and press the couscous on top of that. Have a heavy skillet hot with ¼ inch olive oil. Brown the tuna steaks very well on both sides, and by doing so, they will be medium rare to medium. Place immediately into the following broth.

Broth

Sauté the garlic in 2 tbs. of olive oil, then add the fennel and sprinkle with a little salt and pepper to taste. Stir until the fennel is al dente, then add the olives and tomatoes. Bring to a boil and adjust the seasoning. If you would like a thinner broth, you can add either a little wine or some chicken stock at this point. Ladle into individual serving bowls and place the prepared tuna steak in the center. Sprinkle with some chopped parsley and serve immediately.

This dish was prepared by my son, Chef Rob Cone, while cooking at the Café Lafayette in Madison, CT.

Filet of Sole Rolls with Spinach and Scallop Mousse

6 Sole Filets
2 Egg Whites
½ lb Fresh Spinach, stemmed
3 Shallots, chopped
½ lb Scallops
2 tbs Butter

½ cup Dry White Wine
1 Lemon, juiced
½ tsp each Salt and Fresh Ground
    Pepper
Grating of fresh Nutmeg

Prepare sole by dividing the filets in half lengthwise. Set aside. Sauté shallots in butter until just opaque. Place scallops, spinach, egg whites, half of the shallots, nutmeg and salt and pepper into bowl of processor, process until thick and combined. Lay filets out onto work counter that has been lined with plastic. With a spatula spread each half of filet with the mousse, roll up as a jellyroll. Place swirl side up with sides just touching, into a baking dish that is sprayed with pan spray. Mix the wine and lemon juice with the remaining shallots and pour over the fish. Bake in a preheated 375 degree oven for 15 minutes. Remove from oven and place the rolls onto a warmed serving dish and keep warm by returning them to the oven that has been turned off. Reduce the liquid over medium heat until it reaches a sauce consistency. You can thicken this by whisking in cold butter. Correct seasonings, add more salt, and pepper if needed.

Oven Poached Salmon

2 lbs Fresh Salmon Filet, skinless
½ cup Dry White Wine
¼ cup Lemon Juice

1 tsp Aunt Jane's Crazy Salt®
¼ tsp Dill Weed

Rinse salmon filet and remove all bones with clean pliers (They will pull right out). Place salmon onto a shallow baking pan that has been sprayed with non-stick spray. Pour wine and lemon juice over salmon and sprinkle with Aunt Jane's® and dill weed. Cover with foil and bake in a 400 degree oven for 20 minutes.

Use this method for a whole fish, a whole side or for small filets and steaks.

For a great presentation, prepare a half salmon and chill. Remove from the baking pan when cold by putting several large flat utensils under the whole side and transfer it to a serving platter that has been lined with a dark green leafy vegetable like kale. Garnish with sprigs of fresh dill, half lemon slices and cherry tomato halves. Serve with the *Orzo Salad* and *Cucumber Sour Cream Sauce.*

Prosciutto Wrapped Filet of Atlantic Salmon with **Basil Pesto,** *Whipped Spuds and Roasted Red Pepper Aioli*

4, 8-oz Portions of Atlantic Salmon,
  skin off and rubbed with olive oil
  and black pepper
12 Thin Slices Parma Prosciutto
¼ cup White Wine
1 Lemon, juiced
¼ cup Water

¾ cup **Basil Pesto**, or to taste
6 to 8 Yukon Gold Potatoes, peeled
¼ cup Butter
½ cup Sour Cream
 Buttermilk
Salt and Pepper to taste

Whipped Spuds

Cook potatoes in boiling water until tender, about 35 to 45 minutes. Drain and mash with butter, sour cream and buttermilk. Add the buttermilk gradually to reach the desired consistency. Add salt and pepper to taste and whip until light. Keep warm until salmon is cooked.

Wrap the salmon filets with the prosciutto and sear all sides until golden brown in canola oil. Add the wine, lemon juice and water and finish in a 425 degree oven for 12 to 15 minutes.

Stir ¾ of the pesto into the whipped spuds, place a portion of the potatoes onto individual plates and lean a serving of the salmon against the spuds and drizzle with the following Aioli (a squirt bottle works well for this). Use the remaining pesto for garnish atop salmon and serve immediately.

Aioli

2 Egg Yolks
3 Garlic Cloves, chopped
½ oz Wine Vinegar
½ oz Water
1 tsp Dry Mustard

2 cups Canola Oil
1 cup Roasted Red Pepper
Lemon Juice to taste
Salt and Pepper

Blend roasted peppers until smooth and set aside in separate container.

Combine yolks, garlic, vinegar, water and mustard in blender. Blend 20 seconds. Gradually add oil in a thin stream until incorporated and thickened into a mayonnaise. Stir in roasted pepper puree. Add salt, pepper and lemon juice to taste.

This recipe and the Pan Seared Chilean Sea Bass was created by Brett Rokjer, a very dear friend of the family and an excellent chef who has broadened his talents unbelievably since he began his cooking career at Beverly's some 10 years ago. He likes to say that he has me to thank for his accomplishments, but I have to disagree with him. He has the ability and a natural God-given talent to be the excellent chef that he has become. Thank you Brett!

Rob's New Harbor Mussels

2 doz Fresh Mussels, soaked, brushed and de-bearded
3 cloves Fresh Garlic, minced
½ cup Onion, minced
3 Roma Tomatoes, diced fine
¼ cup Fresh Basil, sliced into thin strips
1 Red Pepper, roasted and julienned
½ cup Red Wine (not sweet) (optional)

¼ Lemon, zest of
1, 15-oz can Cannellini Bean
5 strips Bacon, fried crisp and crumbled
4 oz Chevre (goat cheese)
4 tbs Olive Oil
Salt and Fresh Ground Black Pepper to taste

Use a heavy pot, large enough to hold all the ingredients, place on medium heat and add the bacon. Render bacon, crumble and set aside. Drain the bacon fat from pot and add the olive oil, garlic and the onion. Sauté until they are opaque and slightly brown. Add the wine, tomatoes, red pepper and basil. Simmer for 10 minutes then stir in the beans, bacon and lemon zest. Adjust seasoning. Bring back up to boiling temperature, then add the prepared mussels, cover and continue to simmer until all the mussels are opened. Immediately crumble the goat cheese on top and cover again for 2 or 3 minutes, just until the cheese in melted. Serve immediately, in individual bowls, with lots of crusty bread and wine.

One of my favorite things to do in September, at the end of Track Season, was to rent a house on the coast of Maine for 10 days or so. I always went to the little town of New Harbor. The house was large enough to house my entire family, but I did insist on a few days alone to regain my sanity and strength. On one of these get-a-ways, at one point there were just four of us, my son, Chef Rob, the present chef employed by me at that time, Chef Steve Boardman, my daughter Tammy (also a great cook), who was dating Steve at the time, and myself. Needless to say, we had some awesome food. Rob created this dish, just by walking through the grocery store, looking for ideas and using the fresh from the ocean mussels that he and I had picked up just that morning at low tide.

✳

Top left: Rob's New Harbor Mussels. Top right: Chef Rob and Chef Steve B. Bottom: Family dinner in Maine.

Saratoga Style Oysters Rockefeller

24 Raw Oysters
1 cup Corn Meal
Salt and Pepper
Oil for Frying

2 cups *Creamed Spinach*
1 cup *Hollandaise*
Horseradish to taste

Prepare **Creamed Spinach** and keep warm. Mix horseradish with the **Hollandaise** and set aside. Drain oysters and sprinkle with salt and pepper, then coat with cornmeal. Have a shallow fry pan hot with oil covering the bottom. Sauté oysters very quickly until golden brown and drain them on a paper towel to absorb some of the fat. Place the hot **Creamed Spinach** into a 3-inch deep baking dish, then arrange the oysters on top, and then spoon the **Hollandaise Sauce** on the top of each oyster. Place under the broiler until all is brown and bubbly.

Thank you to my son Chef Rob Cone for this one.

Sea Bass with Red Grapefruit

6, 6-oz portions Sea Bass
¾ cup Dry White Wine
2 Shallots, chopped
2 tsp Fresh Garlic, minced

Fresh Ground Pepper
Aunt Jane's Crazy Salt®
18 sections Fresh Red Grapefruit,
    reserving juice

Spray or rub each piece of fish with olive oil. Rub the top of each piece with the minced garlic, then place into a sprayed baking dish with skin side down.

Pour wine over fish then sprinkle with the shallots, pepper and Aunt Jane's®.

On each piece of fish, place 3 sections of red grapefruit. Squeeze extra juice from grapefruit membranes over all. Spray top with olive oil or pan spray to prevent drying out. Tent the baking dish with foil by placing foil very loosely on the container, and bake in a pre-heated 400 degree oven for 15 to 20 minutes, depending on the thickness of the fish.

Remove from oven and let set for 5 minutes, and then remove fish from baking pan with a large flat spatula, to prevent fish from breaking up, to a warmed platter. Place foil over fish to keep warm and return to oven that has been turned off. Pour the juices into a skillet and reduce the liquid over medium heat until it reaches a sauce consistency, then pour it over the platter of fish before serving. Or, you can serve each portion on individual plates and top with a little sauce. Because sea bass is so rich, no additional fat is necessary.

One of the many times I have gone on a diet, I created this dish and served it with **Roasted Potato Fans, Steamed Asparagus** and **Braised Red Cabbage**.

A great combination and the eye appeal is awesome.

Shad Roe with Bacon and Onions

1 Pair of Shad Roe per person
¼ cup Chopped Crisped Bacon
¼ cup Chopped Onion

1 tbs Butter
Salt and Pepper
Flour for dredging

Season flour by adding a little salt and pepper.

Melt the butter in a medium hot skillet.

Dredge roe in seasoned flour. Place into the hot skillet, brown on one side and turn it over. At this point, toss the bacon and onions on the top and place into a 375 degree oven for about 12 minutes, depending on the size of the roe. I finish this off in the oven because the little eggs burst and splatter something fierce.

Remove from oven onto a serving plate, and serve with lots of lemon wedges, roasted baby red potatoes and fresh sautéed fiddleheads. What a beautiful spring treat.

When I was very young back in western Pennsylvania, my brothers would go trout fishing in the spring and my mother would always fry the egg sack. I didn't know at that time it was called roe, but I loved it. Many years later, my then husband Walt and I were visiting his brother Charlie and his wife Ruth in Connecticut. We went out for dinner and on the menu was Shad Roe and Shad. I had no idea what either one was, it was then explained to me what roe was. Remembering the wonderful treat of the fresh trout, I tried it and have been a lover of Shad Roe ever since. Unfortunately, it is only available in the spring of the year as are fiddleheads.

Steamed Mussels or Clams

4 or 5 doz Fresh Mussels or Fresh
  Clams
2 Lemons
¼ lb Butter, melted
2 Bay Leaf

1 tbs Fresh Garlic, minced
1 tsp Black Pepper Corns
1 cup White Wine
¼ cup Fresh Parsley, chopped
Herb Butter

Soak clams, or mussels, in cold water for an hour or two. This helps them to discharge the salt water, and clean the inside of sand and replace it with fresh water, which will keep your broth from getting too salty.

With a stiff brush, clean the outside really well to prevent the broth from getting sandy. Place the clams or mussels into a very large flat pan. I like to use the bottom of my lobster steamer. Add the remaining ingredients. Cut lemons in half, squeeze in juice and then place lemon rinds right into the water. Pour the butter on top of everything. I suggest a large flat pan so the shellfish have room to open their shells and also absorb the wonderful flavors of the broth.

From here you can do several things. Serve them as steamed shellfish in individual bowls with lots of hot crusty bread for dunking. Or, you can remove each one from the shell, saving 1 half of the shell to place the body of the shellfish onto. After doing that, pipe on about ½ tsp. **Herb Butter**, then top with a small piece of lean bacon. Bake in 400 degree oven for about 12 minutes or until the butter is bubbly and the bacon is crisp. Serve immediately. This can be served at cocktail parties or as an appetizer before dinner. Serve with lemon wedges, a cocktail fork and hot crusty bread.

❋

Pasta, Rice, Potatoes & Veggies

Pasta, Rice & Potatoes

Dough Balls with Cabbage

2 cups Flour
2 Eggs
⅔ cup Water
½ tsp Salt
1 small head Cabbage, lightly
    steamed

½ cup Butter
½ cup Onion, diced and sautéed in
    butter
Salt and Pepper to taste.
Have a pot of boiling salted water
    ready.

Mix the first four ingredients together with a spoon and place the mixture on a small board or plate. Scrape off bits with a knife, (about the size of a teaspoon), and drop into the boiling water. Boil 5 minutes. Remove with slotted spoon onto a flat pan. Drizzle with oil and gently toss, coating to prevent sticking together.

Combine these with lightly steamed cabbage, butter and sautéed onions. Add salt and pepper to taste. This is one of those comfort foods that you can't get enough of.

One of my best friends Marlene McGrath, from Baltimore gave me this recipe. Her Polish mother-in-law shared her recipe with Marlene, who passed it on to me. Thank you again, Marlene.

Mom's Macaroni and Cheese

This is, without a doubt, the best macaroni and cheese you will ever eat. It's the sauce, and the kind and amount of cheese that makes it so yummy. It's NOT low fat, low cal or low carbs. It's just delicious!

2 lbs Elbow Macaroni
2 lbs Sharp Cheddar Cheese,
    coarsely shredded, use a good
    grade

1 *Recipe White Sauce*
2 cups Milk

Cook the macaroni according to directions on package. Drain well and toss with a little oil. Brush a baking pan or casserole dish with *Pan Grease*. Cover the bottom with a thin layer of *White Sauce*. Place a layer of macaroni, then cheese, and then White Sauce again. Continue these layers until all the products are used up or until the pan is full. Reserve some of the cheese for the top. Pour milk over all until it comes to the top layer of macaroni. You DON'T want to cover it entirely with milk. This extra milk will make the dish a little moister than it would be without it. Sprinkle the top with the reserved cheese.

Place the pan into a 375 degree, preheated oven. Do not cover. Bake until it is bubbly, brown and crispy on top (about 45 minutes to an hour). Serve immediately.

The "Thank You" for this goes to my mother, Mary. Although we were fairly restricted in the finance department, my mother never skimped on good, healthy food. Besides, this was very filling and satisfying for a large family. If she couldn't afford enough good cheddar to make it tasty, she wouldn't make it at all.

When we did have this dish, it was always served with her home canned *Pickled Beets.* They just went together. Enjoy this and expect to overeat.

Pasta with Fresh Tomatoes and Feta

1 lb Your Favorite Pasta
¼ cup Olive Oil
6 or 8 Large Ripe Tomatoes, halved, seeded and diced
¼ cup Onions, diced small

2 tbs Fresh Garlic, minced
3 tbs each Fresh Basil and Fresh Parsley, minced
½ lb Feta, crumbled
Salt and pepper

Cook pasta according to directions on package, or to your liking. Drain and toss with a little oil. Heat a large skillet then add olive oil onions and garlic. Sauté until transparent. Add tomatoes, salt, pepper, basil and parsley. Heat just to boiling. Add cooked pasta. Toss to combine and to reheat pasta. Place onto serving plates, top with crumbled feta. Sprinkle edge of plate with parsley and serve immediately.

Pasta Primavera

1 lb Your Favorite Pasta
¼ head Broccoli Florets
¼ head Cauliflower Florets
1 Carrot, peeled and sliced diagonally
½ cup Onion, julienned
½ cup Olive Oil
1 tbs Fresh Garlic, minced

1 ea small Zucchini and Yellow Summer Squash, sliced diagonally
½ cup Parmesan
¼ cup each Fresh Basil and Fresh Parsley
¼ cup Dry White Wine
Salt and Fresh Ground Pepper

Prepare pasta according to package directions, or to your liking. Blanch cauliflower, then carrots and then broccoli. In a large skillet, sauté onions and garlic in the olive oil. Add vegetables, salt and pepper, parsley, basil and white wine. Toss together to heat and coat the vegetables. Add pasta and parmesan then toss to combine. Place onto serving plates. Sprinkle with additional parmesan and a sprinkling of chopped parsley. Serve immediately.

Polenta

6 cups Water
2 cups Corn Meal
2 tbs Butter

1 cup Parmesan
⅓ cup Fresh Parsley, minced
Salt and White Pepper

Pour 2 cups of the water over corn meal. Stir to combine. Bring the remaining 4 cups water to a boil along with the salt and butter. Very slowly pour the corn meal mixture into the boiling water, stirring constantly. When the mixture has come to a boil again, reduce heat to a simmer. Stir constantly until it is very thick. Remove from heat. Adjust seasoning. Stir in parmesan, pepper and parsley. Serve immediately or pour out onto a buttered sheet pan. Chill, then cut into desired shapes. When ready to serve, brown the polenta shapes, in hot butter, on each side. Sprinkle with a little parmesan. Serve immediately.

This can be varied by adding chopped sun dried tomatoes, sautéed mushrooms, roasted red peppers, broccoli florets or just about anything you can find in your refrigerator. Have fun with it; let your creativity urges flow.

Potato Pancakes

4 cups Raw Potatoes, grated
1 Lemon, juiced
6 Eggs
3 tbs Flour
2 tsp Salt

2 tbs Onion, grated
¼ tsp Nutmeg
¼ tsp Black Pepper
½ cup Parmesan, grated
　　(optional)

Squeeze lemon juice over potatoes and mix thoroughly; drain well, then place grated potatoes on heavy kitchen towel and squeeze liquid out. Mix the remaining ingredients together, then add potatoes and mix just to combine.

Heat a heavy skillet with enough olive oil or vegetable oil to cover the bottom. Drop the potato mixture by the tablespoons full into the hot skillet. They will flatten out. Brown very well on one side then turn over and brown on the other. Repeat this until all the batter is used. Keep warm by placing them on a platter that is lined with a paper towel and into a warm oven until ready to be served.

They can be made ahead of time and re-heated in a 400 degree oven until hot. They are great for a cocktail party too; just make them smaller than dinner size. I always serve these with *Applesauce* and *Roast Pork.*

Roasted Reds with Garlic and Onions

3 lbs Red Potatoes, cleaned and
   quartered
2 tsp Fresh Garlic, minced
1 Green or Red Pepper, julienned

1 lg Onion, julienned
¼ cup Olive Oil
2 tsp Aunt Jane's Crazy Salt
Fresh Ground Pepper

Toss all ingredients together to completely coat with oil. Place into a baking pan that has been sprayed with nonstick spray and is large enough to allow the mixture to be spread out in a single layer. Place into a preheated 400 degree oven for 1 hour, stirring every 15 minutes. Serve hot.

Sometimes I will use the purple, red and yellow potatoes to give it a little different appearance.

This is a wonderful potato dish that works very well on a buffet table, and it is very easy.

Reinhardt's Spaetzle

4 cups Flour
4 Eggs
1 tsp Salt

¼ tsp Fresh Grated Nutmeg
1 qt Club Soda

Place the first four ingredients into a mixing bowl. Add club soda, a little at a time, stirring until dough is consistency of very thick glue. Stir very well until all the flour is incorporated. Continue to stir until the dough becomes elastic and shiny. The dough should not be too stiff. It should be sticky but not runny. Allow to rest for about 2 hours. Every 15 or 20 minutes stir it well. This time allows the club soda to work and the chemical reaction to take place. Use the same method for cooking as in the other *Spaetzle* recipe.

The winter of 2000, I spent in Key West and worked as a housekeeper/cook for an interior decorator, David Dresey. Houseguests, Gerta and Reinhardt, arrived from Connecticut. Reinhart was a chef from Germany. I was so excited and we had so much fun cooking together. This method of making spaetzle came from him.

Rice Pilaf

1 cup each Brown, Wild and White
    Rice
½ cup Butter
½ cup Spanish Onion, minced
1 med Carrot, diced

1 rib Celery, diced
½ cup Frozen Peas
Chicken Base OR Chicken Bouillon
    OR Chicken Stock
Salt and pepper

I like to sauté the rice in a little butter before adding the liquid. This will give you a very different flavor. Cook the rices separately according to package directions. They each have different cooking times. If you have chicken stock, use it instead of water. If using water, season it with the base or bouillon. Sauté vegetables in the butter until tender. When rices are cooked, combine all ingredients together. Season with salt and pepper to your taste. Serve immediately.

Risotto

2½ cups Arborio, Italian rice
8 cups Water, Chicken or Beef
    Broth, hot
¼ cup Dry White Wine

1 Leek, the white root sliced thin
    rinsed thoroughly and drained well
¼ cup Butter
1 cup Parmesan
Salt and Fresh Ground Pepper

In a heavy pan, place half the butter and leeks. Sauté until leeks are somewhat wilted. Add the rice stirring to coat for 5 minutes. Add one cup of the liquid and the wine, stirring constantly until the liquid is absorbed. Repeat again and again until the rice is creamy on the outside and firm on the inside (about 20 minutes). Remove from heat. Add the remaining butter and parmesan. Stir to combine. The consistency should be creamy but not runny and definitely not dry. Adjust the seasoning with salt and pepper.

There are so many variations to this. Again, let your creative urges go. I believe the most important guide lines to follow are the adding of the liquid, in increments, the constant stirring and not overcooking.

    This is a comfort food to top all the rest!

Roasted Garlic Mashed Potatoes

8 Potatoes, cleaned and quartered
½ stick Butter
1 to 2 cups Milk or Half and Half

1 bulb Garlic, roasted and skinned
Salt and White Pepper

Cover potatoes with water. Sprinkle with 1 tsp. salt. Cook until fork tender. Drain well. Add butter, *Roasted Garlic* and pepper. Mash with a potato masher. Add half of the milk. Mix well. If too dry, add milk until the desired consistency is reached. Adjust seasoning. Serve immediately.

Roasted Olive Mashed Potatoes

8 Potatoes, cleaned and quartered
1 cup Mixed Olives with pits
1 tbs Olive Oil

¼ cup Butter
1 to 2 cups Milk OR Half and Half
Salt and Fresh Ground Black Pepper

Coat the olives with olive oil. Place into a baking pan that is just large enough to have olives in one layer. Roast for 20 minutes, in 375 degree oven, or until olives are tender. Place olives on a work surface and press down with a flat object to force out seed. Chop very fine. Set aside. Place potatoes into a pot with enough water to cover completely. Add 1 tsp. salt, cover and bring to a boil. Reduce heat. Simmer until potatoes are fork tender. Drain completely. Return to a low heat. Add butter and 1 cup milk. Mash with potato masher. Add the prepared olives and pepper. Add milk as needed to reach the consistency you desire. Check before adding more salt because the olives are a little salty.

Another one of my favorite chefs, at Beverly's, was Steve Boardman. He came to me from one of the large hotels in Tahoe and is a very talented chef who taught me an enormous amount about techniques and ideas. Thank you, Steve for this tasty version of mashed potatoes.

Roasted Potato Fans

1 good sized baking potato per
   person
A good brand of Olive Oil

Aunt Jane's Crazy Salt
An oil spritzer for your convenience.

160)

Peel the potatoes. Lay potato on a work surface lengthwise. With a very sharp, thin bladed knife, slice the potato almost all the way to the bottom every ¼ inch, to within ½ inch of the other side, cutting across not lengthwise. Place into cold water for 1 or 2 hours. Drain and pat dry with paper towels. Coat the entire potato with olive oil then the salt. Place on a baking pan about 2 inches apart, cut side up. Bake in 400 degree oven for at least 1 hour. Every 10 minutes spray the fan side with oil spritz. As the potato bakes, it will open up into a fan and the slices will get very crisp.

The presentation of this potato is very interesting and unusual, but most importantly, it's delicious.

*

Spaetzle

4 Eggs	½ tsp Baking Powder
1 cup Water	3 cups Flour
1 tsp Salt	Sprinkle of Nutmeg

Whisk eggs and water together. Mix remaining ingredients together and then add to egg mixture. Mix with wooden spoon until well blended. The dough should be sticky and wanting to run off the plate. If you have a ricer or a spaetzle mill that is wonderful, but if you don't, place ¼ of the dough onto a plate or a wooden board.

Have a pan of boiling, salted water ready. With a spoon or a flat knife, scrape the dough off into the boiling water, by half teaspoons. If you keep the spoon or knife wet, the dough will not stick to it. When all the dough of the first quarter is scraped into the boiling water, cook for about 3 minutes. Remove with slotted spoon onto a flat pan. Don't stack them or they will stick together. At this point I drizzle a little oil over the cooked spaetzle to prevent them from sticking together. By the time the next batch is done the first one will be cool enough to add the next batch. Repeat the process until all the dough is used up.

Coming from a German background, this is one of my favorite dishes. I always serve it with *Roast Pork, Homemade Applesauce, Braised Red Cabbage* and a *Winter Squash Bake*. You can find these recipes elsewhere in this cookbook. This is a good winter menu and your guests or family will love you for it.

*

Spaghetti with Brussel Sprouts, Mushrooms and Cheese

½ lb. Brussel Sprouts, cleaned, quartered and steamed lightly	½ tsp Dill Weed
½ cup Spanish Onion, chopped medium	½ tsp Tarragon
½ lb Mushrooms, sliced	½ tsp Dry Mustard
2 tbs Butter	1 cup Mild Cheddar, shredded
1 tbs Flour	2 tbs Fresh Parsley, chopped medium
1 cup Milk, heated	Salt and Pepper to taste
1 tsp Horseradish	1 lb Spaghetti, cooked according to package

Cook pasta. Drain and mix with a little oil to prevent sticking. Sauté onions and mushrooms in butter until onions are transparent. Sprinkle in the flour, mix and cook for 3 or 4 minutes. Slowly add the milk, stirring all the while to prevent lumping up. Reduce heat, cover and gently simmer for about 5 minutes. Add the horseradish, dill, tarragon and dry mustard. Blend well. Add the shredded cheese continuing to stir until cheese melts. Add the well-drained brussel sprouts and stir gently to coat. Serve this over warm spaghetti and garnish with the chopped fresh parsley.

Jane Hubbell from Margaretville, NY, gets a big thank you for this recipe. Janey and my daughter Kimberlie were very good friends and graduated from high school together. Her mother, Carolyn, used to baby sit Melissa and Rob while I worked. She was loved very much by all the kids and is still loved by all who meet her. Her husband, Bob, still makes maple syrup and presses apples for cider. They live on the Hubbell Farm in Halcott Center, NY. What a great homestead. It has been in the family for well over 100 years. If you ever get to that area, drive by and take a look.

❈

Spanish Rice

1 cup White Rice	2 Cloves
1 cup Spanish Onion, diced	1 tsp Salt
1 cup Green Pepper, diced	¼ tsp Black Pepper
¼ cup Butter	19 oz Canned Chopped Tomatoes
1 Bay Leaf	

In a heavy pan, sauté rice, onion and pepper in butter until the rice begins to brown slightly. Add the remaining ingredients. Stir to combine. Cover, reduce heat and simmer until the rice is soft. Stir every 15 minutes with a fork to combine and allow for even cooking.

To mellow out a spicy Mexican meal serve this dish.

My friend Marie Ruhe will take "Thanks" for this one.

❈

Stuffed Baked Potato

8 Baking Potatoes	1 tbs Fresh Parsley, minced
2 tbs Olive Oil	1 to 2 cup Half and Half
Course salt	1 cup Cheddar Cheese, shredded or
½ cup Butter	½ cup cream cheese
1 tsp Fresh Garlic, minced	Salt and White Pepper (be careful
¼ cup Onions, minced	this is strong stuff)
1 tbs Fresh Chives, minced	1 cup Crab Meat (optional)

Wash potatoes. Rub with olive oil and sprinkle with course salt. Bake in a 400 degree oven until fork tender. Remove from oven. Sauté onion and garlic in butter.

When potato is cool enough to handle, slice in half, lengthwise. Scoop out center, leaving enough potato around the outside to stabilize or reinforce the skin. Place the scooped out potato into a mixing bowl. Add the sautéed onion and garlic, half of the cream, half of the cheese, chives, parsley, salt and white pepper. Mash with potato masher. If too dry, add more half-and-half. Adjust seasoning. At this point add crabmeat, if desired. If using crabmeat, substitute the cheddar with ½ cup cream cheese added in the mashing process. With a spoon, place the potato mixture back into the shell. Sprinkle the top with the other half of the cheddar. Place into a preheated 400 degree oven until heated through and the cheese is melted.

White Vegetable Lasagna

1 Eggplant	½ cup Olive Oil
1 Zucchini	½ lb Mozzarella, shredded course
1 Yellow Summer Squash	½ lb Provolone, shredded course
½ lb White Mushrooms, sliced	16-oz Ricotta
1 cup Onions, diced	1 cup Parmesan
2 tbs Fresh Garlic, minced	1 lb Lasagna noodles
2 Fresh tomatoes, diced and drained	Salt and Pepper
¼ cup Fresh Basil, minced	1 Recipe *White Sauce*
¼ cup Fresh Parsley, minced	

Cook lasagna noodles just until they can bend. DO NOT over cook. Drain and mix with a little oil to prevent them from sticking together. Lay out flat. Slice eggplant, zucchini and yellow squash ¼-inch-thick. Drizzle with olive oil, season lightly with salt and pepper. Grill either on grill or in a skillet until light brown on each side and cooked through. Keep separate. Sauté onions, garlic and mushrooms together until transparent then season lightly with salt and pepper. Keep separate.

Combine provolone and mozzarella in a bowl. Set aside. Combine basil and parsley in a bowl, set aside. Spray a baking pan with nonstick spray. Line up the ingredients for convenience in assembling lasagna. Cover bottom of pan with white sauce.

Lay one noodle on work surface and spread with ricotta. Place it on layer of white sauce. Repeat until bottom of pan is covered with one layer of noodles. Place a layer of squash, then cheese mixture, then sauce, sprinkle with parmesan. Sprinkle a little basil-parsley mix on each layer. I like to use a different vegetable on each layer. Repeat until all the vegetables are used up and the pan is full. Top with sauce. Sprinkle with the remaining cheeses. Cover with foil that has been sprayed with nonstick spray. Place into a 375 degree oven. Bake for at least one hour. Remove foil and return to oven for 10 minutes to allow cheese to brown a little.

Beans and Greens

1 head Escarole
1, 15-oz can Cannellini Beans OR
   White Kidney Beans
2 tbs Olive Oil
¼ Onion, cubed

1 tbs Fresh Garlic, minced
4 slices Bacon, cut into small strips
½ cup Water
Hot Pepper Flakes (optional)
Salt and Fresh Ground Pepper

Soak and rinse escarole *very* well to remove all sand and grit. Drain. Cut into large cubes. Sauté bacon in olive oil until crisp, then remove and set aside. Add garlic and onions to the skillet and sauté until the onions are transparent. Place cut escarole into skillet and sprinkle with salt and pepper. Add water then cover and steam for 5 minutes. Remove lid and stir to blend. At this point, add the bacon and beans and stir until combined. Cook for another 10 or 15 minutes to blend flavors. Serve immediately with hot crunchy bread. It can be a meal in itself.

You may think that a whole head of greens will be too much, but it wilts down.

My friends Rocky and Mary Ann can take the credit for this one.

Braised Escarole or Broccoli Rabe with Garlic

2 bunches Escarole or Broccoli Rabe
2 tbs Fresh Garlic, sliced

¼ cup Olive Oil
Salt and pepper

Cut core off end of escarole. Separate and soak in cold water for 30 minutes. Wash very well. Drain completely. Chop very course. For rabe, cut in 4 to 5-inch lengths and wash as above. In a very large skillet, sauté garlic in olive oil for 2 or 3 minutes. Add escarole or rabe then sprinkle with salt and pepper. Cover and steam 10 minutes. Remove cover and mix well to allow for even cooking. Continue to cook and stir until it is wilted, bright green and tender. Serve immediately.

Braised Fennel

2 Fresh Fennel Bulbs
¼ cup Butter

Salt and Pepper
to taste

Trim fennel stems down to the bulb. Slice ½-inch-thick, lengthwise. Melt butter in a large flat skillet. Rinse fennel and place into melted butter. Sprinkle with salt and pepper. Add just enough water to cover bottom of skillet to create steam. Cover and bring to a boil, reduce heat and simmer for 10 minutes. Remove cover then continue to cook allowing the liquid to evaporate. Braise in the butter that remains until fork tender.

❄

Braised Red Cabbage

1 head Red Cabbage
1 Spanish Onion, diced
¼ cup Butter, Oil OR Bacon
   Drippings

½ cup Brown Sugar
½ cup Cider Vinegar
Salt and Pepper to taste

Remove the outer wilted leaves from cabbage. Cut into quarters and remove core. Slice thin. In a large skillet, sauté onions in the fat for 5 minutes, stirring to cook evenly. Add cabbage, salt and pepper. Cover, reduce heat and steam for 15 minutes. Remove lid and stir to distribute the uncooked cabbage. Continue this process until all the cabbage is wilted and tender. Add brown sugar and vinegar at this point. Stir to combine. Continue to cook with lid off for another 15 to 20 minutes. Test to suit your taste for salt, sweetness and tartness. Adjust seasonings as needed.

Serve this dish with your favorite German dishes or *Garlic Roasted Pork, Spaetzle* and *Homemade Applesauce*.

❄

Broccoli Au gratin by Louise

2, 10-oz pkgs Frozen Broccoli,
   chopped
1 can Mushroom Soup
1 cup Hellmann's® Mayonnaise

½ cup Onion, chopped
2 Eggs, beaten
1 cup Cheddar, grated
Ritz® Crackers

Cook broccoli for 5 minutes, then drain. Fold in the remaining ingredients and place into greased baking dish. Top with crushed Ritz crackers and dot with butter. Bake in 350-degree oven until it is bubbling and the crackers are browned (about 30–35 minutes).

This is a great item for a buffet or as a side dish for any meal.

Thank you Sister Louise, for one more!

❄

Calico Corn

½ Green Pepper, diced
½ Red Pepper, diced
1 medium Onion, diced
1 tsp Fresh Garlic, minced
3 strips Bacon, diced, rendered and drained

6 ears Fresh Corn, cut from cob or one can of
2 tbs Butter
¼ cup Water
Salt and Fresh Ground Pepper

Sauté peppers, onion and garlic in butter. Add water, rendered bacon and corn. Mix and season with salt and pepper. Cover, reduce heat and steam for 10 to 15 minutes.

Coffeed Carrots

2 lbs Carrots, peeled and sliced diagonally ½-inch-thick
¼ cup Butter
1 cup Brown Sugar

½ tsp Cinnamon
¼ cup Coffee
Salt

Blanch carrots to al dente and drain well. In a cast iron or heavy skillet, melt butter. Add brown sugar, coffee and cinnamon, stirring until sugar melts and has turned into syrup. Add carrots and continue to simmer for 10 to 15 minutes, stirring to coat carrots well and allowing them to finish cooking. Serve immediately.

When my husband turned 50, some years ago, I threw a large surprise party for him. With 75 guests in and around my kitchen and not knowing the catering business too well at that point, I was putting the finishing touches on the meal. One of the dishes I was preparing was glazed carrots. In my haste and indulgence in a bit of wine, I mistakenly poured coffee into the carrots instead of hot water, which were both right in front of me. Realizing my mistake too late, I tasted them. To my surprise they were the best glazed carrots I had ever made. Everyone wanted to know how they were prepared, and I told them. I haven't served plain glazed carrots since. Sometimes I will add orange zest or fresh grated ginger.

Corn Pudding

½ cup Sugar	1, 13-oz Can Evaporated Milk
3 tbs Cornstarch	Butter
2 Eggs	Grease baking dish
1, 1-lb can Cream Style Corn	Salt, Pepper & Nutmeg to taste

I always use the corn that I have frozen myself, but the canned is good also. Combine sugar and cornstarch in a bowl, then add eggs, milk and corn and mix well. Pour into baking dish and dot with butter. Bake for about 1 hour in a 350 degree oven until firm in center.

Thanks to Jane Golden, one of my mother's step daughters-in-law, this is the best baked corn I have ever tasted.

❋

Creamed Spinach

2, 1-lb bags Spinach	2 or 3 cups *White Sauce*
½ cup Spanish Onion, diced small	¼ tsp Nutmeg
2 tbs Butter	

Wash spinach and drain *very* well. Pull stems off and discard. Chop coarsely.

Sauté onion in butter, then add nutmeg and spinach, stirring until it wilts. Immediately add it to the *White Sauce* that has been heated separately. Stir to combine. Serve hot. The secret to this dish is in the sauce. The amount of spinach can be adjusted to more or less.

Try this topped with pouched eggs for brunch. It's a big hit at Beverly's.

❋

Fried Green Tomatoes—not the movie

6 Green Tomatoes	¼ tsp Garlic Powder
1 cup Flour	¼ tsp Onion Powder
¼ cup Corn Meal	½ cup Milk
1 tsp Salt	Oil for frying
¼ tsp Black Pepper	

Wash tomatoes. With a sharp pointed paring knife, remove the stem. Slice ¾-inch-thick. Mix dry ingredients together. Dip each slice of tomato into milk and then into the dry mixture, coating each side very well. Apply pressure to secure breading. Immediately fry in hot, large, heavy skillet, with ¼ inch oil until brown. Turn each slice over to brown the other side. Serve immediately while still crisp. The tomatoes should be crispy on the outside and tender on the inside.

As a child growing up, I couldn't wait until the tomatoes were large enough to pick from our garden for this favorite, however, we had to have a few red ones before we were allowed to pick the green ones. If you've never had Fried Green Tomatoes, you will really enjoy their tart, unusual flavor.

Garliced Vegetable Medley

½ head Cauliflower, broken into florets

½ head Broccoli, broken into florets

2 Carrots, peeled and sliced diagonally ¼-inch thick

1 Yellow Summer Squash, sliced diagonally ½-inch thick

1 Zucchini, sliced diagonally ½-inch thick

1 med Onion, julienned

1 tbs Fresh Garlic, minced

½ cup Olive Oil

Salt and Pepper to taste

Blanch the cauliflower, then broccoli and then carrots. The carrots will take a little longer than the broccoli and cauliflower, but you still want them crunchy. By doing it in this order, you can use the same water. Drain and set aside. In a large skillet, sauté the garlic in olive oil just until it begins to change color. Add the onion and both squashes. Toss gently until all is cooked. Add the blanched veggies and season with salt and pepper, tossing to combine and heat through. Serve immediately. Sprinkle with chopped fresh parsley for a little extra color.

This makes a tasty, colorful dish for a buffet table.

Green Beans Cacciatora

1 qt Canned Green Beans OR Fresh that have been blanched

1 cup Onion, cubed

1 Green Pepper, cubed

1 tbs Fresh Garlic, minced

4 Fresh Tomatoes OR one 28-oz canned

¼ cup Olive Oil

Salt and Pepper to taste

¼ cup Parmesan

Sauté onion, green pepper and garlic in the olive oil, then add tomatoes and season to your taste. Simmer for 15 minutes Add green beans, mixing well. Place into a baking dish, sprinkle with parmesan and place into a 375 degree oven for 30 minutes.

I created this recipe when my children were small. When Michael was in second grade, his class made a small cookbook, which was tied together with yarn. All the mothers submitted a recipe. This was mine, and he was very proud of that. I still have that cookbook; it was the first time I was in print.

Actually, having 6 children I have boxes of momentos made by their little hands. It's fun to go through them to recall those memories. Where did time go, and oh, so quickly?

Grilled Summer Vegetables

1 ea Zucchini, Summer Squash,
   Eggplant,
Yellow and Red Pepper
1 Red Onion
1 cup Olive Oil

¼ cup Balsamic Vinegar
Kosher Salt
Fresh Ground Pepper
Garlic Powder

Slice the zucchini, summer squash and eggplant into ½-inch-thick slices.

Cut the ends off the pepper, (saving for another use), then cut it into quarters.

Place the cut vegetables, except the onion, in a large bowl with the vinegar, olive oil and seasoning, tossing to coat. Be careful not to allow the eggplant to be in the oil long as it will act like a sponge. Place onto a hot grill. Cut the onion into ½ inch slices. Gently, coat both sides with the oil and very carefully place them onto the hot grill. The onions are not as easy to grill, but are oh so delicious. Grill both sides of vegetables until browned and flavorful. Remove from grill and arrange onto a serving platter. Serve hot or at room temperature.

What a great side dish for a cookout, and it also makes a wonderful sandwich. Just add some fresh mozzarella or goat cheese.

Melissa with stray bird and fresh from the garden zucchini.

Plum Tomatoes-Roasted or Grilled

2 lbs Ripe Plum Tomatoes, washed
    and cut in half lengthwise
½ cup Olive Oil

¼ cup Balsamic Vinegar
1 tsp Fresh Garlic, minced
Salt and Fresh Ground Pepper

Mix all the ingredients together, except the tomatoes. Add the tomatoes and marinate for 30 minutes or so. Place on a hot grill, cut side down for 5 minutes. Turn and grill the skin side until brown but still has its shape. Serve hot or room temperature.

    This is great for a steak cook out, along with grilled red onions.

To roast in oven: Marinate as above. Arrange tomatoes cut side down on a baking sheet that has been sprayed with nonstick spray. Place into a hot 450 degree oven. Roast until the skin is browned. This gives them a wonderful flavor and can be added to pasta or served as a side dish.

❋

Ratatouille

1 Large Eggplant
2 Med Zucchini
2 Med Yellow Summer Squash
2 Med Spanish Onions
2 Green Peppers

8 or 10 Ripe Tomatoes
3 tbs Fresh Garlic, minced
½ cup Olive Oil
Salt and Pepper

Cut strips of skin from eggplant about 1 inch wide. Wash the vegetables very well and cut all into 1-inch cubes. In a baking pan large enough to hold all, place the olive oil and garlic. Sauté for 5 minutes, then add the remaining ingredients, stirring to combine. Place into a 400 degree oven, uncovered, until they are cooked but still crunchy. This allows for reheating. Stir every 15 minutes. Adjust the seasoning.

    If this seems like a large quantity, just use equal parts of all the vegetables and prepare as above.

This is a perfect dish to help use up those summer vegetables. Walter Keller from Binnekill Square Restaurant served this au gratin with Swiss cheese and hot bread. It makes a great lunch and can also be used in quiche, in omelets or as a side vegetable.

❋

Roasted Garlic

Break bulb apart. With flat side of knife, press each garlic clove between knife and work surface to release skin. Peel skin off. Place garlic cloves into a bowl and coat with olive oil. Place garlic in a baking pan just large enough to hold the garlic in one layer. Roast in a 350 degree oven until garlic is tender (about 15 minutes).

An alternative method is to cut a thin slice off the top of a full bulb to expose the cut edge of each clove. Drizzle olive oil into the cuts. Place onto a baking pan and roast until tender (about 20 to 25 minutes).

After roasting, the garlic can be used for salad dressing, bruschetta or just spread on crusty bread, with olive oil, parmesan cheese and fresh ground pepper.

❊

Roasted Red Peppers

6 Fresh Red Peppers
3 tbs Olive Oil

1 tsp Fresh Garlic, minced
½ tsp Fresh Ground Black Pepper

Wash and dry the peppers. Rub each one with oil. Place peppers onto a baking pan.

Place into a preheated 475 degree oven for 35 to 45 minutes or until they are very brown. Check about every 15 minutes and turn as needed for uniform browning.

Remove from oven and cover tightly with foil. Allow to steam and cool for 30 minutes. Remove stem, seeds and skin, reserving the liquid. The skin should peel off very easily. Place into a flat container. Mix the liquid with 2 tbs. olive oil, garlic and pepper. Pour over the peppers. Refrigerate until ready to use.

This is a wonderful addition to a sandwich.

❊

Steamed Asparagus

This is so simple you'll wonder why you didn't think of it, or maybe you have!

2 bunches Fresh Asparagus
2 tbs Butter
½ cup Water

sprinkle Aunt Jane's Crazy Salt®
Fresh Ground Pepper
Fresh Lemons cut into wedges

Break the tough part from the asparagus. Wash and place into a large skillet with a tight fitting lid. Cut the butter into pats and place around on top of asparagus. Sprinkle with salt and pepper. Add water then cover and bring to a boil. Turn off heat and allow to set in steam for 10 minutes or until you are ready to serve. You may also microwave. Place asparagus into a microwave proof dish with ¼ cup water, butter, salt and pepper, then cover tightly with plastic wrap and cook on high for 4 minutes. Allow to set in steam until ready to serve. Place onto a serving platter, surrounded with fresh lemon wedges. Serve immediately. Or serve chilled with the Arugula and Pear Salad.

Sweets

Candy

Caramel

2 cups White Sugar
¾ cup Light Karo® Syrup
½ cup Butter

1 cup Cream
½ cup Walnuts or Pecans, chopped
medium

Toast nuts for 10 minutes in a 350 degree oven. Toasting the nuts improves the flavor.

Butter an 8-inch square dish or pan. Sprinkle with chopped nuts.

Put sugar, syrup, butter and 1 cup of the cream into a heavy sauce pan, place over medium heat, stir to combine and bring to a boil. Add the remaining cup of cream. Stir frequently until mixture begins to thicken. Continue to cook until mixture reaches 255 degrees on a candy thermometer.

Pour into prepared pan. Spread out evenly. Allow to cool until able to cut into desired size squares. Remove from pan. Separate before the caramels set up together. Wrap separately with waxed paper or store in an airtight container by placing waxed paper between layers.

This is another wonderful Holiday treat. Years ago my friend, Eleanor Messner, from Akron, Ohio, and I would get together quite often. While our children were playing, we would make holiday cookies and candies or iron our bushels of cotton children's clothes, eat egg sandwiches with *Home-made Relish* and drink tea. It was so enjoyable; I will never forget the times we had together. As I'm writing these recipes that she and I used to make together, it brings back many memories. I can see her home so plainly and the children playing as if it were just last week. I can almost smell the candy, relish, pickles or egg sandwiches and tea we enjoyed together. I miss her very much. Friendships and making memories are important.

Easter Eggs

4 Eggs Whites, room temperature.
4 cups White Sugar
1 cup Water
1 tsp. Cream of Tarter
¼ cup White Karo® Syrup

2 cups Coconut or
2 cups Candied Fruit or
2 cups Nuts of your choice or any
combination of the above.

Except the coconut, candied fruit or nuts, and egg whites, place all the ingredients into a heavy saucepan. Stir over medium heat until sugar dissolves. With a pastry brush that has been dipped in water, wash the sides of pan down to remove any sugar crystals.

Continue to cook until it reaches the hard crack stage when a little dropped in cold-water cracks like glass. While the sugar mixture is cooking beat egg whites with electric mixer until they become firm but not dry. When sugar mixture reaches the correct temperature, pour it slowly over egg whites with mixer running. Continue to beat until it stands in stiff peaks. With a rubber spatula or wooden spoon, fold in the desired addition. Butter your hands and form into desired sized eggs. Place onto cooling rack that has been placed on a cookie sheet or waxed paper. Pour melted tempered chocolate over eggs, or you can dip them into melted chocolate, if you are more comfortable with that procedure. Allow coating to dry. The surface will change from a shiny gloss to a dull finish. Decorate with icing flowers or to your liking.

Another one of my childhood memories is making these eggs with my mother. Being the youngest, it seems that my niece and I were the only children participating, because the next two older siblings were boys and they probably weren't interested. And, the two oldest were already gone from home. In any case, it is a good memory and a delicious Easter treat.

Beverly with the Easter Bunny.

Mills Family Fudge

2 cups Sugar	½ stick Butter
4 tbs Cocoa	½ tsp Salt
1 cup Milk	Peanut Butter to taste

Combine sugar, cocoa, salt, milk and butter into a heavy bottomed saucepan.

Place on medium heat, stirring to dissolve sugar. Continue to cook until mixture, when a little dropped in cold water forms a soft ball. Remove from heat; add peanut butter, stir until fudge starts to thicken and turns creamy. Pour into buttered pan. When partially cool cut into desired size squares.

Just recently, my mother told me that Aunt Martha has always used the same recipe they used as children and that was 80 years ago. I think you will agree it's one of the best.

Peanut or Cashew Brittle

2 cups Sugar	1 tsp Baking Soda
2 cups Light Corn Syrup	1½ lbs Raw Blanched Nuts, peanuts
2 tbs Butter	or cashews
1½ tsp Salt	

Place corn syrup into a 3-quart pan with a thick bottom. Add sugar, salt and butter. Stir over medium heat until sugar is dissolved. Add nuts. Stir together and continue to cook until peanuts are golden brown. Remove from heat and stir in the baking soda completely until the mixture is foamy. Immediately pour onto a buttered marble slab or a buttered flat pan. Spread the mixture out to about ½-inch-thick. Allow to cool but not completely. Slide a thin knife under the brittle to loosen. Turn it over and crack it with the handle of a knife. When completely cool, store in an airtight container, if there is any left after tasting. It's like potato chips, you can't eat just one piece.

When I was a child, during the Christmas Holidays, my mother would always make this. I'm not sure where she found the blanched, raw peanuts or where the recipe came from but we all enjoyed it and thought it was such a special treat but it was handed out with restrictions and rationing. That probably made it even more special. Our house wasn't very large but my mother could always hide things from us and get away with it. This has been a seasonal tradition for my family now and I have sold many, many pounds to my customers.

When I sold the hard sesame bread sticks by the pound, I would save the fallen sesame seeds for sesame seed brittle. You can also make coconut brittle by cooking the sugar mixture to the light brown color, *before* adding the coconut. Experiment and enjoy!

Peanut Butter Balls

1 lb + 1 cup Powdered Sugar
1½ cups Peanut Butter
1 cup Butter

½ lb. Dipping Chocolate, you can find this with candy making supplies

Mix the first three ingredients together with a mixer. Chill. Form into balls the size of a nickel.

Melt the chocolate in a small metal bowl over hot water. You want the bowl to be small around, but deep. Place a ball on a two or three-pronged fork, dip into chocolate, allow excess to drip off then place onto waxed paper. Allow to cool and dry thoroughly before moving them to a serving plate or into a canister. If you like peanut butter and chocolate, you will love this.

One day around Easter time, I got the idea of forming these into Easter eggs before dipping. I made them larger, I think about 3 ounces, dipped them as above, and decorated them with pastel buttercream flowers and green leaves. Usually 2 or 3 small flowers on the top made them look really sweet. I first did this for my own children but then when I had a bigger audience, I made them for my customers as well. The demand was much greater than the available supply. Your children or grandchildren will enjoy these as much as mine did, I'm sure. It's a quick and easy treat that will go a long way in the points department.

❄

Poppy Cock

4 qts Popped Popcorn
2 cups Brown Sugar
1 cup Butter
½ cup Corn Syrup

1 tsp Vanilla
1 tsp Baking Soda
8 oz Peanuts (optional)

Bring the brown sugar, butter and corn syrup to a boil. Continue to boil for 5 minutes. Remove from heat, then add vanilla and soda and stir to combine. Stir mixture into popped corn, mixing well. Place into a large roasting pan that has been sprayed with a non-stick spray. Bake in a 275 degree oven for 1 hour, stirring every 15 minutes. Remove from oven onto buttered sheet pans, spreading out to cool. This can be stored in airtight containers for several weeks.

A large thank you to my daughter, Tammy, for this one. I'm not sure where it originated but it has become a Christmas tradition in our family. I hope you enjoy it as much as we have.

❄

Potato Fondant Peanut Butter Roll

1 or 2 White Potatoes
Powdered sugar

Peanut Butter of your choice, it
doesn't matter
A little Salt

Peel the potato and cut into 1½ -inch cubes. Place in small saucepan, cover with water, add the sprinkling of salt and cook until very tender. Drain well. Mash until smooth. I suppose you could add a little vanilla if you wish to make it seem a little less primitive. Start by adding powdered sugar slowly and mixing until smooth after each addition. The mixture will get very runny in the beginning. Continue to add sugar until the mixture is the consistency of silly putty or play dough.

Sprinkle a flat surface with powdered sugar. Roll the potato mixture out with rolling pin to about ⅓-inch-thick. Spread the surface with your favorite peanut butter. Roll up as a jellyroll. Allow to chill thoroughly then slice into ½-inch slices. THIS is delicious.

When my oldest brother, Paul, went to the Korean War, he wrote home and asked for some of this candy. He said he was so hungry for something from home and this was his favorite. So of course it was sent to him along with a home canned chicken and home-made cinnamon buns. Well the candy arrived in much better condition than the chicken did, and it smelled a lot better, too. I can't imagine the cinnamon buns surviving either. But my brother did and he also survived Vietnam!

Baked Goods & Misc

Pan Grease

2 cups Vegetable Oil
4 cups Flour

2 cups Crisco®

Place all ingredients into bowl of mixer. With paddle mix until mixture reaches the consistency of whipped cream. With a pastry brush, apply to baking pans before filling with batter.

I learned this trick in my first cake decorating class. What a great product to have close by. Keep at room temperature for easy application.

Bailey's® Carmel Sauce

2 cups Sugar
⅔ cup Bailey's®

2 cups Heavy Cream
⅓ cup Butter, cold

In a heavy pan or skillet, caramelize the sugar by stirring over medium heat to a medium brown color. Remove from heat, whisk in Bailey's, mixing well, then whisk in heavy cream and butter. Mix very well. Serve at room temperature on **Chocolate Torte** or vanilla ice-cream.

Blackberry Dumplins

1 qt Blackberries
½ tsp Salt
1 cup Sugar
1 tsp Lemon Zest
1½ cup Flour

1 tbs Sugar
2 tsp Baking Powder
¼ tsp Nutmeg
⅔ cup Milk
Cream or **Whipped Cream**

Combine blackberries, sugar, salt and lemon zest in a heavy pot. Bring to a boil and simmer for 5 minutes. In the meantime, combine in a bowl the flour, baking powder, nutmeg, 1 tbs. sugar and a little salt. Add milk, stirring just to combine—don't overmix. Dough will be thick. With pot still simmering, drop dough by heaping teaspoons into the hot berry mixture. At this point, either cover lightly and simmer about 15 minutes, or top with a layer of dough, lattice style. Sprinkle with a little sugar and pop in a 375 degree oven until the top crust is golden brown.

Serve warm with cream, whipped cream or vanilla ice cream.

This is a southern dish but given a chance it will be loved by the Yankees too. It's the absolute best cobbler ever.

Bourbon Sauce

4 cup Sugar
4 Eggs
2 cups Bourbon

1 lb Butter, unsalted, cut into chunks

Using a stainless steel pan only, heat bourbon and sugar, almost to boiling, but do not boil. Stir until sugar is melted and clear. Add ⅔ of the butter and whisk until melted. In a mixing bowl, whisk ⅓ butter and eggs. While whisking, slowly add hot liquid and then return to pan. Heat to very hot, but not boiling. Store in glass container only.

Serve as desired. Or with the *Apple Bourbon Cake*.

When Michael was living in New York City, he worked at the Empire Diner, where this sauce was served on one of their desserts. He thought it would go nicely on the Apple Bourbon Cake, so I have him and the Empire Diner to thank for this wonderful sauce.

Empire Diner

Brown Sugar Butter Sauce

1 cup Brown Sugar
1 cup Water
½ cup Butter

2 tbs Corn Starch
2 tbs Water
Sprinkling of salt

Dissolve the cornstarch in the 2 tbs. of water to make a slurry and set aside. Place brown sugar, 1 cup of the water, salt and butter into a small saucepan. Bring it to a boil and very slowly add the slurry until it reaches the thickness you desire.

This sauce was made by my mother for **Mom's Gingerbread** and of course topped with whipped cream. Try it on Apple or Raisin Pie.

✸

Chocolate Almond Pâté

½ cup Sugar
½ cup Water
4 lg Eggs
½ cup Almond Paste
2 tbs Amaretto

12 oz Semi Sweet Chocolate,
  chopped medium
2 cups Whipping Cream, chilled
1, 10-oz. Frozen Raspberries with
  sugar

Line 9×5×2½-inch loaf pan with plastic wrap or foil. Stir sugar and water in a heavy saucepan over low heat until sugar dissolves. Bring to a boil and set aside. Blend egg yolks and almond paste together with mixer. Gradually beat in the hot syrup you've just made. Set bowl over saucepan of simmering water and beat until candy thermometer reaches 160 degrees (about 5 minutes). Remove bowl from heat. Add amaretto and beat until cool. Stir chocolate in top of double boiler until melted and smooth. Fold melted chocolate into yolk mixture. Beat cream into stiff peaks then fold into chocolate mixture. Pour mixture into prepared pan. Cover and freeze overnight. Puree raspberries. Strain into bowl, cover and chill until cold.

Turn loaf out onto platter. Peel off plastic and cut into slices. Spoon a tablespoon of raspberry sauce onto individual plates and place a slice of paté on each. Garnish with fresh raspberries, sugared almonds and a fresh mint sprig.

✸

Chocolate Ganache

2 cups Heavy Cream

1 lb Semi Sweet Chocolate

Cut chocolate into small pieces, place in a metal bowl and set aside. Heat cream to the boiling point, pour over chocolate and let stand for 5 minutes. Then whisk to a smooth consistency. If you wish to add a flavor such as hazelnut, almond or raspberry, now would be the time to do so. Allow to cool for 10 to 15 minutes before pouring over the dessert of your choice.

To coat a torte with ganache, place the torte on a cooling rack that is sitting on a baking sheet or waxed paper. Pour the ganache over the torte, allowing the excess to drip off. When this is finished, place the torte onto a serving plate and garnish. Refrigerate until 30 minutes before serving. Chocolate is much better if served at room temperature.

❈

Chocolate Glaze

12 oz Semi Sweet Chocolate
(I always use Callebaut®)
¾ cup Half and Half or Heavy Cream

3 oz Butter
¼ cup Liquor of your choice

Place chocolate, cream and butter in top of double boiler. Do not allow the top pan to touch the hot water in the lower pan. Turn heat down to a simmer until all is melted (be careful not to overheat as it will separate), whisking lightly to incorporate. Remove from heat, add liquor and stir to mix. Allow to cool to a pouring consistency or to a more firm, spreadable type frosting.

Use on your favorite rich dessert. This is a very eloquent creamy rich glaze.

❈

Chocolate Mousse

12 oz. Semi Sweet Chocolate, such as Callebaut®
6 tbs Strong Coffee
4 tbs Sugar

2 tbs Vanilla
6 Eggs, separated and at room temperature
1 pint Heavy Cream

Using a double boiler, place chocolate, coffee and vanilla over hot water to melt. Stir to combine. When totally melted, set aside to cool. While chocolate is melting, whip all the other products as follows. Beat egg yolks until very thick and lemon color. Fold into above and mix well. Beat egg whites until soft peaks, and then add sugar slowly while continuing to beat until glossy, stiff peaks are formed and sugar is melted. Fold egg whites gently into chocolate mixture. Whip cream and gently fold into chocolate mixture and chill thoroughly.

This seems like a complicated project, but once you get started it all comes together quite nicely.

Using a dark chocolate cake, slice into thirds across, fill each layer with the mousse, and cover with *Ganache*. Garnish with fresh raspberries or nuts. This is a wonderfully rich and elegant dessert.

❈

Chocolate Sauce

2 cups Heavy Cream
2 tbs Butter
2 tsp Vanilla

½ cup Sugar
½ lb Semi Sweet or Bitter Sweet
      Chocolate, cut into small pieces

Place chocolate into bowl. Heat all other ingredients to boiling to dissolve sugar. Pour hot liquid over chocolate. Let stand for about 5 minutes. Stir to melt chocolate. Serve warm or at room temperature.

❋

Chocolate Curls

1 Chocolate Bar or block of chocolate

Have a chocolate bar or block of chocolate at room temperature or a little warmer. With a vegetable peeler, shave off curls of chocolate, or grate on course side of a grater. Use as a garnish or sprinkle on top of desserts of your choice. If you want a wider curl, melt chocolate in double boiler and spread onto sheet pan. Allow to just set up but not too cold. With the back of a spatula or pancake turner upside down, place onto chocolate pushing down and away from you. You should see some nice curls forming. Place in a container and chill.

❋

Crumb Topping

1 lb Butter, cold cut into ½ inch
    cubes
4 cups Flour
2 cups Brown Sugar

2 cups Sugar
2 cups Oats
2 tsp Cinnamon
1 tsp Salt

Place all ingredients into bowl of mixer and mix until blended into a crumby consistency. Be careful not to over-mix, as the mixture will start to stick together.

This is a great topping for crumb pies, muffins or coffee cakes.

❋

Butter Cream Frosting—Vanilla or Chocolate

1 cup Crisco®
1 cup Butter
4 lbs Powdered Sugar
1 tsp Vanilla

¾ tsp Salt
1 cup Water, room temp
¾ cup Cocoa (optional, for
    Chocolate Butter Cream)

Sift powdered sugar (and cocoa). Cream butter and Crisco® together, just to combine completely. Scrape sides. Place salt and vanilla into water. Stir to dissolve salt. Place powdered sugar (and cocoa) into mixer bowl with creamed mixture. Pour water mixture over sugar, turning mixer on and off on low until the sugar is moistened. Scrape sides and mix to combine. If making **Chocolate Butter Cream**, you may have to add a little more water.

A recipe from my cake decorating class, which is very tasty; works great for birthday cakes, all occasion cakes and cupcakes.

❄

Cream Cheese Frosting

2 lbs Philadelphia Cream Cheese®
1 cup Butter

4 lbs Sifted Powdered Sugar
1 tsp Vanilla

Cream butter and cream cheese together until completely blended. Add sugar and blend. Add vanilla and mix thoroughly.

❄

Cooked Fluffy Frosting

1¼ cups Sugar
⅓ cup Water
1 tbs Light Corn Syrup
⅛ tsp Salt

¼ tsp Cream of Tartar
3 lg Egg Whites
1 tsp Vanilla

Make sure that all your equipment and utensils are free of any grease, as it will hinder the frosting from whipping up properly. In 2002, when I was baking at Putnam Market, I made this icing several times and it was perfect. Then all of a sudden, it stopped working. I realized one sleepless night that it was because the pan I was using was being stored too close to the stove and a very small amount of grease was splattering into it. I was excited to have finally found the answer to the problem.

Place sugar, water, corn syrup and salt into a small heavy pan. Place over medium heat and stir to dissolve sugar. Cover with a lid and allow the steam to wash the sugar from sides of pan. Remove lid and continue to boil until syrup spins a thread when hot mixture is dropped from spoon above pan or when it reaches 223 to 234 degrees if using a candy thermometer. In the mean time, whip the egg whites and cream of tartar with whisk of mixer until firm peaks form. When the syrup has reached the correct temperature, pour it very slowly into egg whites with mixer running. Continue to whip until it is very stiff and shiny. Add vanilla, mix well and use immediately on your favorite chocolate cake.

A wonderful and beautiful thing is to make small cakes or cupcakes, frost with this icing and cover all with coconut. Great taste! Remember the snowballs we used to buy?

This can also be used for meringue. Just arrange it on the pie and place in a preheated 425 degree oven until browned to your liking. Watch carefully as it will brown very quickly.

Gingerbread House Frosting

⅔ cup Water
4 tbs Meringue Powder
12 cups Powdered Sugar, sifted
1¼ cups Shortening

¾ tsp Salt
½ tsp Almond Flavoring
½ tsp Clear Vanilla

You will be able to find the meringue powder and clear vanilla at a cake-decorating store.

Place all ingredients into mixer bowl and mix until completely blended.

This icing is tasty and works extremely well for holding together that *Gingerbread House* that can be so aggravating. I once donated one which was auctioned off for $125.00.

This icing is also used for making icing flowers for cake decorating. It is very much edible but it dries hard.

I acquired this recipe in my cake decorating classes. I would sit by the hours, in the evening, while I was

Auctioned Gingerbread House

watching TV, making all kinds of flowers, putting them on the buffet, dining room table or side board to dry. We had a little black Pomeranian Poodle named She She, who always found a way to get to my flowers before they dried. She lived to a ripe old age of 17 so I guess they weren't too bad for her.

Lemon Curd

2 cups Sugar
12 Egg Yolks, slightly beaten and
    strained

1 cup Lemon Juice
½ lb Butter, cut into chunks
2 tbs Lemon Rind, grated

Combine sugar and yolks in a stainless steel saucepan. Gradually add lemon juice, whisking all the while. Cook over low heat, whisking constantly until mixture coats spoon (just below the boiling point). Remove from heat, whisk until slightly cooler and add butter, a chunk at a time, until all is added and melted. Add lemon rind and stir to combine. Chill, covered with plastic wrap which is placed directly on curd. Use as desired.

Pastry Cream

2 cups Half and Half
2 cups Milk
¾ cup Sugar
½ cup Cornstarch
4 Eggs

2 tbs Butter
2 tsp Vanilla
2 oz Semi Sweet or Dark Chocolate
    cut into small chunks (optional)

Whisk together the cornstarch and sugar to break up any lumps in cornstarch. Add eggs and whisk until all is combined and mixture becomes somewhat liquid.

In the meantime, heat milk and cream to just the boiling point. Very slowly, whisking all the while, pour in the egg-sugar mixture. It will start to thicken immediately. When mixture comes to a boil again, remove from heat. Stir in vanilla. At this point, if you are making chocolate pastry cream, add the chocolate chunks, mixing until all the chocolate is melted. Add more or less chocolate, depending on your taste. Pour into a glass or stainless steel flat container. Cover with plastic wrap or waxed paper, pressing it directly onto the hot cream to prevent a film from forming. If the plastic wrap is not directly on the pudding it will form moisture and cause the pudding to become thin.

Puff Paste

1 cup Flour, sifted before measuring	1 cup Milk
⅛ tsp Salt	⅓ cup Butter
1 tbs Sugar	4 to 5 Eggs, depending on size (room temperature)

If you are going to use these puffs for a savory filling, omit the sugar.

Mix dry ingredients together and set aside. Place milk and butter into a heavy pan on medium heat. When mixture boils, add dry ingredients in one fell swoop, stirring quickly with a wooden spoon while still on heat. It looks rough at first, but suddenly it becomes smooth, at which point you stir faster. In a few minutes the paste becomes dry, does not cling to the spoon or the sides of pan. Remove from heat immediately and let it rest 2 minutes. Add eggs one at a time, beating vigorously after each addition. Continue to beat each addition until the dough no longer looks slippery. The dough is of perfect consistency if a small amount stands erect when scooped up and is now ready to bake.

To make cream puffs, spoon the batter onto a sheet pan that has been lined with parchment paper. To make éclairs use a pastry bag with a ½-inch opening. Pipe dough onto sheet pan holding the tip parallel with the pan, squeezing out the batter to 1½-inch wide and 4-inch long pieces. Pull the tip up and release the pressure to stop. With a wet finger, gently press down the points of dough to make the puff uniform. They can be made smaller for hors d'oeuvres. Place into a preheated 400 degree oven for 10 minutes. Reduce the heat to 350 degrees and bake for about another 25 minutes or until they are quite firm to the touch. Cool on a rack away from a draft.

Eclair Christmas Tree

If filling with **Pastry Cream** you can either cut off the top and spoon in the filling or you can fill with a pastry bag and tip. Sprinkle them with powdered sugar or drizzle with a chocolate icing. If using for savory filling, slice off top and fill with your favorite chicken, ham, turkey or smoked fish salad. This may seem a little difficult but it really isn't, you just have to be careful with the procedure. When I first took an interest in baking, this was my favorite thing to make. Later I graduated to experimenting with different fillings. One of my favorites was to fill the puff with vanilla ice cream and top with fresh sugared strawberries or peaches and then a dollop of whipped cream, naturally.

❈

Pumpkin Roll by Diane

3 Eggs
1 cup Sugar
⅔ cup Pumpkin

¾ cup Flour
1 tsp Soda
½ tsp Cinnamon

Grease 15×10-inch cookie sheet with sides. Cover with waxed paper then grease waxed paper. Mix all ingredients together completely. Spread out into prepared pan. Bake in 375 degree oven for 13 minutes (no longer). Turn out onto a clean dishtowel that has been dusted generously with powdered sugar. Sprinkle cake with powdered sugar also. Roll cake and towel lengthwise. Let cool, unroll and spread with the following.

Filling

8 oz Cream Cheese
2 tbs Butter

1 cup Powdered Sugar
1 tsp Vanilla

Roll cake back up, cover with plastic wrap and refrigerate until cold. Slice diagonally and serve with a dollop of cinnamon whipped cream. To make cinnamon whipped cream, just add a little cinnamon to regular whipped cream.

Thank you Diane Warinner for this recipe.

❀

Crusts, Pies & Tarts

Almond Crust

10 oz Almonds, toasted
½ lb Butter, unsalted
⅓ cup Sugar

3 cups Flour
1 Egg

Place first 4 ingredients into bowl of processor with steel blade. Process to a fine texture.

Add egg, process to a crumbly consistency. Divide in half, press into a 9-inch spring form tart pan.

Chill 30 minutes. Bake in 350 degree oven for 15 to 20 minutes until golden brown. This is a great crust for those Fresh Fruit Tarts.

Pie Dough

2 cups Flour
1 cup[scant] Crisco®, only

1 tsp Salt
5 or 6 tbs Iced Water

Place flour, Crisco® and salt into bowl of processor with steel blade. Turn processor on and off 5 times. Drizzle ice water over flour mixture, making sure not to put it all in one spot. Pulse processor until dough starts to come together. Turn out onto lightly floured work surface. Knead slightly with hands until it comes together. Divide in half, form each halve into a flat ball. Wrap and chill completely. Be careful not to overwork dough, as that will make it tough. This recipe will make 2, 9-inch pie shells or 1 double crust 9-inch pie.

To make pie shells, using 1 ball, roll out on floured pastry cloth with a rolling pin that has the pastry sock in place, to a circle large enough for pie tin. Lift one corner of cloth to help place the rolled dough onto the rolling pin. Transfer dough to center it into pie tin. Crimp edges by turning excess dough under slightly then push dough with the thumb of one hand in between the thumb and index finger of the other to form the scalloped edge. Continue all the way around the shell. Prick bottom of shell with fork. Place a piece of waxed paper or paper pan liner in shell. Cover the paper with dried beans or rice to prevent crust from bubbling up or sliding down on sides. Bake at 375 degrees for 10 minutes. Remove the paper with the rice or beans. Continue to bake for another 10 minutes or until crust is light brown.

Chocolate Pastry Dough

1 cup+2 tbs Flour
2 tbs Sugar
3 tbs Cocoa

¼ tsp Salt
½ cup Butter, cold, cut into chunks
2 or 3 tbs Iced Water

Place dry ingredients into bowl of processor with steel blade. Add butter, process on and off until the mixture is the consistency of very course corn meal. Drizzle water over mixture, pulse on and off until dough comes together. Turn out onto work surface, press together. Wrap with plastic wrap. Chill thoroughly. Roll out to desired size on floured cloth. To move pastry to pan, lift corner of cloth to place dough over rolling pin. Move dough, on pin, to pie tin rolling the dough off onto pan. Crimp edges by pinching together with fingers. If this shell is baked before filling, be sure to weight the bottom with rice or beans that have been placed in shell on waxed paper or a paper pan liner. Bake 12 minutes, remove paper, continue to bake for 10 more minutes until crisp.

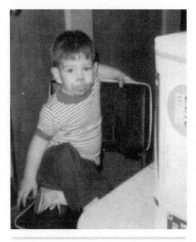
Chef Rob Cone

Graham Cracker Crust

1 sleeve Graham Crackers
¼ cup Brown Sugar

⅓ cup Butter, room temperature
1, 9-inch pie tin

Place all ingredients into processor bowl with steel blade. Process until it starts to come together and everything is completely blended. Pour out into a 9-inch pie tin. Press with fingers to cover entire surface and make the crumbs into a firm crust. Place into a preheated 350 degree oven for 12 minutes or until it begins to turn light brown.

Sweet Tart Crust

1, 10-inch Tart Pan with removable
   sides
2⅓ cups Flour
3 tbs Sugar

14 tbs Butter, chilled, cut into
   chunks
pinch Salt
2 Egg Yolks
5 tbs Iced Water

Whisk yolks and water together. Set aside.
   Place first 4 ingredients into bowl of processor with steel blade; process to course corn meal consistency. With processor running, slowly add egg and water mixture. Process just

191

until dough starts to come together. Turn out onto floured work surface. Work dough with hands to press together. Form a flat ball, wrap with plastic wrap, chill. Roll out on floured cloth to desired size. This will line a 10-inch tart pan. Press dough into fluted edges flattening top with thumb. If baking before filling, prick bottom of shell with fork, line with waxed paper or paper pan liners and rice or beans to prevent crust from bubbling up. Bake for 10 minutes, remove paper and beans, continue to bake for an additional 10 minutes or until slightly brown in color. Remove from oven onto cooling rack.

Banana Cream Pie

1 Baked 9-inch Pie Shell   3 Bananas, peeled and sliced
2 cups Pastry Cream   1 recipe Whipped Cream

Layer pastry cream and bananas beginning with pastry cream and ending with bananas. You should have two layers of each. Top with whipped cream. Serve chilled.

Buttermilk Pie

1 Unbaked 9-inch pie shell   4 tbs Cornstarch
2 cups Buttermilk   3 tbs Lemon Juice
1 cup Sugar   1 tsp Lemon Rind, grated
½ tsp Salt   2 tbs Butter, melted
3 Eggs   1 tsp Vanilla

Mix dry ingredients, then stir in eggs and buttermilk. Add melted butter, lemon juice, lemon rind and vanilla and mix thoroughly. Pour into prepared pie shell. Bake in preheated 350 degree oven until filling is set and crust is brown (about 35 to 40 minutes). Remove from oven. Chill before serving.

My daughter Melissa and I were traveling through Williamsburg, VA, where we stopped at a quaint little place for lunch. For dessert, we ordered a piece of buttermilk pie, which was outstanding. Being a baker, before leaving, I spoke with the manager telling him how wonderful the pie was and about Beverly's in Saratoga Springs. I told him that I was Beverly, did all the baking, and would appreciate it if they would share the recipe with me. I assured them I would not, in any way be competition for them. They declined! So I came home, put on the apron, tried and tested until I was satisfied that I had come as close to that buttermilk pie as I could possibly get without having the actual recipe. So if anyone wants to open a restaurant in Williamsburg, VA, you have my permission to use this recipe. I think you will enjoy it as much as I do.

Chocolate Chip Pie

1, 9-inch Unbaked *Chocolate Crust*	½ tsp Salt
2 Eggs	2 tbs Butter
½ cup Flour	2 tbs Cocoa
½ cup Brown Sugar	1 tsp Vanilla
½ cup White Sugar	1 cup Chocolate Chips

With the electric mixer, mix very well the flour, sugars, butter, salt and cocoa. Add eggs and vanilla and mix until blended. Stir in chocolate chips. Pour into prepared pie shell. Bake in preheated 375 degree oven until set (about 45 to 50 minutes).

Another original from Beverly's kitchen.

❉

Chocolate Cream Pie

1, 9-inch Baked Pie Shell	1 *Recipe Whipped Cream*
2 cups *Chocolate Pastry Cream*	*Chocolate Shavings*

Fill baked pie shell with chocolate pastry cream and top with whipped cream. Sprinkle with chocolate shavings. Serve chilled.

To make chocolate shavings have chocolate at room temperature or a little warmer. With a vegetable peeler, shave off curls of chocolate, or grate on course side of a grater.

❉

Chocolate Walnut Pie

1 cup Brown Sugar	1 cup Walnuts or pecans, use broken
2 tbs Cocoa	pieces of broken halves
½ tsp Salt	1 tsp Vanilla
2 tbs Butter	1, 9-inch Unbaked *Chocolate Shell*
3 Eggs	or *Regular Pie Shell*
1 cup Corn Syrup	

Place brown sugar, salt, cocoa and butter into mixer bowl and mix very well. Add eggs, corn syrup and vanilla and mix thoroughly. Add nuts, stirring just to blend. Pour into prepared pie shell. Bake in preheated, 375 degree oven for 45 to 50 minutes or until center is cooked. Serve chilled or warmed with ice cream.

Quite a few years ago, I was doing some desserts for Chez Pierre and this was one of them. I adapted this recipe from the pecan pie filling. If you are a chocolate nut lover, you will love this dessert.

❉

Coconut Cream Pie

1, 9-inch Baked Pie Shell
2 cup *Pastry Cream*

1 cup Sweetened Angel Flake
   Coconut®
1 recipe *Whipped Cream*

Mix pastry cream with coconut. Place into baked pie shell. Top with whipped cream and sprinkle top with some toasted coconut. Serve chilled.

Grandma Minnies Apple Cream Pie

1, 9-inch Unbaked pie shell
2 Apples, peeled, sliced into
   eighths
⅓ cup Sugar

2 tbs Flour
¼ tsp Cinnamon
1 cup Milk or Half and Half
2 tbs Butter

Prepare pie shell. Mix sugar and flour in a small bowl and sprinkle on bottom of unbaked shell. Arrange apples in a decorative fashion in the shell. Pour milk over all. Sprinkle cinnamon on top and dot with butter. Bake in 350 degree preheated oven about 40 minutes or until apples are tender and slightly browned.

This is another heirloom recipe from my mother's mother which I wouldn't part with, but I'm glad to share with you.

My grandmother never measured any of these ingredients so I had to figure this out on my own. I can remember her making this pie, in particular, because we loved it so. It's fairly easy to make and doesn't take many ingredients. It's a winner.

This was a big hit at Beverly's and whenever it is served.

Grandma Minnie

Grandma Steffey's Custard Pie

3 Eggs
3 tbs Sugar
1 tsp Vanilla
2 cups Milk

1, 9-inch Unbaked Pie Shell
Sprinkling of Fresh Grated Nutmeg
on top

Prepare pie shell.

Whisk eggs completely. Add remaining ingredients. Pour into pie shell then bake in pre-heated 375 degree oven for 30 to 45 minutes. When a thin bladed knife inserted in center comes out clean, the pie is done. Be careful not to over cook as it will become watery.

You may add ½ cup coconut to the mixture, if desired. Or, if it is just baked custard you are looking for, butter ramekins or baking dishes, fill with mixture and bake in a water bath.

This recipe has been in our family for a hundred years or more. I can still see my father's mother, Grandma Steffey, doing her baking on Saturday mornings. Now this was after she had cleaned her house, taken her bath and set her hair, with a silk scarf wrapped around her pink curlers. She always used a heavy canvas cloth to roll her pie dough on, and a stretchy cover over the rolling pin. I found a set of these at a craft store and they really work. But how did my grandmother know this so many years ago? If we only knew what they knew!

Grandma Steffey and Grandma Minnie

Lemon Meringue Pie

I have tried for 40 years to make a perfect Lemon Meringue pie. This is as close as it's going to get and I have to thank Jean Richards, a customer at Beverly's, for saving me from a tortured life of weeping meringue. It's in the baking. I even tried a torch to brown the meringue only to have it weep all over the counter, ending up just a puddle of syrup with a small meringue puff in the center of the pie. Try this!

1, 9-inch Baked Pie Shell	⅛ tsp Salt
Filling:	¾ cup Sugar
1 tbs Lemon Peel, grated	1½ cup Water
½ cup Lemon Juice	4 Egg Yolks
⅓ cup Cornstarch	1 tbs Butter

Whisk sugar and cornstarch together to break up any lumps in cornstarch. Add salt and egg yolks, while whisking. Add a little lemon juice at a time until all is incorporated.

Bring water to a boil in either a glass or stainless steel saucepan. [Aluminum will discolor the filling because of a chemical reaction with the eggs and lemon juice.]

Slowly pour the egg mixture into the boiling water, whisking all the while. Allow the mixture to come to a boil for 1 minute. Remove from heat. Stir in lemon peel and butter. Pour into baked pie shell. Allow to cool on rack for 30 minutes.

Meringue

4 Egg whites, have at room temperature	¼ tsp Cream of Tartar
	½ cup Sugar

With the electric mixer, whip egg whites and cream of tartar until foamy. Add sugar, 1 tbs. at a time, whipping for 1 minute after each addition until all sugar is used, and it has become very glossy and stiff and the sugar grains are all but unnoticeable. Immediately top the pie with meringue being careful to seal the meringue to the edge of pie shell. Be as decorative as possible by pulling up on the spatula to create swirls and tips. Place into a preheated 375 degree oven until golden brown. About 15 to 20 minutes. Remove from oven onto a cooling rack away from all draft. Avoid chilling until it is completely cool. This pie is definitely best if eaten the same day.

❋

Pumpkin Pie

I have tried many pumpkin pie recipes and this is, hands down, the best! I've even tried changing it, but there is no need. You cannot make it better. Well actually, the only way you can make this pie better is to use my *Pie Dough* recipe.

2, 9-inch unbaked Pie Shells
4 Eggs
1, 29-oz Canned Pumpkin, I only
   use Libbys®
1 cup White Sugar
½ cup Brown Sugar

1 tsp Salt
2 tsp Cinnamon
1 tsp Ginger
½ tsp Clove
2, 12-oz cans Evaporated Milk

Prepare pie shells. Beat eggs slightly. Add remaining ingredients, whisking to mix well. Divide into the pie shells. At this point I always place a turkey or pumpkin on top of filling, in the center, that has been cut from scrap pie dough.

Bake 15 min

   Place in preheated 425 degree oven, then reduce heat to 350 degrees. Bake for 35 to 40 minutes or until there is no more jiggle in the center. It will be firm when pie is shaken slightly.

What is Thanksgiving or Christmas Dinner without pumpkin pie?

Neapolitan Cream Pie

1 Baked 9-inch Pie Shell
1 *Vanilla Pastry Cream*
1 *Chocolate Pastry Cream*
1 Banana, peeled and sliced
6 to 8 Fresh Strawberries, washed,
   dried, stemmed and sliced

½ pint Whipping Cream
2 tbs Powdered Sugar
1 tsp Vanilla
Chocolate Shavings

Spread chocolate pastry cream on bottom of baked pie shell. Arrange prepared strawberries in a layer on top of the chocolate pastry cream. Next spread the vanilla pastry cream on top of the strawberries, place the sliced bananas on top of the vanilla pastry cream, then top all with whipped cream. Sprinkle with chocolate shavings. Serve Chilled.

   (Make Whipped Cream by placing the whipping cream into chilled bowl of mixer, adding vanilla and sprinkling in powdered sugar, a little at a time. Continue to whip until soft peaks form. Be careful not to over-whip or you will have butter.)

A few years ago, Gary Zack, who is a local glass blower and the owner of Symmetry, came into Beverly's kitchen where I was making pies to fill orders for Easter. Gary asked if I could make a pie for him. Being late in the day, the day before Easter, this is what he received because I only had left over filling and a pie shell. He was lucky! He returned to say it was outstanding and enjoyed by all.

Old Fashioned Apple Pie

1 Recipe Pie Dough
6 Apples,* peeled, cored and sliced
1 cup Sugar
1 tsp Cinnamon

⅛ tsp Nutmeg, I prefer freshly
    grated, if I don't have that I
    don't use any.
¼ cup Flour
a pinch Salt

*Use some tart apples but not all. I like to use a variety of apples, but never use Red Delicious because they won't cook up and are too sweet. I don't use Macintosh because they cook up too much. There are so many wonderful apples on the market now, but some of my pie favorites are, Jonathan, Golden Delicious, Ida Reds, Cortlands, Northern Spys and Jonareds, just to name a few.

Place sliced apples into a mixing bowl, Mix the dry ingredients together and sprinkle on top of apples. then mix gently with a rubber scraper. Place immediately into prepared pie shell. Cover either with top crust or with *Crumb Topping*.

    If using a top crust, trim the bottom crust to about ½-inch overhang all around the pie plate. With a pastry brush, brush the edge with water. Place apple mixture into shell (it will be filled high, but as it cooks will come down) and place the top rolled dough over apples. Trim the top crust a little smaller than the bottom. Fold the bottom crust edge up over the top edge and crimp together with thumb on one hand, thumb and index finger on the other. By wetting the edge, it helps it to stick together and will prevent losing a lot of the juice.

I like to brush the top with a mixture of egg white and milk, and then sprinkle with a little sugar. When baked this gives a nice golden brown crunchy crust. Why do I do this? Because my grandmother always did it. With a sharp knife slash some decorative marks on the top to allow the steam to release.

Place immediately into a 425 degree preheated oven for 15 minutes, reduce heat to 375 degrees for another 30 minutes. Don't let the fruit stand to long before baking as the sugar will turn to liquid before it has a chance to thicken with the flour.

❄

Pecan Pie

1 cup Brown Sugar
1 tbs Butter
3 Eggs
1 tsp Vanilla

1 cup Corn Starch
1½ cup Pecans
1 Unbaked 9-inch pie shell

Cream brown sugar and butter together, then add eggs and mix very well. Stir in salt, vanilla and corn syrup. Add pecans, combine completely. Pour mixture into prepared pie shell. Place into preheated 375 degree oven for 40 to 45 minutes or until the center is cooked.

This has been a Holiday standard at our home since I lived in Baton Rouge, LA, years ago. My sister-in-law, Dot McCollister, will get credit for this one. She was and still is a wonderful southern cook.

❈

Rhubarb Custard Pie

3 Eggs
3 tbs Milk
2 cups Sugar
¼ cup Flour

¾ tsp Nutmeg
4 cups Rhubarb, cubed in ½ inch
    pieces
1, 9-inch unbaked pie shell

Prepare pie shell. Beat first 5 ingredients together. Add rhubarb. Stir to combine and pour into unbaked pie shell. You can either leave the pie open or place lattice pie dough over all. Bake in preheated 375 degree oven for 50 to 60 minutes or until filling is completely cooked. Check with a thin bladed knife. If it comes out clean, the pie is cooked.

My dear friend, Eleanor Messner, gave this recipe to me years ago. We had been friends since our camp meetin' days as teenagers working in the dining hall. She was one of the funniest people I ever met.

❈

Apple Yogurt Tart

3 tbs Sugar
1 tbs Flour
2 cups Yogurt, low fat
½ cup Sugar
⅓ cup Flour
¼ tsp Cinnamon

Grating Fresh Nutmeg
3 large Apples (not red delicious or Macintosh) peel and slice each quarter into thirds
1, 10-inch **Sweet Tart Shell**, unbaked

Mix first 3 tbs. sugar and 1 tbs. flour together, then sprinkle evenly over bottom of crust. Arrange apples in a decorative pattern on crust. Mix yogurt, ½ cup sugar, ⅓ cup flour, cinnamon and nutmeg. Pour back and forth over apples making sure all are glazed. The mixture will run to the bottom, but that is okay. Bake in a preheated 375 degree oven for 40 to 45 minutes. Serve warm.

This is a variation of **Grandma Minnie's Apple Cream Pie**. You will love this, it's tasty and light.

❋

Fresh Fruit Tart

1, 9-inch Baked Tart Shell prepared either from **Almond Crust or Pie Dough** recipes.
1 oz Semi Sweet Chocolate
1 tbs Cream
1 cup **Vanilla Pastry Cream**

1 cup Fresh Raspberries
1 cup Fresh Blueberries
1 pint Fresh Strawberries
½ cup Red Currant Jelly, melted
1 tbs Water

Prepare the crust of your choice. Melt red currant jelly with water, whisking to combine. Melt chocolate with the cream, mixing thoroughly. Brush bottom of prepared crust with chocolate mixture. Distribute pastry cream on the chocolate.

Arrange prepared fruit in a decorative manner on top of pastry cream. Brush fruit with red currant jelly. Serve chilled.

This tart can be made without the pastry cream, and you could actually use any kind of fresh fruit in season. Some suggestions: Mango, Kiwi, Pineapple, Peaches or any combination you desire.

❋

Peach or Plum Tart

1 cup Flour, sifted
½ cup Sugar
¼ tsp Salt
¾ tsp Baking Powder

½ stick Butter 1 Egg Yolk
Grated Rind of 1 Lemon
3 to 4 Fresh Plums or Peaches

Combine first five ingredients with pastry blender. Add grated rind of lemon and the beaten egg yolk. Knead with floured hands. Grease layer tin and push in dough to cover sides and bottom pan. Arrange peeled, sliced peaches or plums on top in a decorative manner. Sprinkle with cinnamon and sugar, then dot with butter. Put into a 350 degree oven for approximately ½ hour.

Another thank you goes to my friend Marie Ruhe for this gem.

Pear Frangipane Tart

1, 9-inch tart shell made from *Sweet Tart Dough* recipe, unbaked, and chilled

Frangipane

1 cup Almonds that have been
    toasted and ground fine, measure
    after grinding
½ cup Butter, unsalted
½ cup Sugar
1 Egg

3 tbs Amaretto
1 tbs Flour
1 tsp Almond Extract
3 or 4 Pears, pouched
1 cup Water
½ cup Sugar

Cream butter and sugar together with mixer. Add egg, flour, Amaretto and extract, beating until smooth. Combine with almonds and pour mixture into prepared shell. Refrigerate while preparing pears.

Combine water and sugar in saucepan and simmer. Peel pears, cut in half and remove core. Poach pears in simmering water and sugar for 2 or 3 minutes. Remove pears, slice each half crosswise and keep together. Place sliced pear halves onto frangipane mixture, in a decorative fashion. Depending on size of pear, you could place 5 halves around the outside and one in the center. Bake 45 minutes in a preheated 400 degree oven. Remove from oven onto a cooling rack. When cool remove outside ring of tart pan. Serve slightly warm or chilled with ice cream or whipped cream.

Beverly

Apple Bourbon Cake

1½ cup Vegetable Oil
3 Eggs
2 cups Sugar
2 tsp Vanilla
1 tsp Orange Extract
3 cups Flour
1 tsp Baking Soda

2 tsp Cinnamon
1 tsp Nutmeg
3 cups Tart Apples, peeled and
   sliced
3 tsp Orange Rind, grated
1 cup Walnuts, chopped medium
½ cup Bourbon

Brush a 12-cup bundt pan, liberally, with **Pan Grease**. Sift dry ingredients together, set aside. Cream oil, eggs, sugar, vanilla and orange extract until very light and fluffy. Gradually add dry ingredients. Mix until thick and sticky. Add apples, walnuts and orange rind, mixing for about 2 minutes or until completely blended, scraping sides of bowl at least 3 times. Spread batter into prepared pan. Bake in preheated 350 degree oven for 60 to 75 minutes or until toothpick comes out clean when inserted into center of cake. Remove from oven, immediately pour bourbon over cake while still in pan. Allow to cool for 10 minutes, Remove from pan onto a cooling rack. Serve warm with **Bourbon Sauce**.

This recipe came from Lonnie and Erika in Monroe, CT, great customers of mine at Cheese Etc.

❋

Banana Cake

2¼ cup Cake Flour
½ tsp Salt
¾ tsp Baking Soda
½ tap Baking Powder
½ cup Butter

1½ cup Sugar
2 Eggs
¼ cup Buttermilk
1 cup Ripe Banana, mashed
1 tsp Vanilla

Brush two 9-inch cake pans with **Pan Grease**

Sift dry ingredients together and set aside. Cream butter and sugar together until light and fluffy. Add eggs, continuing to cream until very light in color. Mix buttermilk and banana together. Add alternately with dry ingredients, in three additions. Scrape sides of bowl after each. Divide between two cake pans. Bake in 350 degree preheated oven for 20 to 25 minutes. Check with toothpick in center of cake. If comes out clean, the cake is done. Remove from oven onto a cooling rack. After 5 minutes remove from pans onto cooling rack.

✳

Beverly's Own Cheesecake

1 cup Cottage Cheese
2 lbs Philadelphia Brand Cream
    Cheese®
1 tsp Vanilla
½ tsp Salt
2 tbs Flour

1 tbs Orange Juice Concentrate
¾ cup Sugar
4 Eggs
½ cup Sour Cream
1 recipe **Graham Cracker Crust**

Brush a 9-inch spring-form pan with **Pan Grease**, dust with unbaked **Graham Cracker Crust** crumbs. Press the remainder of the crumbs onto the bottom and bake for 7 minutes in a 350 degree oven. Set aside.

Have cream cheese at room temperature.

Place cottage cheese into bowl of processor and process until smooth and then place into bowl of mixer. Add cream cheese and mix to combine. Add vanilla, salt, flour, orange juice concentrate and sugar. Mix for 2 minutes on low speed, stop mixer and scrape sides of bowl and repeat. Scrape bowl again and add eggs one at a time mixing well after each addition. Scrape bowl and fold in sour cream. Pour mixture into prepared spring-form pan; place it into a pan that is large enough for it to fit into then place the two pans into a larger pan that is large enough to hold water to create a hot water bath in the outside pan.

Bake in a preheated 350 degree oven for 45 to 50 minutes or until the center of cake is firm when shaken. Remove from oven and place the inside pan onto a cooling rack until *completely* cool. Gently remove the ring from the outside. Place a piece of plastic wrap on top of cake, then a flat cardboard cake round and invert. Gently remove the bottom of the pan and place your serving plate on top (which is really the bottom). Turn over, remove the wrap and cake round from top. Place in the refrigerator until completely cold; preferable about 12 hours. Serve cold with your favorite fruit.

To cut a cheesecake use a thin bladed knife that has been dipped in hot water and dried after each cut.

※

Black Magic

3½ cups Flour	2 cups Buttermilk
2 cups Sugar	4 Eggs
1½ cups Hershey's® Cocoa	1 cup Vegetable Oil
4 tsp Baking Soda	2 tsp Vanilla
4 tsp Baking Powder	2 cups Strong Hot Coffee
1 tsp Salt	

This cake is best baked in a sheet pan because the batter is thin which makes a very soft cake. The layers after baking shouldn't be more than 1½-inch high. Adjust the cake pan size accordingly.

Sift dry ingredients into bowl of mixer. Place the wet ingredients, EXCEPT the coffee, into a pitcher large enough to hold all. With mixer running, slowly but continuously, add both the wet mixture and the hot coffee. Scrape sides of bowl and mix until free of any lumps (about 3 minutes). Bake in preheated 350 degree oven for 25 to 30 minutes, depending on size of pan.

A **Chocolate Butter Cream** is great on this.

This recipe probably will produce the moistest chocolate cake you will ever have. If you don't already have a recipe like this, here it is. It's the best! I have used it for years for everything from a sheet cake to a wedding cake. When Jeff and Dru, from the Old Bryan Inn, got married some 16 years ago, I made this cake into an all chocolate wedding cake. It was iced with a dark **Chocolate Butter Cream Frosting** and decorated with a cascade of hand-made chocolate roses, chocolate dipped strawberries and raspberries. It was gorgeous and delicious.

※

Cream Cheese Pound Cake

1½ cup Butter	3 cups Cake Flour
3 cups Sugar	1 tsp Baking Powder
6 Eggs	1 tsp Salt
18 oz Cream Cheese	1 tbs Vanilla

Sift baking powder, salt and baking powder together and set aside. Cream butter, cream cheese and sugar until light and fluffy. Add eggs, one at a time, and beat well after each addition. Add vanilla and mix well. Add dry ingredients, stirring to combine very well. Bake at 325 degrees until golden brown. Check with a toothpick in center to insure doneness.

A family treasure. Moist and delicious.

❋

Good Ole Yellow Cake

3 Eggs	4 tsp Baking Powder
1½ cup Sugar	1 tsp Salt
1 cup Butter, unsalted	3 cups Cake Flour
1 tsp Vanilla	1½ cup Milk

Brush two 9-inch pans with *Pan Grease.* Sift dry ingredients together and set aside.

Cream sugar and butter until lemon-colored, very light and fluffy. Add eggs, 1 at a time and continue beating until very creamy. Add dry ingredients alternately with milk and vanilla in three additions, scraping sides of bowl each time. Pour batter into prepared pans making sure to distribute batter equally over pan to insure a level cake and one that bakes evenly. Bake in a preheated 350 degree oven until a toothpick inserted in center of cake comes out clean.

This cake is delicious with *Chocolate Butter Cream Frosting*.

❋

Lazy Daisy Oatmeal Cake

1¼ cup Boiling Water	1 tsp Vanilla
1 cup Uncooked Oatmeal OR you can use 1½ cups cooked left over oatmeal	2 Eggs
	1½ cup Flour
½ cup Butter	1 tsp Baking Soda
1 cup Brown Sugar	½ tsp Salt
1 cup Sugar	¾ tsp Cinnamon
	¼ tsp Nutmeg

Pour boiling water over dry oats, cover and let stand for 20 minutes, or use leftover oatmeal. Cream butter and sugar until light. Add vanilla and eggs. Continue beating until very light and fluffy. Add oat mixture and mix well. Sift the remaining dry ingredients together. Add to creamed mixture, mixing to combine. Pour batter into prepared 9-inch square pan. Bake in 350 degree oven for 50 to 55 minutes. Remove from oven, spread with topping and broil until bubbly.

Topping

¼ cup Butter, melted
½ cup Brown Sugar
3 tbs Cream

⅓ cup Ground Nuts
¾ cup Coconut

Combine all ingredients. Spread evenly over cake and place under broiler until bubbly.

This recipe was given to me by an employee we had at *The Blairsville Dispatch*. This is a great keeper, because it is such a moist cake. It can also be baked in a slightly larger pan and cut into bars. I like the bars for my Holiday Cookie Trays.

Lemon Poppy Seed Pound Cake

3 cups Flour
2 cups Sugar
¼ cup Poppy Seed
1 cup Butter, softened
1 cup Buttermilk
4 Eggs

½ tsp Baking Soda
½ tsp Baking Powder
½ tsp Salt
4 tsp Grated Lemon Rind
½ tsp Vanilla

Brush 12-cup bundt pan with **Pan Grease**. Place all cake ingredients into bowl of mixer. Beat at low speed, scraping bowl often, until all ingredients are moist. Beat at high speed, scraping bowl often, until smooth (1 to 2 minutes). Pour batter into prepared pan. Bake in a preheated 350 degree oven for 55 to 65 minutes or until a toothpick inserted in center comes out clean. Cool 10 minutes, remove from pan. Cool, completely upside down on cooling rack. Place onto serving plate, drizzle with glaze.

Glaze

1 cup Powdered Sugar

1 to 2 tbs Lemon Juice

Mix and drizzle onto cake.

Milkless-Eggless-Butterless-Cake

2 cups Brown Sugar
2 cups Water
⅔ cup Lard or Oil
3 cups Raisins
½ tsp Nutmeg
1 tsp Cinnamon

½ tsp Cloves
4 cups Flour
2 tsp Baking Powder
1 tsp Soda
1 tsp Salt

Boil together the brown sugar, water, oil, spices and raisins for 3 minutes.

Set aside to cool. Mix flour, baking powder, baking soda and salt together, then add to cooled mixture. Bake in greased and floured 9×13-inch pan in preheated 350 degree oven for about 1 hour or when tested with toothpick, it comes out clean. Remove from oven and cool completely. Glaze with a simple powdered sugar frosting.

Frosting

1½ cup Powdered Sugar

1 tsp Vanilla

Just enough milk to reach a spreading consistency.

Do you remember the Spanish bar from the A & P? Well this cake tastes very much like it. My mother made this cake, when we were children, and we loved it.

Mom's Gingerbread

1¼ cup Crisco®
3 Eggs
1¼ cup Sugar
2½ cup Molasses
6¼ cup Flour
2 tsp Baking Soda

½ tsp Cloves
¾ tsp Nutmeg
1 tbs Ginger
2 tsp Cinnamon
1¼ tsp Salt
2½ cups Boiling Water

Brush a 12×15-inch cake pan with **Pan Grease.** Sift dry ingredients together. Cream Crisco®, sugar and eggs together until very light and fluffy. Add dry ingredients alternately with hot water in three additions, scraping sides of bowl after each. Pour into prepared baking pan. Bake in preheated 350 degree for 25 to 30 minutes. Check for doneness by inserting a toothpick into center of cake. If it comes out clean, the cake is done. Serve hot with **Butter Rum Sauce.**

When I was a child, my mother would make this in the winter, but, being a tee-totaler, we never had rum in the house, so she would make a **Brown Sugar Butter Sauce**, which was very good also. The gingerbread was always served hot with the hot sauce poured over it, then a dollop of whipped cream or a scoop of vanilla ice-cream. This is soooooo delicious!

Old Fashioned Blueberry Cake

1 cup Sugar	2 cups Flour
½ cup Butter, softened	2 tsp Baking Powder
1 Egg	1 tsp Salt
1 cup Milk	2 cups Blueberries

Brush a 9-inch baking dish with **Pan Grease**. Mix flour, salt and baking powder and set aside. Cream sugar, butter and egg together. Add dry ingredients and milk. Mix thoroughly. Fold in blueberries, turn out into the prepared baking pan. Bake in 350 degree oven for 20 to 25 minutes or until toothpick inserted in center of cake comes out clean.

One Bowl Honey Cake

1 cup Sugar	1 tsp Nutmeg
3 cups Flour	1 cup Honey
1½ tsp Baking Powder	1 cup Strong Coffee, cooled
1½ tsp Baking Soda	¾ cup Vegetable Oil
1 tsp Salt	1 tsp Vanilla
1 tsp Cinnamon	3 Eggs
1 tsp Allspice	½ cup Raisins
1 tsp Clove	½ cup Nuts, chopped medium

Generously brush a tube or bundt pan with **Pan Grease**. Sift all dry ingredients into a large bowl. Make a well in center. Add all liquid ingredients. Thoroughly whisk together. Stir in raisins and nuts. Pour into prepared pan. Bake in preheated 350 degree oven for 45 to 60 minutes. Test center with toothpick.

Several years ago, on a Jewish Holiday, Shirley asked me to make a honey cake. Since I don't have the recipe, she supplied one. I've made this delicious treat many times.

Thank you, Shirley, for sharing this recipe. I'm sure many of you know her. She used to work at MacFinns Pharmacy.

Pumpkin Cake

1½ cup Vegetable Oil	1 tsp Baking Soda
3 cups Sugar	1 tsp Salt
4 Eggs	1 tsp Nutmeg
2 cups Canned Pumpkin	1 tsp Cinnamon
4 cups Flour	1 tsp Ginger
2 tbs Baking Powder	1½ cup Milk

Brush 9×13-inch baking pan with **Pan Grease**. Cream eggs, sugar and oil together until light and fluffy. Sift remaining dry ingredients together. Add alternately with milk to creamed mixture, in three additions, scraping sides of bowl after each. Distribute batter in baking pan, making sure batter is pushed into corners and level on top. Bake in preheated 350 degree oven for 50 to 60 minutes. Test center with toothpick for doneness. Remove from oven onto cooling rack. When completely cool, top with topping.

Topping

5 tbs Flour	1 cup Sugar
1 cup Milk	1 tsp Vanilla
1 cup Butter	Chopped Walnuts

Combine flour and milk in saucepan and cook until thick, stirring constantly. Allow to cool. Cream butter, sugar and vanilla until light and fluffy. Add cooled milk/flour mixture to butter mixture and beat at high speed until light. Spread onto Pumpkin Cake and sprinkle with chopped walnuts.

Rhubarb Cake

½ cup Crisco	1 Egg
1½ cup Sugar	1 cup Buttermilk
½ tsp Salt	2 cups Flour
1 tsp Baking Soda	3 cups Rhubarb, diced

Brush 9×13-inch baking pan with **Pan Grease.** Cream first five ingredients. Stir in buttermilk. Add flour and rhubarb, mixing completely. Place into prepared pan. Cover with topping.

Topping

⅔ cup Brown Sugar	3 tbs Butter, softened
1 cup Walnuts or Pecans, chopped	½ cup Flour
1 tsp Cinnamon	

Mix until crumbly and sprinkle on top of unbaked cake. Bake in preheated 350 degree oven for 45 minutes. Serve warm with vanilla ice cream.

This is an original from my home town in western Pennsylvania.

The Best Carrot Cake

2 cups Vegetable Oil
3½ cups Sugar
8 Eggs
5 cups Flour
4 tsp Baking Powder
4 tsp Baking Soda
4 tsp Cinnamon

1½ tsp Salt
2 lbs Carrots, peeled and
    shredded small
Optional: ½ cup raisins, coconut,
    drained crushed pineapple
    and/or nuts

This recipe will make 1 full sheet pan or two halves or six 9-inch layers.

Brush pans with **Pan Grease**. Cream eggs, oil and sugar until very light and fluffy. Add dry ingredients, mixing thoroughly. Stir in carrots. At this point, add nuts, raisins or coconut if desired. Pour into prepared pans. Bake in 350 degree oven for 25 to 30 minutes, depending on size of cake. Remove from pans onto cooling racks when cool enough to handle. Put together with **Cream Cheese Frosting**. Sprinkle with nuts

This recipe is one of my originals and it really is "The Best Carrot Cake". I have made this for several local restaurants over the years, and, without a doubt, it has outsold all the desserts I have ever made.

❈

White Pepper, Ginger and Lemon Cake

2 Lemons, rinds of
2 tbs Lemon Juice
3 inches Fresh Ginger, grated
3 cups Flour
¾ tsp Baking Soda
¾ tsp Baking Powder

½ tsp Salt
2 tsp White Pepper
½ lb Butter, unsalted
1¾ cup Sugar
3 lg Eggs
1 cup Buttermilk

Prepare a 10 to 12-cup bundt pan by buttering very generously and dusting it with fine breadcrumbs. Be sure the tube is fully buttered and crumbed. Place the lemon rind, ginger and lemon juice into a small bowl and set aside Sift flour, baking soda, baking powder, salt and pepper together, set aside. In the large bowl of mixer, cream butter and sugar until fluffy. Add the eggs one at a time, mixing well after each addition. Scrape the bowl after each addition. On low speed, add the dry ingredients alternately with the buttermilk in 3 additions. Remove from the mixer and stir in the lemon mixture until totally combined. Pour into prepared bundt pan. Batter will be rather heavy. Make sure to smooth top and distribute evenly in pan. Place onto rack, in the middle of oven. Bake for 45 to 60 minutes at 325 degrees until a toothpick comes out dry when inserted into center of cake. Remove from oven onto a cooling rack for 10 minutes. Place another rack on top of pan, invert the cake onto the second rack. Remove pan and place the cake over a piece of foil. Brush with the following glaze.

Lemon Glaze

⅓ cup Lemon Juice   ½ cup Sugar

This should be mixed as soon as the cake is placed into the oven, to allow the sugar to dissolve. Brush the glaze onto cake until it is all absorbed. Let stand until cool.

With two wide metal spatulas transfer to serving plate. Serve when cool or allow to age for a day or two which brings out the flavors. Serve thinly sliced with raspberry sorbet, a dollop of whipped cream and a sprig of fresh mint.

Several years ago, there was a very talented pastry chef named Paula who baked for me. She always came to work with a large canvas tote full of cookbooks and recipes. This recipe came from that bag but I'm not sure which book. I certainly cannot take credit for this tasty treat, but I will forward it on to you. Before Paula moved out of town, she copied some of her recipes for me. This one has been used many times and in several restaurants in town where I have filled in as baker, Beverly's of course, Sperry's and Putnam Market, to name a few. You will thoroughly enjoy this dessert; it has a flavor you have never tasted before.

❋

Above: Kimberlie and
  Abigail making Christmas
  cookies.
Right: Cookie baking with
  Tammy and Rob.

Almond Citrus Biscotti

1⅓ cup Whole Almonds, toasted
2¾ cup Flour
1⅔ cup Sugar
½ tsp Salt
1 tsp Baking Powder
1 tsp Anise Seed

1 ea Lemon, Orange and Lime,
   grated rind of
3 Eggs
3 Egg Yolks
1 tsp Vanilla

Grate rind of lemon, orange and lime being careful not to get into the white, set aside.

Crack eggs and yolks into a small bowl, add vanilla and grated rinds, set aside.

Combine flour, sugar, salt, baking powder and anise seed in bowl of mixer.

While mixer is running, add egg mixture and then almonds. Mix just to combine. DO NOT OVER MIX.

Divide dough in two. Place each half onto a cookie sheet that has been lined with baking paper. Press out to 4 to 5 inches wide and the length of the sheet pan gradually sloping the side edges down.

Bake in preheated 350 degree oven until golden (about 25 minutes).

Remove from oven and cool. When completely cool, slice diagonally 1½ to 2-inches-thick. Place the cut biscotti back onto the cookie sheet, not allowing the cookies to touch. Return to oven for another 15 to 20 minutes or until the biscotti is completely dry.

Authentic Short Bread

1¼ cups Flour
7 tbs Castor Sugar

8 tbs Butter, cold and
   unsalted

Cut butter into very small pieces, add to flour and sugar.

Mix and then spread out onto a surface that has been sprinkled with bread crumbs. Knead together with hands to make a paste

Press into 5-inch circles, ⅓-inch-thick. Place onto ungreased cookie sheets. Score the *top* into six wedges with back of knife. Bake for 30 minutes in a preheated 300 degree oven or until they reach a rich golden brown.

A little English Nanny by the name of Julie will get the credit for this wonderful rich shortbread. Julie was in Saratoga working as a nanny, and she dined frequently at Beverly's. While talking one day, she offered to call her Mum for this recipe. I hope you enjoy it as much as I have.

By the way castor sugar is a superfine granulated sugar, which may be substituted cup for cup with granulated sugar as we know it.

Triple Chocolate Biscotti

1¾ cup Hazelnuts, skinless, toast
2⅔ cup Flour
1 cup Dutch Processed Cocoa
1½ tbs Baking Soda
¼ tsp Salt
2 cup Sugar

1½ tbs Coffee, instant
⅔ cup Chocolate Chips
5 Eggs
1½ tsp Vanilla
12 oz White Chocolate

Crack eggs into bowl, add vanilla, set aside. Place flour, cocoa, baking soda, salt, sugar and coffee into bowl of mixer. Add chocolate chips and nuts. With mixer running, slowly add eggs and vanilla, mixing just to combine; DO NOT OVER MIX.

Line two cookie sheet pans with baking paper. Divide the dough between the two. Press the dough out to 4 to 5-inches-wide and the length of the pans. Slightly slope the side edges down. Place into a 325 degree preheated oven for 25 minutes. Remove from oven and cool completely.

Cut diagonally into 1 to 1½-inch-thick pieces. Place back onto sheet pan with the biscotti not touching, return to oven for another 20 to 25 minutes or until they are dry and crisp. When completely cool, dip or spread half of each biscotti with melted white chocolate.

❋

Black and White Chocolate Chunk

1 lb Butter
1½ cup Sugar
1 tbs Vanilla
1 tsp Almond Extract
1 tsp Salt
4 cups Flour

¾ lb Semi Sweet Chocolate, cut into ½-inch cubes
¾ lb White Chocolate, cut into ½-inch cubes
1½ cups Walnuts, large pieces, or macadamias

Cream butter, sugar, vanilla and almond extract together until very well mixed, scrap bowl often.

Add dry ingredients mixing thoroughly. Stir in chocolate chunks and nuts.

Scoop with ice cream scoop and place onto ungreased cookie sheet. Flatten just a little and bake in 350 degree oven for 15 to 17 minutes or until edges turn slightly golden brown.

I always use Callabaut® chocolates, but any fine chocolate will work, and you could certainly use all dark chocolate, also.

Paula, a very talented pastry chef that was once employed at Beverly's, gave this recipe to me.

❋

Chocolate Nut Balls

½ cup Butter
⅓ cup Sugar
1 tsp Vanilla
1 cup Flour

¼ cup Cocoa
1 cup Nuts, roasted
Confectioner's sugar

Cream sugar, butter and vanilla. Mix flour and cocoa together; add to creamed mixture. Stir in nuts. Roll into 1-inch balls and place on greased cookie sheet. Bake in 350 degree oven for 12 to 15 minutes. Cool on cookie sheet, then roll in confectioners' sugar while still slightly warm.

❉

Chocolate or Vanilla Shortbread

1½ cups Butter
1½ cup Sugar
2 Eggs
1 tsp Vanilla

4 cups Flour
½ tsp Baking Powder
½ tsp Salt
4 tsp Cocoa

Sift dry ingredients together and set aside. Add cocoa for chocolate dough, omit for vanilla dough. Cream butter and sugar until fluffy. Mix in eggs and vanilla. Mix dry ingredients into butter mixture. Shape or spread flat on sheet pan to make shortbread crumbs. Or layer chocolate and vanilla dough, shape into log, chill, slice into ½ inch pieces, place on ungreased baking sheet, bake in 350 degree oven for 8 to 10 minutes. Remove from sheet onto cooling rack.

❉

Chocolate Peanut Butter Chip

1 cup Butter
1½ cup Sugar
2 Eggs
2 tsp Vanilla
2 cups Flour

⅔ cup Cocoa
¾ tsp Baking Soda
½ tsp Salt
2 cups Peanut Butter Chips

Cream butter, sugar, eggs and vanilla until light and fluffy. Combine dry ingredients and add to creamed mixture. Stir in chips. Drop by spoonsful onto sprayed cookie sheet.

Bake in 350 degree preheated oven for 8 to 10 minutes. Cool 1 minute before removing to cooling rack.

❉

Coconut Butter Balls

1 cup Butter
½ cup Sugar
2 tsp Vanilla
2 cups Flour
¼ tsp Salt

2 cups Pecan Halves, toasted
1 Egg White
1 tbs Water
¾ to 1 cup Coconut

Cream butter, sugar and vanilla until well mixed and creamy.

Add flour and salt. Stir until blended. If dough is sticky, chill for an hour.

Whisk water and egg white together.

Wrap 1 tsp. dough around a pecan half. Dip in egg white mixture then in coconut. Continue until dough and pecans are used.

Bake on parchment paper in 325 degree oven for 12 to 15 minutes or until golden brown.

It's a little tedious but really worth the effort.

Date Pin Wheels

2 cups Brown Sugar
1 cup Crisco®
3 Eggs

4 cups Flour
½ tsp Salt
½ tsp Baking Soda

Cream Crisco® and sugar together. Add eggs and continue to cream until sugar is well mixed. Add dry ingredients and stir just to combine. Scrape bowl very well as you go. Cover with plastic wrap and chill for at lease 1 hour.

Filling

2½ cups or 1 lb. Chopped Dates
1 cup Water

1 cup Sugar
1 cup Walnuts, chopped fine

Combine dates, sugar and water. Cook over medium heat until dates are softened and mixture is thickened. Remove from heat, add nuts, mix well and set aside to cool. After dough has chilled and filling is cool, divide dough into 6. On a floured surface roll the dough out into a rectangular shape about ⅓-inch-thick. Spread a layer of the filling on the dough about the same thickness. Roll jelly roll style and refrigerate until dough is very firm. Slice into ½-inch-thick slices. Place onto cookie sheets that have been sprayed with pan spray, about 2 inches apart, as they will spread. Bake in a 375 degree oven until slightly firm to touch (about 12 to 15 minutes).

This cookie is well worth the effort and is my daughter Kimberlie's favorite.

Double Orange Cookie

1½ cup Sugar
1 cup Butter
1 cup Sour Cream
2 Eggs
6 oz Orange Juice Concentrate

4 cups Flour
1 tsp Baking Powder
1 tsp Baking Soda
½ tsp Salt
2 tbs Orange Rind, grated

Cream sugar and butter together until light in color. Add eggs and beat well. Add sour cream and orange rind then combine. Add flour, salt, baking powder and baking soda alternately with thawed orange juice. Mix well just until ingredients are combined. Drop by teaspoonful onto sprayed cookie sheets leaving room for cookies to spread. Bake in 350 degree preheated oven until firm to touch, about 12 to 15 minutes. Remove cookies from sheet pans onto cooling racks. When completely cool, frost.

Frosting

8 oz Cream Cheese
1 tbs Butter
2 cups Powdered Sugar

1 tbs Orange Rind, grated
1 tbs Orange Juice Concentrate
2 tbs Milk, if needed.

Completely mix cream cheese and butter together. Stir in powdered sugar, orange rind and orange juice concentrate until completely blended to a spreading consistency. If too thick, add a little milk, until spreadable.

Thank you Julie Pratt. This is a great keeper and has been a favorite of our family.

Ginger Snaps

1 cup Sugar
¾ cup Crisco
1 Egg
4 tbs Molasses
2 cup Flour

2 tsp Baking Soda
1 tbs Ginger
1 tsp Cinnamon
½ tsp Cloves

Cream the sugar, Crisco®, egg and molasses together. Add dry ingredients and mix to combine well. Cover and chill dough for at least an hour. Remove from the refrigerator, roll into walnut size balls, and then coat with granulated sugar. Place about 2 inches apart (as they will spread) onto a cookie sheet that has been sprayed with pan spray.

Bake in preheated 350 degree oven for 10 to 13 minutes or until golden brown and the surface is crackled. Remove from oven and place cookies onto a cooling rack. The cookie will be slightly soft when hot, but should be very crisp when completely cooled.

This recipe came from Lucille Rentz, a lifelong friend of my mother's. At this writing, they are both very healthy and in their nineties. I think you will agree that it is a cookie worth adding to your holiday cookie list. You won't need a room deodorizer when you bake these cookies.

Gingerbread House Dough

1 cup Butter
1 cup Crisco®
2 cups Sugar
2 Eggs
1 cup Molasses
4 tbs Lemon Juice
6 cups Flour

2 cups Whole Wheat Flour
3 tbs Ginger, ground
2 tsp Allspice
1 tsp Nutmeg
2 tsp Baking Soda
1 tsp Salt

Combine dry ingredients and set aside. Place butter and Crisco® into mixer bowl then mix to combine. Add sugar and continue to beat until fluffy. Add eggs, molasses and lemon juice. Beat until well blended. Gradually add dry ingredients to butter mixture. Beat well.

Divide into 2 pieces. Wrap each in plastic wrap and refrigerate for at least 1 hour. Grease back of cookie sheets. Roll dough out right on the back to ⅓-inch-thick. Cut into desired sizes and shapes. Remove excess dough and bake for 10 to 12 minutes in 375 degree oven. Let cool on pan for *only* 1 minute and then remove to cooling rack.

I'm not sure where I found this recipe, but it is wonderful for Gingerbread Houses. It's very easy to work with both baked and unbaked. It's so delicious, and wait until you smell that aroma. Look in the *Dessert Misc*. Chapter for the frosting.

Grandma Bowman's Oatmeal Cookies

1 cup Crisco®
1 cup Brown Sugar
½ cup Sugar
2 Eggs
4 tbs Milk
2 cups Flour
1 tsp Baking Soda

1 tsp Salt
2 tsp Cinnamon
½ tsp Nutmeg
2 cups Raisins
2 cups Oats
1 cup Nuts, chopped (optional)

Mix dry ingredients together and set aside. Cream shortening, sugars, eggs and milk together, scraping bowl several times.

Stir in dry ingredients completely, then add oats, raisins and nuts until combined. Drop by spoonfuls onto sprayed cookie sheet. Bake in preheated 375 degree oven for 12 to 15 minutes. Remove from baking sheet to cooling rack.

This is a down-home style cookie that everyone will love. Grandma Bowman was my first husband's mother. What a saint! She had nine children and she was a great cook. This recipe was hers, and when she made them, they always came out soft, chewy, and delicious.

Linzer Hearts

¾ lb Sweet Butter-softened
1¾ cups Confectioners' Sugar
1 Egg
2¼ cups Flour, all purpose, sifted

¾ cup Cornstarch
2 cups Almonds, toasted, finely
ground
½ cup Raspberry Jam

Sift the flour and cornstarch together and set aside. Cream butter and 1 cup of the sugar until light and fluffy, add egg and mix well. Add dry ingredients, blend well, add nuts and thoroughly mix. Form dough into a ball, wrap in waxed paper, and chill for 4 to 6 hours. Roll dough out to ¼-inch-thick. Using a small heart-shaped cutter, cut cookies and place on an ungreased cookie sheet. With a smaller heart cutter, cut the centers out of half of them after placing them on the baking sheet and before baking. Chill cookies for 45 minutes. Bake in a 325 degree preheated oven for 10 to 15 minutes, or until they are evenly and lightly browned. Remove and cool on a rack. While they are still warm spread half of them with warmed jam. Handle carefully as they are very tender. Top each one with a heart that has the center cut out. Sift the remaining sugar into a bowl and dip the tops and bottoms into the sugar to coat. Makes 4 doz.

Linzertorte Cookies

1 cup Almonds, toasted
1 cup Rolled Oats
1 cup Whole Wheat Flour
¼ tsp Cinnamon

pinch of salt
½ cup Pure Maple Syrup
½ cup Corn Oil
Raspberry Jam

Place dry ingredients into bowl of processor, grind very fine. Mix the syrup and oil together and then combine with dry ingredients. Form into walnut size balls (approximately 16). Place onto oiled cookie sheet. Press thumb gently into center to create a small well. Place ½ tsp. jam into each well.

Bake at 350 degrees for 10 to 15 minutes. Turn pans half way through for even browning. They should be slightly soft and golden brown. They will firm up as they cool.

Macaroonies

2 Eggs
½ tsp Salt
¾ cup Sugar
½ cup Flour
1 tbs Butter, melted

2 cups Coconut, flaked
1 cup Chocolate Chips, mini
1 tsp Lemon or Orange Rind, grated
1 tsp Vanilla

Beat eggs and salt until foamy. Gradually add sugar, continue to beat until thick and ivory colored (5 to 7 minutes). Fold in the flour and butter. Stir in coconut, chocolate chips, grated rind and vanilla. Drop by teaspoon onto lightly greased cookie sheet or a sheet pan that has been lined with baking paper. Bake in preheated 325 degree oven for 12 to 15 minutes until browned. Cool 1 minute. Remove from cookie sheet onto cooling rack. Cool completely before storing.

Thank you to Rose Stahl from Roxbury, NY.

Mocha Pecan Balls

1 cup Unsalted Butter, room temperature
½ cup Granulated Sugar
2 tsp Vanilla
1 tbs Instant Espresso Powder
¼ cup Unsweetened Cocoa Powder

¾ tsp Salt
1¾ cup All-purpose Flour
2 cups Pecans, finely chopped
Confectioners' sugar for coating the cookies

Cream butter and sugar together until mixture is light and fluffy. Add vanilla, espresso powder, cocoa powder and salt. Beat mixture until combined well. Add flour and mix just until combined. Mix in pecans. Cover with plastic wrap and chill dough for at least 2 hours or overnight. Roll dough in 1-inch balls and arrange on cookie sheet 1 inch apart. Place cookie sheet in middle of preheated 375 degree oven and bake for 12 to 15 minutes or until just firm. Remove from oven and cool for 5 minutes on sheets pans. Remove to cooling rack for another 5 minutes, then toss in confectioners' sugar to coat well. Makes about 95 cookies.

This cookie is a great keeper and can be stored up to 2 months in the freezer. You better hide them well because they disappear quickly.

Molasses Cookies by Kate Young

5 to 6 cups Flour, sifted
2 tsps Baking Soda
2 tsps Ground Ginger
1 tsp Salt
1 cup Butter or Lard

1¼ cup Sugar
1 Egg
1 cup Molasses
1 cup Sour Milk

Sift dry ingredients (except sugar) together; set aside. Cream butter and sugar until light and fluffy. Add egg and molasses, beat very well. Add dry ingredients alternately with milk, mixing well.

Roll out on floured surface to ⅓-inch-thick. Cut into 3-inch rounds; place onto lightly greased baking sheet, sprinkle with sugar. Bake in 350 degree oven for 12 to 15 minutes or until firm to the touch. Remove to a cooling rack.

Kate Young was a childhood neighbor and always had something delicious to give us. When we had used up all of our homegrown corn, we would buy it from them for 25 cents a dozen. Of course milk was 25 cents a gallon, too, and it came right from the farmer with the top third of it dark yellow cream. It wasn't kept in refrigeration, only in the spring house to keep it cool, so you had to get it fresh. Whipped cream just doesn't taste the same without that "fresh" cream.

✻

Orange Pecan

2 tbs Orange Juice
2 tsp Grated Orange Rind
1 cup Pecans, coarsely chopped
1 cup Butter, unsalted at room temp
½ cup Light Brown Sugar

½ cup Sugar
1 Egg
2¾ cup Flour
½ tsp Salt
½ tsp Baking Soda

Cream butter and sugars. Beat in egg, then add orange juice and rind. Combine flour, salt and soda. Add to egg mixture and gently stir in nuts. Chill for one hour. Divide dough in half. On a lightly floured surface, form dough into two rolls about 1½ inch in diameter. Wrap each roll in waxed paper, refrigerate for 4 hours or overnight. Slice dough into ½-inch slices, place on lightly greased cookie sheet or on a parchment paper-lined baking pan. Bake in 350 degree oven for 8 minutes.

These cookies are great as is or may be glazed with an orange glaze by mixing a little orange juice with confectioners' sugar.

✻

Peanut Blossoms

½ cup Peanut Butter, Creamy
½ cup Crisco®
½ cup Sugar
½ cup Brown Sugar
1 Egg

1 tsp Vanilla
1¾ cup Flour
1 tsp Baking Soda
½ tsp Salt
1 lb Hershey® Kisses, Unwrapped

Mix flour, salt and baking soda together, set aside. Cream Crisco® and peanut butter together. Add sugars, cream very well. Add egg and vanilla, cream well again. Add flour mixture and combine thoroughly. Chill dough for 1 hour.

Roll into walnut sized balls, coat with granulated sugar and place on cookie sheet 1½ to 2 inches apart. Bake in preheated 375 degree oven for 10 minutes. Remove from oven. Press a Hershey's® kiss into the center of each cookie. Return to oven for an additional 3 to 5 minutes or until edges begin to turn golden brown.

What a great combination!

❈

Pumpkin Cookies

½ cup Crisco®
1¼ cup Brown Sugar
2 Eggs
1 tsp Vanilla
1½ cup Libby's® Pumpkin
2½ cup Flour

4 tsp Baking Powder
½ tsp Each: Cinnamon, Nutmeg,
    Salt
1 cup Raisins
1 cup Nuts, chopped

Sift dry ingredients together and set aside. Cream Crisco®, brown sugar, eggs and vanilla together until light in color. Add pumpkin, scrape bowl several times while mixing to combine completely. Stir in dry ingredients and mix thoroughly. Add raisins and nuts mixing well. Drop by spoonfuls 2 inches apart onto greased cookie sheet. Bake in preheated 350 degree oven for 12 to 14 minutes or until firm to touch. Remove from sheet to cooling rack. When cool, sprinkle with powdered sugar or top with a little powdered sugar frosting.

Because of the pumpkin, this is a very moist cookie and a wonderful addition to your holiday cookie trays.

❈

Russian Tea Cakes

1 cup Butter, unsalted
½ lb Powdered Sugar
1 tsp Vanilla
2¼-cup Flour

¼ tsp Salt
¾ cup Nuts of your choice, finely
chopped

Toast the nuts in 350 degree oven for about 10 minutes. Cream butter, powdered sugar and vanilla together just until mixed. Add flour and salt, mixing until combined. Add nuts and mix well. Chill dough for at least 1 hour. Form into 1-inch balls. Place on ungreased cookie sheet and bake 10 to 15 minutes or until golden brown. Remove from cookie sheet onto a cooling rack. When almost cool, toss in powdered sugar.

There are several different names for this cookie but, regardless of what it's called, it is still an all-time favorite.

Snickerdoodles

1 cup Crisco®, room temperature
1½ cup Sugar
2 Eggs
2¾ cups Flour, sifted
2 tsp Cream of Tarter

1 tsp Baking Soda
½ tsp Salt
2 tbs Sugar
2 tsp Cinnamon

Mix dry ingredients (except the 2 tbs. sugar and 2 tsp. cinnamon) together and set aside. Cream Crisco® and sugar together. Add eggs and continue to cream scraping sides of bowl several times. Add dry ingredients and mix well just to combine. Chill dough for 1 hour. Mix the 2 tbs. sugar and 2 tsp. cinnamon together in a medium size bowl.

Roll the dough into walnut sized balls, coat with cinnamon and sugar mixture. Place 2 inches apart on ungreased cookie sheet. Bake in a preheated 400 degree oven for 8 to 10 minutes. Cookie will flatten out and become very crisp when cool.

Cookie trays would not be the same without these. (They make great dunkers!) I remember loving this as a child, and this could very well be the first cookie I made or even the first thing I ever baked. This recipe has been around a very long time.

Soft Sugar Cookies

2 cups Butter	2 tbs Baking Powder
3 cups Sugar	2 tsp Baking Soda
4 Eggs	2 tsp Salt
2 cups Buttermilk	1 tbs Vanilla
8 cups Flour	½ tsp Nutmeg (optional)

If using salted butter, use only 1 tsp. salt. Cream together the butter, sugar and eggs, until very light in color. Mix dry ingredients together. Add alternately with buttermilk and vanilla. Scrape bowl several times in the course of mixing. Chill dough for at least 1 hour. Divide dough into 4 parts, working with one part at a time. Place dough onto floured surface, fold over and pat out several times. Dough will be quite soft but that will make a tender cookie.

   Roll dough out to ⅓ to ½-inch-thick. Cut with your favorite floured cookie cutters. Place onto a sprayed cookie sheet, bake in a 350 degree oven for 10 to 15 minutes or until cookie feels firm to touch. You can sprinkle cookies with decorations before baking, or ice with a powdered sugar icing in different colors after baking.

This is a little more time consuming than a spritz or drop cookie but will be very much worth the effort, making it a great holiday cookie, which keeps quite well in an airtight container in the freezer. I'm sure it will become one of your family's favorites as it has ours.

My mother always used this recipe, and I can't tell you where it came from, but I do remember her souring the milk with a tablespoon of vinegar per cup of plain milk to make her own buttermilk.

✻

Spritz—Lemon or Almond

1 cup Crisco®	2 tsp Lemon or Almond Extract
1 cup Butter, unsalted	4½ cup Flour
1½ cups Sugar	½ tsp Salt
2 Eggs	1 tsp Baking Powder

Cream butter and Crisco® until soft. Add sugar gradually, continuing to cream until light and fluffy. Add eggs and extract of your choice and beat.

   Sift flour, salt, baking powder together. Add in 3 additions and beat well after each addition, scraping bowl after each. Chill dough 10 minutes.

   Pack into cookie gun, press into desired shapes onto ungreased cookie sheet.

   Bake 8 or 10 minutes in 400 degree oven, or until golden brown. Makes 14 dozen, depending on size. You may also color the dough if you wish.

Years ago I bought a Wear-ever® Cookie Gun and this recipe came with it. Trying many other spritz cookie recipes, I have decided that this is the best one for just a simple butter cookie.

✻

Strawberry Tart Cookies

3 cups Flour	1½ cup Butter
1 cup Sugar	2 Egg Yolks
½ tsp Salt	1 cup Strawberry Jam

In bowl of mixer, mix the flour, sugar and the salt. Add the butter and blend the mixture until it resembles coarse meal. Stir in the egg yolks and blend the mixture until it forms a dough. Wrap the dough in plastic wrap and chill for 2 hours. Let the dough soften slightly then roll level teaspoons of it into balls. Arrange about 2 inches apart on lightly greased baking sheets.

Using your thumb, make an indentation in the center of each ball.

Fill each indentation with ½ tsp. strawberry jam and bake in 350 degree preheated oven for 12 to 15 minutes or until edges are pale golden. Let cookies cool for 2 minutes before transferring to cooling racks.

Cookies may be made 1 month in advance and kept frozen.

Christmas Sugar Cookies

1¼ cup Butter	4 tsp Baking Powder
2 cups Sugar	1 tsp Nutmeg, freshly grated
2 Eggs	½ cup Milk
5 cups Flour	2 tsp Vanilla
1 tsp Salt	

Mix dry ingredients, except sugar, together and set aside. Cream butter and sugar together, add eggs and continue to cream until light. Add dry ingredients alternately with milk and vanilla. Scrape bowl several times and continue to mix until combined. Chill dough for 1 hour. Roll out on lightly floured surface to ¼-inch-thick. Cut into your favorite shapes. Place on ungreased baking sheet pan, then into a 350 degree preheated oven for 8 to 10 minutes or until slightly firm to touch.

This dough can be tinted with food coloring and sprinkled with colored sugar or nonpareils before baking or can be iced or glazed after baking and cooling.

This recipe is firmer and easier to work with than the soft sugar cookie dough. They do have different flavors but both are excellent.

Chocopeaban Bars

2 Eggs
1 cup Vegetable Oil
1½ cups Sugar
1 cup Banana, pureed
½ cup Peanut Butter
2 cups Flour

1½ tsp Baking Powder
1 tsp Baking Soda
½ cup Nuts, of your choice,
   chopped med
1 cup Chocolate chips

Prepare a 13×9-inch baking pan by coating with *Pan Grease*.

    Cream eggs, oil and sugar together. Add bananas and peanut butter, mixing to incorporate. Mix dry ingredients together and add to creamed mixture. Mix well. Stir in nuts and chips. Pour into prepared pan. Place into 350 degree oven on middle shelf and bake for 20 to 25 minutes or until a toothpick comes out clean when inserted into center of bars. Remove from oven and cool on a cooling rack. Frost with *Cream Cheese Frosting* and sprinkle with nuts.

This is a moist, tasty treat. One day I was looking through my freezer and found several whole bananas. I always loved peanut butter and banana sandwiches, so I thought I would try making a bar and adding some chocolate chips and nuts. It worked! Enjoy!

Congo Squares

1 cup Butter
1 lb Brown Sugar
3 Eggs
2½ cup Flour

1½ tsp Baking Powder
1 small pkg Chocolate Chips
1 small pkg Butterscotch Chips
1 cup Nuts

Preheat oven to 325 degrees. Brush a sided cookie sheet with *Pan Grease*.

    Melt butter, add sugar. Let cool slightly, add eggs one at a time, beating after each addition. Add flour and baking powder in three additions, mixing well after each. Add nuts and chips mixing thoroughly.

    Spread mixture onto prepared pan. Place into oven and bake for 20 to 25 minutes. Cut into bars or squares before completely cool.

A family favorite!

Lemon Delights

2 cup Flour
1 cup Butter
½ cup Sugar

Filling

1 tsp Salt
4 Eggs
2 cup Sugar
2 tsp Grated Lemon Rind

6 tbs Lemon Juice
4 tbs Flour
1 tsp Baking Powder
½ tsp Salt

Blend flour, butter, ½ cup sugar, cornstarch and salt together to a crumby consistency. Press into a half sheet pan with 1 inch sides which has been sprayed with a nonstick spray. Make sure to bring the dough up the sides of pan. Bake 15 to 20 minutes or until lightly browned. Mix eggs and sugar together, then add the remaining ingredients and mix well. Pour this mixture into the baked crust. Return to oven and continue to bake at 325 degrees for 20 minutes or until mixture is totally set. Remove from oven. When cool sprinkle with powdered sugar. Cut into bars or square. These freeze very well in air-tight containers.

Another family favorite.

Pumpkin Bars

4 Eggs, beaten
1 cup Vegetable Oil
2 cups Sugar
1 cup Pumpkin, I prefer Libby's®
2 cups Flour
½ tsp Salt

2 tsp Cinnamon
1 tsp Baking Soda
1 tsp Baking Powder
½ cup Raisins
½ cup Walnuts

Combine all ingredients and pour into a cookie sheet that has been brushed with **Pan Grease**. Bake at 350 degrees for 20 to 25 minutes. Frost while warm.

Frosting

3 oz. Cream Cheese, softened
6 tbs Butter
¾ lb Powdered sugar

1 tsp Vanilla.
1 tsp Milk

Mix together with mixer. Spread over warm pumpkin bars. Good luck and happy eating!

Aunt Emma, who is 95 at this writing, gave this recipe to me many years ago. It is still in her handwriting and exactly as she wrote it. The walnuts and raisins are optional. Make sure the cookie sheet is a pan with sides, like a half sheet pan.

Aunt Emma and Uncle Bob

Pumpkin Streusel Squares

3½ cup Flour
⅔ cup Brown Sugar, packed
¾ cup Granulated Sugar
2 cups Butter, cold and cubed
2 cups Walnuts, chopped course
4 cups Pumpkin, I prefer Libby's®

2 cans Condensed Milk
4 Eggs
2 tsp Cinnamon
½ tsp Allspice
1 tsp Salt

Preheat oven to 350 degrees. Prepare a half sheet pan by greasing or spraying with a non-stick spray. Place the flour, brown sugar, granulated sugar and the butter into a bowl. Mix until it is the consistency of course corn meal or when squeezed in fist it forms a ball but breaks apart easily.

Add walnuts and mix. Press onto bottom and sides of pan; reserving 1 cup for the top. Mix the remaining ingredients together and pour into prepared dough-lined pan. Sprinkle with reserved crumbs. Bake until golden brown and set about 25 to 30 minutes. When cool cut into desired size.

This is a great product and is enjoyed by many people especially by my daughter Melissa.

The Family Pantry

Top left: Beverly, Mother,
  Tammy and Michael
Top right: Mother and Diane
Bottom: The apple butter pot

Preface to Canning Chapter

Before you begin *any* canning, preserving or pickling project, read the recipe to make sure you have all the ingredients. If the product needs to be peeled, chopped, blended, pitted or ground, do it just prior to starting. You want the products to be as fresh as possible. It is extremely important to gather all of your equipment and supplies before starting. Make sure all the jars and utensils are freshly washed, sanitized and free from any chips or rust. Pre-measure all ingredients and set aside to have at your fingertips.

I always use Sure Jell® or Certo® and Heinz® Vinegar.

Apple Butter—Old Fashioned

9 bushels Apples, variety for cooking
50 to 75 lbs Sugar
2 lbs Cinnamon
¼ cord Fire Wood
1 lg Copper Apple Butter Pot
1 long Wooden Stirrer
About 150 pint jars
A handful of new pennies (minted in the current year)

Several pots of coffee, hot cider or tea
Several lbs hot dogs and fixin's, depending on the number of participants
Hot dog roasting sticks
Warm clothes and several days to dedicate to this project

Pick a day in the fall that you hope and pray will not be rainy, snowy, and blustery or too hot, you may want a little coolness though. Start several days before this perfect apple butter day to prepare your apples by doing the following:

Cut the apples into quarters or eighths. Place them into a pot, add water to about ½ to ¾ full. Cook the apples until they are mushy. Put apples through a food mill to remove skins and seeds. Place the applesauce into buckets or containers. Place in a cool place. Repeat this process until all the apples are cooked. Depending on the amount of helpers, this could take 1 to 3 days.

On the day you actually want to make the apple butter, gather all your friends and relatives for a nice "quality time" day. Bribe them, promise them anything just to get their help.

Build a nice fire not too far from the kitchen. Roast and eat a hot dog. Get your pot cleaned (a good thing to clean the copper kettle with is vinegar and salt). Place the kettle rack over the fire, the kettle in it and pour about half of the applesauce into the kettle. Throw in the pennies and start stirring. The pennies keep the sauce from sticking to the bottom of the kettle. You have now begun the apple butter making process. The sauce has to be stirred at all times. That's one reason you will need all the help you can find. As the sauce cooks down, add more sauce. Don't make it too full as it will boil over and put out the fire, not to mention the loss of product. Roast and eat a hot dog. When the sauce reduces in volume by almost half, start adding the sugar. Mix the cinnamon with some of the sugar before adding to the sauce, to assure proper blending of the cinnamon. Now the sauce will get thin again because of the melting of the sugar, so put another log or two on the fire, fill your mugs with whatever liquid you prefer, and continue to stir sauce for a few more hours. Roast and eat a hot dog. When the mixture becomes very thick and dark in color, you are ready to start jarring it. Now you should taste it to make sure it is sweet enough and spicy enough for your taste. If not, add more cinnamon and sugar and then cook it down a little longer.

At this point you won't have time or energy to cook another hot dog. If there are any of your friends and relatives remaining, you'll need them at this time. Using clean jars pour the hot apple butter mixture into the jars and seal them as quickly as possible. Take time to wipe the top of the jars clean of any of the apple butter before putting on the lid. Have someone wipe the jars, if the apple butter is allowed to dry you may never get it off. Continue to jar as fast as possible, because the mixture will cook down very fast. When it gets a few inches from the bottom of kettle, remove it from the heat. When all is jarred, clean the kettle immediately. Apple butter is very hard to remove as it has been adhering to the kettle all day.

Now share the wares of the day with your helpers, enjoy your accomplishments and if you're still hungry, order a pizza, delivered.

❋

Dilly Beans or Cauliflower

2 lbs Fresh Green Beans, straight	4 Heads Fresh Dill *or*
1 tsp. Cayenne Pepper	2 tsp Dried Dill
4 Cloves Garlic	2½ cups Water
	2½ cups Cider Vinegar
	¼ cup Salt

Wash beans and pack lengthwise into 4 prepared pint jars, as tightly as possible, leaving ¼-inch head space. Top each jar with one clove garlic, ¼ tsp. cayenne and 1 head dill *or* ½ tsp. dried dill.

In a stainless steel saucepan combine salt, water and vinegar. Bring to a boil and immediately pour over the beans. Seal jars. Process pints for 10 minutes in a boiling water bath: this means to place jars on the rack, in a canner, fill with hot water, bring to a boil and simmer for 10 minutes.Let stand 2 weeks before tasting to allow flavor to develop.

What an outstanding substitute for a pickle! Actually, I prefer this to a pickle. Another recipe from my mother, but I go one step farther. After I have consumed the beans from the brine, I reheat it and do the same process with fresh cauliflower florets. I don't process it, I just refrigerate it. However, I have done the same process and it came out a beautiful shade of lavender, maybe it was the type of cauliflower I used.

When all the children were home, I was a frequent customer of Shaul Farms in Fultonham, NY. I would buy produce, by the bushel, that I didn't have space to grow. What a great time I had canning and preserving, but the children enjoyed only the *finished* product.

❋

Hot Pickled Vegetables

1 peck Hot or Medium Hot Peppers
1 head Celery
¼ cup Oregano
¼ cup Vegetable Oil
¼ cup Olive Oil
⅓ cup Salt
4 cups Water

4 cups Heinz® Cider Vinegar
1 head Cauliflower
½ lb Baby Carrots
2, 15-oz cans Black Olives
1 bulb Fresh Garlic, peel and crush
    but leave whole cloves

Cut the vegetables into bite-sized pieces. Mix oregano, salt, oil, water and vinegar together. Pour over vegetables, let stand overnight at room temperature.

Have jars clean and hot. Spoon vegetables into jars, bring brine to a boil, pour over vegetables and seal with hot lids.

This is a wonderful item. I can't tell you where I got it, but it is well worth doing.

Zucchini-Apricot Jam

6 cups Zucchini, seeded
    and grated
1 cup Crushed Pineapple, drained

½ cup Lemon Juice
6 cups Sugar
1 lg Apricot Jello®

Simmer zucchini over low heat for 6 minutes, drain. Add the pineapple, lemon juice and the sugar, boil for 10 minutes. Add Jello®, mix very well to dissolve Jello®. Pour into small jelly jars and seal.

An interesting substitute for the real thing!

Jelly—Cider

4 cups Sweet Cider
7½ cups Sugar
1 package Certo®

Have 10 to 12, 8-ounce jars washed
    and sanitized.

Combine sugar and cider in a heavy 4 or 5-quart pot. Stir over medium heat until mixture boils. Continue to boil for 1 minute. Add Certo® and again bring it up to a full rolling boil for 1 minute. Remove from heat and skim with metal spoon. Immediately pour into prepared jars and seal.

    If you prefer a little spice in your life, or your apple jelly, add cinnamon, allspice and cloves to taste in the beginning.

During our time in Roxbury, NY, we became friends with Bob and Carolyn Hubbell who had a huge cider press. What an operation, it was 3 stories high. The apples were shoveled onto a conveyor belt, which took them up to the top and into a grinder. The ground apples then came out a shoot into a large square frame, which was lined with a heavy canvas. The frame was filled with ground apples. The fabric was then folded over the top, the huge press came down and squeezed out the juice, which then went into a container that was emptied into a metal tank, by a large rubber pipe. You put your jug under the spigot at the bottom of the tank and you would get the freshest, best tasting cider you could ever imagine. This farm is located in Kelly Corners, NY, on Route 30 between Roxbury and Margaretville. This recipe came from the Hubbells. You will enjoy it, I'm sure.

Jelly—Hot Pepper

5 lbs. Sugar
3 cups Cider Vinegar
4 to 6 Hot Peppers, green *or* red

5 large Green *or* Red Bell Peppers
2 boxes Certo®

Remove seeds from peppers. If you have extremely hot peppers, wear rubber gloves. Process medium fine.

Prepare and have ready to fill, 10 to 12 8-ounce canning jars.

Place sugar, vinegar and peppers into a heavy 4-quart pan. Bring to a boil, stirring constantly. Boil 4 minutes. Remove from heat, add 2 boxes [4 envelopes] Certo®. Return to boil for 1 minute. Remove from heat, allow to set 2 or 3 minutes, stir and pour into prepared jars, sealing immediately.

What a great condiment for roast beef, ham, chicken or even lamb. Ask Rob, he can eat a whole jar at one meal. It is also outstanding on cream cheese with crackers for your cocktail party. Just put a 3 or 6 oz brick of cream cheese on a serving plate, top with this jelly, place your crackers around it and serve.

Jelly—Shallot, Garlic or Onion

5 lbs. Sugar
3 cups Cider Vinegar
¼ lb Fresh Shallots, Garlic or
    Onions, peeled and minced fine

2 Boxes Certo®, that would be 4
    envelopes

Mix vinegar, shallots and Certo® together. Place over medium heat in a heavy 6-quart pot. Bring mixture to a full rolling boil, Add sugar, stirring to combine. Bring mixture to a full boil and allow it to boil for 1 minute or until thick. Remove from heat allow it to set for 2 or 3 minutes. While the mixture is still very hot, stir well and pour into prepared canning jars, either 8 or 16-ounce. I prefer 8-ounce. Place lid on immediately to seal. This should fill 12 8-ounce jars.

    This recipe is a spin-off from the hot pepper jelly we have all tried at one time on another. I have also used this for garlic jelly and onion jelly. These are great condiments for meat sandwiches and especially good with country paté as hors d'oevres or with cream cheese on crackers.

Orange Marmalade

8 Thick Skinned Oranges
4 Lemons
¼ tsp Baking Soda
5 cups Water

11 cups Sugar, measure and set
    aside
2½ pkgs Sure Jell®

This recipe can be cut in half by using just one package of Sure Jell® and halving all the other ingredients.

    To prepare fruit, cut a slice off each end. Stand on one end and with a sharp knife trim rind off fruit in a downward slice turning the fruit, as you go, being careful not to cut too deep into the white. After all the peels are removed, slice the peels into ½-inch wide strips. Set aside. Remove all the white membrane from outside of fruit and discard. Slice fruit across and remove all seeds. Place fruit only in processor and process until very fine. Set aside reserving all the juices. Place the rinds, baking soda and water into a heavy, 10-quart, stainless steel pot, bring to a boil. Reduce heat, cover and simmer 20 minutes. Add processed fruit along with its juice and simmer 10 minutes.

    Place 8 cups of prepared fruit mixture along with the Sure Jell into the pot. Bring to a full boil. Boil for one minute. Stir often to prevent sticking. Add sugar all at once. Stir to combine and continue to stir until sugar is dissolved. Bring mixture back to a full rolling boil for 1 minute. Stir often. Make sure the pot is large enough to prevent boiling over.

    I always use a wooden spoon. If the mixture comes off the spoon in small thick drops, it is right. If it seems thin, continue to cook for a few more minutes. Remove from heat and allow to set for 2 or 3 minutes while stirring to combine fruit with liquid. Pour into prepared 8-ounce jars and seal immediately. This will take about 2 weeks to totally set up after sealing.

This is a very time-consuming project but if you like orange marmalade, you will absolutely love this and will never buy the commercial brands again. Any kind of jams or jellies I make, except the savory ones, I always use Sure Jell®, because it is sure to jell and because that is what my mother always used.

When I opened Beverly's, it was suggested to me, by my daughter, Tammy, to place on each table a plate of flavored butter, jams and marmalades. Thinking this was a great idea, I proceeded to make my own which turned out to be quite a task to keep on top of, but very rewarding. The customers loved that little touch.

❅

Relish—Confetti Corn

3 qts Fresh Corn, cut from cob
1 lg Green Pepper
1 lg Red Sweet Pepper
2 cups Spanish Onion
6 cups Sugar
1 qt Cider Vinegar

2 tbs Mustard Seed
2 tbs Celery Seed
1 tsp Turmeric
1 tbs Course Ground Black Pepper
Salt to taste.

Measure corn after cutting from cob. Remove seeds from peppers. Dice peppers and onions into pieces about the size of corn kernels. Combine vegetables and set aside.

In a large stainless steel pot, combine the remaining ingredients. Bring to a boil, add the vegetable mixture, come back to a boil, reduce heat and allow to simmer, stirring often, for 20 minutes.

Place into prepared pint jars. Seal and process in a hot water bath for 20 minutes. Remove from hot water, turn lid to tighten. Cool on rack.

This is a variation of Grandma Steffees Barbecue Relish. I like the crunch of it and the flavor is excellent.

❅

Relish—Cranberry Orange Walnut

1 lb Fresh Cranberries, I prefer
  Ocean Spray
1 cup Sugar
1 cup Water

1 Orange
½ cup Walnuts, toasted and
  chopped medium (optional)

Cut orange, remove seeds and process to medium chunks skin and all.

Combine cranberries, sugar and water in a stainless steel saucepan. Bring to a boil, stirring until sugar is dissolved. Reduce heat and continue to cook, stirring occasionally until mixture reaches a saucy consistency and the berries are opened and cooked. Remove from heat, add processed orange, and walnuts if you wish, mixing well. If you want to preserve this in jars, the mixture should be brought up to boiling again and immediately put into prepared jars and sealed while mixture is hot.

To make a cranberry mold, make sure the cranberries are cooked to a fairly thick consistency. Then pour into desired shape mold. It will jell more when chilled and will hold in the refrigerator for several weeks.

Our Thanksgiving and Christmas Holidays would not be complete without this relish. And even in between times it goes quite nicely with roasted chicken, pork, ham steaks or turkey sandwiches.

Relish—Grandma Steffey's Barbecue

1 qt Green Tomatoes, measure after
  grinding
1 qt Yellow Onions, measure after
  grinding
1 doz Green Peppers

½ doz Red Sweet Peppers
½ doz Large Cucumbers, if seeds
  are large, remove
Salt to taste

Dressing

6 cups Sugar
1 qt Cider Vinegar
2 tbs Mustard Seeds

2 tbs Celery Seeds
1 tsp Turmeric

Remove seeds from peppers and from the cucumbers, if seeds are large. Cut all vegetables into pieces small enough to fit into a grinder. Grind small to medium into a large stainless steel bowl. Mix well. Add salt to taste. Cover and let stand overnight. Drain into colander. Pour cold water over to remove any excess salt. Drain for 2 hours.

When the 2 hours are almost up, combine the dressing ingredients in pan large enough to hold both the vegetable mixture and the dressing. Heat the dressing to boiling. Add the drained mixture and stir to combine. Bring to boil again and cook for 20 minutes. Spoon into prepared jars, wipe tops and seal immediately.

This project takes some time but it is worth all the effort.

As long as I can remember this relish has been in our family's larder, starting with my Grandma Steffey's. That would be my father's mother. This recipe actually came from her kitchen. We have used it for many things. To name a few, I suppose # 1 would be hot dogs, or would it be an egg and cheese sandwich. I served it on a baked ham and havarti sandwich at Beverly's. Try it in ham salad. *You* try it and let your taste buds and imagination lead you.

※

Grandma Steffey

Salsa

⅓ Bushel Ripe Fresh Tomatoes
5 lg Green Peppers, or red and
    green
4 lg Spanish Onions
2 Bulbs Garlic
8 to 10 Jalapenos
2 small Cans Tomato Paste

3 oz Fresh Cilantro Leaves
1 tsp Ground Cumin
3 Lemons, juice only
2 Limes, juice only
Salt, Black Pepper, White Pepper
    and Cayenne to taste

Scald and skin tomatoes. Cut in half across the fruit. Squeeze seeds into a colander. Discard seeds. You could reserve this juice to use for cooking something else. (I can it and use it for cooking rice or soup.) Cut the tomatoes into large dice. Again, allow the juice to drain off chopped tomatoes. Add this to the other juice, if desired.

Remove seeds from the sweet peppers, cut into medium dice, along with the onions.

Using rubber gloves, remove the seeds and membrane from the jalapenos. Cut into small dice. You can add more or less of these, depending on your taste for hot fare.

Peel and mince garlic. Chop cilantro coarsely.

Place all ingredients *except the cilantro,* into a large stainless steel pot. Bring to a boil, stirring occasionally and simmer for 30 minutes. Add cilantro, combine well and place mixture into prepared pint jars. Seal and process in a hot water bath for 30 minutes on simmer.

Grandson Jonathan

September 2001, we celebrated my mother's 90th birthday, in western Pennsylvania. My sister-in-law, Leona, from Spokane, WA, brought some of her home-canned salsa for us to try. Thank you, it was wonderful.

I've been making fresh salsa for many years but never thought of preserving it for later use, but here is my version of it. If you don't want to jar it, cut the measurements down and use it as a fresh salsa. When I do that, I omit the tomato paste. I hope you enjoy this as much as my family and friends have.

Spiced Pickled Beets

From the best of my memory, this is a procedure handed down from my Granddad Mills. I don't believe there was ever a written recipe, I just do it until it tastes right. Therefore, this one is from my taste buds but it tastes pretty close to the beets my mother used to make.

If you like beets, you will love this!

Fresh Beets	Salt
Heinz® Cider Vinegar	Pepper
Sugar	Cinnamon Sticks or Ground
Water	Cinnamon
	Jars and lids for canning

Use fresh picked beets. Wash and cut stems off but leave at least 3 inches of stem. This prevents the beets from bleeding and loosing all of their color. Use as many beets as you think you can use over the course of the year. Place the beets into a large pot that has a lid, Cover with warm water, and place over high heat until the water boils. Cover with lid, reduce heat and continue to simmer until beets are fork tender, which will probably take well over an hour. When satisfactorily cooked, drain and rinse with cold water until cool enough to handle. While still in water, and beets are still warm, remove skins. Skins should peel off very easily with the pressure of your fingers. (If you don't want your hands to be stained, you should wear rubber gloves.) This process has to be done while still warm and wet. If the skin gets dry, it will be very hard to remove. After skinning the beets, cut them into desired size pieces.

In another large pot, place *equal* parts of Heinz® cider vinegar, sugar and water. Add enough salt and pepper to taste remembering the beets will absorb some of the salt. At this point, you can add either stick or ground cinnamon. I use the ground because I always have it and it is not a special purchase. I like to use quite a bit of pepper because we like them spicy. Bring this mixture to a boil, add the beets, return to boiling and simmer for 20 minutes. Place into clean hot jars, wipe top of jar of anything, cover with new clean, hot lids and turn to seal. Place onto a cooling rack and allow to cool completely before putting away. The lids will pop when they seal. If one doesn't seal, just place into the refrigerator and use when you wish. These are great with home made *Macaroni and Cheese*.

When I was quite young, one day I was helping my mother with the pickling of the beets. We got to the part where we put them on the stove to cook until tender. Well she put them in the large pressure canner, thinking the rubber seal was removed from the lid. We put them on the stove and went upstairs to take a little nap. We were all settled in for awhile, when all of a sudden there was a huge explosion downstairs. Of course, my mother ran down to see what it was and I was right behind her. Well, the seal in the lid of the pressure cooker was not removed, and the pressure got so great that it blew the lid off and made a very large hole in the ceiling. Do you remember how I told you in the beginning of the book about the kitchen ceiling being low and the whole kitchen always shined with a fresh coat of white enamel? Well it wasn't exactly white anymore. There was purple beet juice everyplace you looked and even where you couldn't see. It was quite a mess, but a blessing we were not in the kitchen.

Good luck and please don't use a pressure cooker.

❋

Sauerkraut

1, 10-gallon crock
1 Sauerkraut cutter or electric slicer

20 lbs Green Cabbage
(approximately 1 bushel)
1 lb Kosher Salt

Slice fully mature cabbage thin (about ⅛ inch thick). If you have a sauerkraut cutter, you can place it directly over the crock, slicing the cabbage right into the crock. Layer the sliced cabbage, 2 to 3-inches-thick, and sprinkle with 1 tbs. salt, pounding down each layer with a mallet or your hands. The cabbage and salt will create a juice. Repeat this procedure until all the cabbage is used. Place a dinner plate, upside down, directly on top of the cabbage, weighing it down with a gallon container of water. Cover all with plastic and place into a corner of your kitchen for about 2 weeks. When fermentation begins, move to a cooler place (65 degrees or lower). Remove scum daily. Kraut is cured and ready to use in 4 to 6 weeks. When it is cured, it is a creamy yellow white and completely free of the white cabbage appearance.

This may be frozen or canned. To process, pack into jars and place into cooker with cold water up to shoulders of jars. Bring to a boil, reduce heat and process for 45 minutes. Remove from boiling water and turn lids to insure a tight seal.

Being of German descent, we had sauerkraut quite often. I learned to make this as a child, but Grandma Mills and my mother always talked about how they made sauerkraut in a very large wooden barrel and kept it outside on the back porch in the winter. When some was needed, it had to be dug free because of the ice in it. How we now enjoy all the modern niceties and conveniences, taking them for granted most of the time! I think that sometimes it would have been great to live back then.

The Mills connection at Mother's 90th birthday.

Miscellaneous & Useful Hints

Apple Sauce

3 lbs Apples, for cooking
or baking

1 to 2 cups Sugar, or to taste
Cinnamon, for sprinkling

Use any kind of apples that will cook up. Do not use red delicious or granny smith. A mixture of any of the other apples makes a great tasting sauce.

Peal and core apples, cut into eighths, place into a stainless steel saucepan. Add enough water to half full. Cover, bring to a boil, and reduce heat to a slow cook. Continue to cook until apples are tender. Stir often to break up apples. When apples are totally cooked and sauce-like remove from heat, add sugar to taste. Pour into a serving bowl and sprinkle the top with cinnamon, serve warm or cold.

Basil Pesto

10 cloves Fresh Garlic
½ lb Fresh Basil
¼ lb Pine Nuts, toasted
2 cups Olive Oil

2 cups Vegetable Oil
½ lb Imported Parmesan, grated
1 tbs Fresh Grated Black Pepper
1 tsp Salt

Remove the basil leaves from stems, wash and drain well. Place all ingredients into processor bowl except the vegetable oil. Process finely. Add vegetable oil if desired to reach a thinner consistency.

Serve with pasta, pasta salads, crustinis, a roasted red pepper and fresh mozzarella sandwich or whatever your imaginations tells you.

Ben's Chili Seasoning

5 oz Ancho Chilies
2 Bay Leaf
5 oz Ground Cumin
4 oz Ground Coriander
4 oz Onion Powder
6 tbs Paprika
¼ cup Salt

2 tbs Seasoning Salt (like Aunt
Jane's Crazy Salt®)
1 tbs Oregano
2 tbs Garlic Powder
1 tbs Cayenne Pepper
1 tbs Black Pepper

Place ancho chilies and bay leaves into processor and process until very fine.
Add remaining ingredients, processing just to combine.

I once had a wonderful chef work for me for much too short a period. His name was Ben. What a talented chef he is. He left Saratoga Springs to be a chef at a yacht club off the coast of North Carolina. I miss him terribly, but he left me with some wonderful recipes and ideas. This is one of them, I'm sure you will enjoy the flavor and zing this adds to your chili or Mexican dishes.

Bread Stuffing

2 lbs Stale White Bread, cut into
   ½-inch cubes
1 cup Corn bread (optional)
1 cup Butter
1 cup Onion, diced

¾ cup Celery, diced
¼ cup Fresh Sage, chopped finely
2 tsp Salt
1 tsp Black Pepper
½ lb Breakfast Sausage (optional)

Prepare the bread and add crumbled corn bread, if desired. Sauté the onions and celery in the butter. Fry the sausage crisp and drain very well, if you decide to use it. Place all the ingredients together in a large bowl, toss to combine. Add just enough water to hold the mixture together when squeezed together gently. Taste and adjust the seasoning to your own liking. Use to stuff any kind of fowl, pork chops, meat loaf or flank steak.

Caramelized Red Onions

4 Large Red Onions, julienned thin
⅓ cup Honey
¼ cup Grenadine
¼ cup Brown Sugar

½ cup White Wine
½ cup Butter
1 Lemon, juiced
Salt and Black Pepper to taste

Melt butter in large skillet. Add the onions and sprinkle with brown sugar. Toss to coat onions with sugar; this will help them to caramelize. Toss over med high heat until the onions wilt. Add the remainder of the ingredients and stir until all is mixed. Reduce heat and simmer until the onions have reduced to the consistency of jam. This is also delicious served with any kind of grilled fish or chicken.

My son Rob gets the credit for this one. He did this at Beverly's with a grilled salmon and got rave reviews. Try it on *Crustinis* with brie and pop under the broiler for a minute or two.

Croutons

Day-old Bread, cut into 1″ cubes
Olive Oil
Garlic Powder
Onion Powder

Aunt Jane's Seasoning Salt®
Paprika
Black Pepper

Use day-old French bread, baguettes or any firm bread. Cut into 1-inch cubes and lay out to dry. Toss with enough olive oil to totally coat the cubes. Then sprinkle with garlic powder, Aunt Jane's Seasoning Salt®, onion powder, paprika and black pepper. Toss again to completely coat. Place onto a sheet pan in a single layer and place into a 250 degree oven, stirring every 15 minutes, until they are completely dried and crisp. When cool, place into a air-tight container.

✲

Crustinis

Homemade baguettes   Olive Oil

I try to use homemade baguettes for this, but store-bought ones will work also. Slice diagonally across the bread into slices no more than ½ inch thick. Brush with a good quality olive oil, bake in a 375 degree oven until crisp and slightly brown. Remove from oven, cool and store in airtight container.

✲

Fondue—Cheese

¾ lb Emmenthaler, shredded   ½ tsp Salt
¼ lb Swiss Gruyere, shredded   ¼ tsp Fresh Grated Pepper
1 tbs Flour   1 clove Fresh Garlic, mashed
¼ tsp Fresh Grated Nutmeg   1 cup Dry White Wine

Place the cheeses, flour, salt, pepper and nutmeg into a bowl then toss to coat the cheese with the flour. Set aside. Place wine into a non-stick pan with the garlic clove. Bring to a boil and simmer for 2 minutes. Remove the garlic. While whisking, add the cheese mixture to the hot wine mixture a handful at a time. Allow the cheese to be incorporated before adding another handful. Continue this procedure until all the cheese is used. Bring to a boil and serve immediately in a fondue pot with sterno heat underneath.

Serve with lightly toasted French bread cubes, bite sized cubes of apples and lightly steamed vegetables of your choice.

I learned to make this from my friend and chef, Walter Keller. He always served it with just the bread and lots of wine. The apples and vegetables are my idea, but they are a great addition and make for a more balanced meal. I sometimes serve cornichons or my **Dilly Beans** with it.

✲

Garlic Bread

2 loaves Italian Bread or Baguettes
¼ lb Butter
½ cup Olive Oil
2 cloves Fresh Garlic, minced

Paprika
Fresh Ground Parmesan
Parsley Flakes
Fresh Ground Pepper

Melt the butter in a small saucepan, then add the olive oil and garlic. Simmer for 2 minutes. Split the bread lengthwise. Brush the cut sides of bread with the butter mixture. Sprinkle with the parmesan first, then the other ingredients ending with the paprika.

Close the bread, wrap with aluminum foil and bake in a 375 degree oven for 15 to 20 minutes, or place the bread open face on a cookie sheet and bake for 10 to 15 minutes.

Grilled Chicken Rub

¼ cup Fresh Rosemary
¼ cup Fresh Parsley
3 cloves Fresh Garlic, minced
¼ cup Onion, minced
¼ cup Whole Grain Mustard

¼ cup Fresh Lemon Juice
¼ cup Olive Oil
1 tbs Kosher Salt
1 tsp Course Ground Pepper

Mix all ingredients together. Rub onto chicken parts or a whole roasting chicken. Allow to stand for at least 2 hours before grilling. Grill to your likeness.

Herb Butter

This butter is the *best* for escargot.

3 lbs Butter, room temperature but
    not melted
½ lb Shallots, peeled
½ lb Garlic, peeled
7 oz Worcestershire Sauce
1 cup Yellow Mustard (I use
    French's®)

2 bunches Fresh Parsley, washed and
    stemmed
1 sm can Anchovy fillets
1 tsp each Salt and Black Pepper
½ cup Marsala Wine
2 tsp Maggi Seasoning

Place shallots, garlic, parsley, anchovies and mustard into bowl of processor. Turn on full speed and process to a fine consistency. Place this mixture and remaining ingredients into bowl of the mixer, that is large enough to hold all ingredients. Whip until it reaches the consistency of whipped butter.

My friend, Chef Walter Keller, is the creator of this recipe, but it is not exactly the same as his. I never saw the exact ingredient list or recipe but, not intentionally, I do remember some of the ingredients. Over the years I have tried to get the exact taste, but not being able to accomplish that, I have come up with something that is very delicious and pretty close to the real thing.

If you ever go to Margaretville, NY, please visit Binnekill Square Restaurant, have the escargot and tell him I said, "Hello".

❋

Jay's Pasta Cheese

5 parts Grated Parmesan
1 part Grated Romano

3 cloves Fresh Garlic
2 Bay Leaves

Peel the garlic and mix all the ingredients together. Place into an airtight container, refrigerate and allow one week for flavors to blend. This mixture can be stored up to a month in refrigeration, or remove the garlic after several weeks and store indefinitely.

This has a wonderful flavor for any of your pasta dishes but mostly just tossed with your favorite hot pasta and a good olive oil.

One of the original Mouseketeers named Michael and his friend, Jay, from New York City, gave this recipe to me some 25 years ago. I met them in Roxbury, NY, at Roxbury Run Restaurant where I worked, and later they become good customers at our little gourmet food shop, The Cheese Barrel in Margaretville, NY.

❋

Mango Salsa

2 Fresh Ripe Mangos, peeled,
    seeded and diced
1 Red Pepper, diced small
1 med Red Onion, diced small
2 cloves Fresh Garlic, minced

¼ cup Fresh Cilantro, minced
1 inch Fresh Ginger, grated
2 Limes, juice
¼ cup Vegetable Oil
Salt, Pepper and cayenne to taste.

Mix all ingredients together and adjust seasoning.
Serve with **Oven Poached Fish.**

❋

249

Mushroom Paste

2 lbs Mushrooms of your choice
½ cup Spanish Onions, diced
2 cloves Fresh Garlic, minced
3 tbs Fresh Shallots, minced

1 stick Butter
2 tbs Fresh Parsley, minced
Salt and Fresh Ground Pepper to
    taste.

Wipe the mushrooms clean with a damp paper towel. If you are using portabellas, discard the stem. Place the mushrooms into the processor and process to a medium fine consistency. Add the onion, garlic and shallots, and process on and off 3 or 4 times.

Melt the butter in a large heavy skillet. Add the processed mixture. Stir over medium heat until all the moisture has evaporated. Add the remaining ingredients. Adjust seasoning to your liking.

What a wonderful, flavorful and versatile item to have. Spread this on *Bruschetta* topped with chevre, use for a coating on one side of a chicken cutlet before breading, or for a coating before the puff pastry in a *Wellington* dish.

❈

Roasted Red Pepper Coulis

3 Roasted Red Peppers
1 cup Heavy Cream
½ tsp Paprika
1 tsp Kosher Salt

¼ tsp White Pepper
¼ tsp Thyme
1 or 2 cloves Fresh Garlic
Hot sauce to taste.

Rub peppers with olive oil. Roast in a 450 degree oven, turning every 15 minutes to brown evenly. Place into container and cover with foil until cool. Remove skins and seeds. Place all ingredients in bowl of processor and process to a medium fine texture. Adjust seasoning to your taste.

Serve with fish or chicken.

❈

Roux

Use equal parts butter and flour.

Melt the butter in a skillet or saucepan. Add the flour and cook about 10 minutes to prevent a floury taste in your soups or sauces. This can be prepared ahead of time for convenience. Use it for thickening sauce, gravy, stew or soup. Have it at room temperature and add it to the hot liquid, a little at a time, stirring to incorporate and thicken the product.

❈

Salsa

10 Ripe Tomatoes
2 Red Bell Peppers
1 Green Pepper
1 Red Onion
1 tbs Fresh Garlic, minced
½ cup Olive Oil

6 Jalapenos, diced small
4 Lemons, juice
1 bunch Fresh Cilantro, chopped
    medium
Cayenne, Salt and Pepper to taste

Dice tomatoes, peppers and onion, then add remaining ingredients and toss together. Let stand for at least 30 minutes to blend flavors. This can be kept refrigerated for up to a week but does loose some of its intensity.

Stock

For this item, you can use fish, shrimp shells, poultry, beef, pork, veal or just plain vegetables.

6 lbs Bones and Trimmings
4 large Carrots
4 ribs Celery
2 large Onions
1 bulb Garlic

¼ cup Olive Oil
5 Bay Leaves
1 tbs Whole Pepper Corns
¼ cup Salt
A large handful Parsley Stems

Wash the vegetables, but there is no need to peel. Cut the onions, celery and carrots into large chunks. Crush the garlic. Toss all vegetables with olive oil.

In a large open roasting pan, place the bones and trimmings of your choice and vegetables. Roast in a 375 degree oven until all are browned and the bones are well roasted.

Transfer from roasting pan to a large stockpot. Cover with water and add bay leaves, peppercorns, salt and parsley stems. Bring the pot to a boil, reduce heat and simmer overnight or at least 6 to 8 hours. Remove from heat and pour through a colander, reserving the stock. Return to heat and continue to reduce to a rich stock. Adjust seasoning to your liking.

This is quite a procedure but well worth the effort, especially for making sauces. Freeze in small containers to use as you wish.

Useful Hints

- Have a small ramekin or dish of Kosher Salt and Fresh Ground Pepper close by.

- To make a roasting rack take a length of foil, scrunch it together and then form it into either a circle or an S shape, spray it with pan spray, place it on the bottom of roasting pan for large pieces of meat.

- Before measuring Crisco®, honey, molasses, or syrup spray the measuring cup with pan spray, or if you have to measure oil and honey, syrup or molasses, measure the oil first; the rest won't stick to the measuring cup.

- When using your non-stick skillets, *always* use a rubber scraper for mixing and stirring.

- Drapery hooks—they are so useful! The last thing I used them for was to attach the icicle Christmas lights to the edge of the roof. If you need a fastener, think drapery hooks.

- To de-vein a shrimp and take the shell off at the same time, all you need is a pair of scissors. I am right handed so, hold the shrimp in your left hand with the legs in your palm and the tail pointing away from you. Insert the scissors into the back top vein where the head was taken off, snip through that thin layer of skin and the shell, down to the last joint before the tail. Break the shell off there and the vein will come with it.

- If you drop a piece of egg shell in with your eggs and you are chasing it with a spoon to no avail, try using the half of eggshell to get it out.

- If you need chopped fresh ginger, use the large side of your grater and shred it.

- Use grated onion instead of chopped onion in your salads and dressings. You get the wonderful flavor of the onion without the large chunks.

- Process garlic or shallots with olive oil, place it into small jars and store in the refrigerator for quick access. Don't do too much at a time, as they will loose they potency.

- Before covering a casserole with foil, spray the foil with non-stick spray.

- To make your own ginger tea just grate some fresh ginger, place it into your mesh ball or teaspoon and place it into your tea to steep for 2 or 3 minutes. You will get a much stronger fresh flavor.

- Before you use any kind of nuts in your baking or cooking, please roast them for at least 10 minutes in a 325 degree oven. You will be amazed at the difference in the flavor, even pine nuts.

- When you are going to heat up something in the oven, try lining the pan with foil and then spraying it. Take off the foil and you have a clean pan. This works especially well for nachos.

- If you are washing sandy vegetables, try putting them in a colander that fits into a bowl. Put the vegetables into the colander which is in the bowl, and fill it with water and swish vigorously; then let set, and all the sand will sift down through the holes in the colander. Repeat until the water is clear.

- To roll out pastry dough, without losing your religion, and still keep the crust tender and flaky, go to your nearest kitchen supply store and buy a rolling pin sock and a pastry cloth. You will be amazed at how easy it makes rolling out the dough.

- Do you know how to blanch vegetables? It's very easy. Have ready a pot of boiling water, a large container of ice water and a large colander. Place the cleaned, cut vegetables into the boiling water just until the color of the vegetables turn a bright color, green, orange, white or whatever. Remove from boiling water immediately with a strainer, place into the ice water until totally chilled, then place into the colander to drain. If you have more than one kind of vegetables to blanch, I always start with the lightest in color to the darkest, that way you don't have to change the water.

- Add ¼ to ½ tsp. almond flavoring to your cherries or peaches when baking a pie. You will be amazed at the flavor.

- Before grilling your favorite fish, spray it with a non-stick spray.

- Freeze tomato paste or tomato sauce in ice cube trays. When frozen, store the cubes in a plastic container or Ziplock® bag in your freezer. When you need a tablespoon or two of this product, you won't have to open a whole can. This also works really well with wine.

❋

Spray for Bugs

¼ cup Cayenne Pepper	¾ cup Boiling Water
	4 Eggs

Mix pepper and water together in a glass jar. Whisk eggs very well, then strain into cooled pepper mixture. Shake very well to mix. Spray on plants for bug control.

❋

Index

To order additional copies of *Beverly's Best Cookbook,* please send a check or money order for $31.65, payable to Beverly Reedy, to:

Beverly's Best
51 County Route 10
Corinth, NY 12822

If it is to be sent as a gift, to a different address, please enclose that name and address. The book will be personalized and a gift card included.